THE PSYCHIC
BATTLEFIELD

THE PSYCHIC BATTLEFIELD

A History of the Military-Occult Complex

W. ADAM MANDELBAUM

St. Martin's Press ✿ New York

THOMAS DUNNE BOOKS.
An imprint of St. Martin's Press.

THE PSYCHIC BATTLEFIELD. Copyright © 2000 by The Reference Works and W. Adam Mandelbaum. All rights reserved. Printed in the United States of America. No part of this book may be used or reproduced in any manner whatsoever without written permission except in the case of brief quotations embodied in critical articles or reviews. For information, address St. Martin's Press, 175 Fifth Avenue, New York, N.Y. 10010.

Book design by Kathryn Parise

LIBRARY OF CONGRESS CATALOGING-IN-PUBLICATION DATA

Mandelbaum, W. Adam.
    The psychic battlefield : a history of the military-occult complex /
W. Adam Mandelbaum.—1st ed.
        p.   cm.
    Includes bibliographical references and index.
    ISBN 0-312-20955-X
        1. Parapsychology—Military aspects—History.   2. Remote viewing
(Parapsychology)—History.   I. Title.

BF1045.M55 M26 2000
133.8—dc21   99-055025

First Edition: February 2000

10   9   8   7   6   5   4   3   2   1

To all those on the night watch.

To all those who have asked how, and why.

To all those who have shined their light in the dark.

To all those who can change their mind.

In the research and preparation of this work, *The Psychic Battlefield*, no information that was classified or restricted in any way was used, nor was access had to same. All facts, theories, suppositions, and prognostications that the reader may find within are based upon the examination of nonclassified or declassified documents only, and interviews with those who imparted information only of a nonclassified or declassified nature.

It is important to note that those men who spent their military service years in the clandestine service and assisted the author in this work still honor their country and their security agreements. Your author has honored and still honors his, and has not divulged any information of a sensitive nature obtained during his period of service.

Any reference to matters that might still be classified or sensitive is purely coincidental.

CONTENTS

ACKNOWLEDGMENTS

Truth is, as they say, stranger than fiction. Sometimes the search for that truth takes the seeker down dark passages around narrow corners, and brings about meetings with remarkable men. In the search for the true history of psychic spying, I have searched through recently de-classified government documents (of which there are too few), read a variety of centuries-old volumes on magic (of which there are too many), and interviewed the top psychic spy the United States Govern-ment was fortunate to have on its side (of which there can be only one).

During this journey into the heart of darkness surrounding psychic spying, I was aided and abetted by my mentor and first-line editor, Harold Rabinowitz, and the competence and persistence of my agent, Alex Hoyt.

Special mention must go to Nancy and Joseph McMoneagle, without whose help this book would not have been one-half of what it is; Mel Riley, who graced this work with his moving foreword, and Dr. Edwin May, for his assistance with respect to the criticism of the American Institute of Research's "Evaluation" of the government remote-viewing program.

Gratitude is herein paid in advance to all those who will have read this history, opened their minds to the potential that is within all of us, and closed their hearts to those in government who would not have this potential be publicly known. Some secrets must be kept in order to maintain national security. Others, in time, must be revealed in order to maintain the dream for a wiser and more perceptive humanity. It is hoped that, in the twenty-first century, this dream, this vision of a new mankind, will be manifested in reality.

FOREWORD

Like many others, I have been a career soldier. Like few career soldiers, however, there were times my duties found me in a realm without borders, without maps, without even a clear idea of where I was, or how I was doing what I was doing. I was a government remote viewer. I was proud to serve in that capacity, since I was first and foremost an American soldier.

Now, as a civilian, I serve a different function, preserving not the territorial integrity of the United States, but the historical integrity of the first Americans—our Native Americans. I am the director of a museum in Wisconsin, where the traditions of the great warriors and shamans of our American past are preserved and studied.

Like the Indian tribes, the American military personnel who served in the government remote-viewing program were representative warriors and shamans—trained to fight if necessary, able to extend their perceptions into different realities in the service of their country's needs.

From its inception in 1978 as "Grill Flame," until its termination in 1995 as "Stargate," the psychic spies of the remote-viewing program were pioneers on the last frontier of this planet, the frontier of the mind. We had no ouija boards to speak of and, except for a civilian or two, no tarot cards. We had a small cadre of highly trained individuals using techniques developed by "hard" scientists in respected laboratories—techniques, methods and protocols designed to bring a new degree of accuracy to psychic perception.

The majority of what was done—the successes and the failures— remains classified. This program, because of its controversial nature, was a bastard child of the military-intelligence complex, and part of what the author calls the military-occult complex. By those who did not know, by those who could not understand, what we did was denied, and when not denied, denigrated.

Those of us who served as remote viewers know the true story. Those of us who served can tell the public this much: remote viewing *works*. Remote viewing has been proven in the laboratory, replicated enough times to satisfy any open-minded scientist. More important, remote viewing has proven its utility in the area of intelligence operations—government-disseminated disinformation notwithstanding.

Psychic spying is not new. It is as old as man's martial traditions. While there have been books on the occult influence in the rise of the Third Reich, books on the remote-viewing program and books by remote viewers themselves (with varying degrees of truthfulness), there has never been, until now, a book that describes and details the entire history of the symbiotic relationship between the paranormal and the military.

The author of *Psychic Battlefield* served in a more traditional intelligence capacity during his stint at Fort Meade, where the remote-viewing operations took place, but his background and familiarity with the paranormal have served him well in this panoramic view of the history of the military-occult complex offered to the reader.

I was one of the initial remote-viewers in 1978, and in 1990 retired from the military, but not from the field of remote viewing. With some dismay, I have seen this perceptual tool turned into tabloid fodder in the media, and prostituted as a fast-buck scam by some who should know better. It is hoped that the current work will present the past, present, and possible future of psychic spying in a purer light, a light that, to the open mind, will shine on the limitless potential that man possesses within the borderless realm of his mind.

—Mel Riley
Scandinavia, Wisconsin

THE PSYCHIC
BATTLEFIELD

CHAPTER 1

INTRODUCTION
The World of the Psychic Soldier

One of the darkly fascinating aspects of man's history on Earth has been his progress, in method and magnitude, in the development of ever more efficient means of destroying his fellow man. Bereft of claw and fang, yet possessed of the most developed brain of all species, man has become the most dangerous predator on the planet.

But this predator, whose feet stalk the ground in search of kill or conquest, has his eyes ever on the stars, in search of, and in supplication to, the extrasensory—what some have called the spirit world, what many still call God. This need to believe walks hand in hand with the need to kill.

As divergent and diametrically opposed as these needs appear to be, they have at times coalesced in a mystical marriage, wherein the warrior is also the wizard, the marauder is also the magician. It is the history of this relationship that concerns us in this work. It is the saga of Psychics and Soldiers—A History of the Military-Occult Complex.

A hunter since the dawn of his time, man, with his opposable thumbs and highly developed cerebral cortex, has progressed from club to spear to flint arrow to flintlock to the summit of destruction, the mushroom cloud producing thermonuclear destruction. He has now reached into the genetic code of life itself to create biological weapons that cannot just kill, but have the potential to be indestructible and irrevocable. As his "technology of thanatology" has evolved, man's concept of the supernatural, the spirit world, has also changed.

The primitive animist became the civilized polytheist. The polytheist became the monotheist. The most recent step is the development of the atheist, a creature with a lesser need to believe in an anthropomorphic deity, but who nevertheless, as we shall see, can still accept the extrasensory spiritual world under a different terminology. The scientific spirit is what now guides him in the paranormal realms.

Whereas the ancient shaman painted cave walls, predicting successful hunts, and danced before tribal fires to contact the spirits, the modern-day magus sits on his CIA-issue couch and sends his government-trained astral body into the ether in search of prey. Even today, what might be called "Private Third Eyes" exist, veterans of the military-psychic spying program. Now, for hefty fees, they will enter the astral world for information, the world's most valuable commodity.

In this survey of psychics and soldiers, the early interaction of the spirit world and the martial world shall be examined. (The word "martial" has its origin in the Roman war god, Mars). We will bear witness to the wonder workings of the Egyptians, who conducted naval warfare in the ether as well as in the real world, and learn the ancient spells to obtain prophetic dreams to predict the outcome of great battles to be fought. Leaving the ancient world, the next stop shall be the frozen north, where the armored Valkyries ride wolves into battle alongside mortal men and weave death on their looms of human guts and skulls.

Our journey across time and space as witnesses to this world of conquest and sorcery reveals the pantheon of war gods and the rituals used to invoke their aid, and the techniques of the samurai and ninja who, as mystic warriors, refined death into an art and a spiritual exercise. Leaving the east and moving through time, we will trek the sands of Jerusalem with the warrior-monks Knights Templars, who started under vows of poverty and chastity to protect the earthly bodies of spiritual pilgrims, and yet became Europe's greedy bankers, then tinder for the stakes of Rome.

Other times and territories shall be revealed in the realm of the psychic and the soldier, until an arrival at the twentieth century. The atheists of the Soviet Union will achieve a TKO (a telepathic knockout) via "remote influence." They will intercept telepathic transmissions and use electro-magnetics to enhance human extrasensory perception.

During the time of Nazi power in Germany are found top-level officers who practiced astrology: The head of the SS conducted "remote influence" experiments and the prophecies of Nostradamus, a converted Jew, were used to further Nazi propaganda aims.

It was the influence of the prewar magical societies that were to give spiritual sustenance to the Nazi movement, and we'll see how some of the world's most famous "sorcerers" were deeply involved in military and intelligence matters during the National Socialist era.

A cast of characters includes such men as Aleister Crowley, a bisexual heroin addict who worked at times for British Intelligence. Jack Parsons, head of a sex-magic cult, who developed solid rocket propellant for the military in World War II. Present also are bogus German aristocrats who, in the years before the war, mixed magic and mayhem as they sought military conquest via magically aided means. Their plans, dreams, and bodies all are now but dust.

More recently, the CIA used superstition to battle insurgents in the Congo, investigated the possibilities of mind control via hypnosis and drugs, and even considered using subliminal persuasion as a behavior modification tool.

The final historical destination shall be at the end of the twentieth century on the eve of the third millenium, in Maryland, sitting alongside CIA-trained psychics who venture out astrally into the ether to spy upon strategic and tactical targets, find downed aircraft, and locate hostages. Interested parties will be able to enroll in a correspondence course in remote viewing, sold over the Internet.

At the end of this work is a special interview with the top CIA psychic, the heavyweight champion of remote viewing, Joseph McMoneagle, and a description of his work, his life, and his predictions for the future, not only for remote viewing, but for the world at large.

But this will be more than a survey of the spirit world and its spies and soldiers. More than a history, this will be, and must be, an analysis, a critique, and finally, in the full spirit of this effort, a prognostication. We must ask *Why? How?* We must know if this mystic marriage of martial and metaphysical ways is a sham wedding, and if not, what is its future?

In addressing the how and why of the psychic soldier, perhaps a partial answer is obtained from the the Hindu god Krishna. In urging the warrior Arjuna on to conquest and the slaughter of his enemies in the Hindu saga, the *Bhagavad Gita*, Krishna details the warrior's qualities: "Heroism, majesty, firmness, skill and not fleeing in battle also.

Generosity and Lordly nature are the natural-born actions of warriors."

This is a description of more than a mere mortal. It is the description of a veritable god of war.

An ancient idealization and idolizing of the warrior. Was it not logical, then, for the warrior to seek divine aid in order to live up to this ideal, and die in accordance with it?

Society calls upon its warriors to act as gods. It empowers them to kill without punishment, destroy without accountability, and it extols the virtue of self-sacrifice. The warrior is our Adonis, our Osiris, our Attis—and, yes, our Jesus too. We demand of him the strength of Hercules, the speed of Hermes and the thundering power of Zeus.

The societies that created the pressure to be as gods, along with these expectations, treated their warriors as if they were gods. Indeed, they *were* higher beings: exempt from mundane occupations, beneficiaries of the sacrifices of grain and gold, they reigned over the other castes and classes. The warrior was the Mercury of mortality, a divine messenger of Death.

It was Death who was the constant companion of the warrior, but historically, death was not a terminus, but a doorway to a better world for the valiant. The Teutonic warrior fallen in battle found his reward in Valhalla. The Saracen whose scimitar fell from his dead hand found his spiritual hand holding a cup of wine, served by a dark-eyed and beautiful houri of Paradise.

The whole existence of the warrior was involved with the mystery of death, the glory of an afterlife, and a temporal exalted status in his society. Not only his function and status, but his way of life also made the warrior comfortable—in the robe of the wizard.

Ritual plays an important rôle in both the military and in magic. A certain cadence in a march, the execution of certain movements, etiquette, are all taught the warrior. In magical ceremonies, a place for everything and everything in its place is a sine qua non for effective evocation. Thus both endeavors were accustomed to formal methods of movement and action.

Symbolism is also found throughout military establishments and magical endeavors, whether it is the five-pointed star on the major general's epaulet, or the five-pointed pentagram on the wizard's breast. The salute is a gesture invoked when confronting a higher-ranking being—both in camp and in coven—although its form may vary with the time and territory.

Hierarchical organization is a major phenomenon in the warrior and magician castes. The sergeant has his captain who has his major who has his general. The priest (who is the intercessor between the material and spiritual worlds) has his bishop who has his cardinal who has his pope.

We have the psychological background in his obligations and status for the warrior to do double duty as a wizard. We have the procedural similarities of ritual, symbolism and structure to facilitate the trip from sword bearer to wand waver. We also have matters of blood ties.

Throughout much of history, the noble families produced the warriors and the priests for their societies. The one who sought adventure in conquest might be a knight. The one who sought learning and the comforts of the cloister, such as they were, might be a priest. Thus, in the ruling classes of nations, where throughout history a theocratic form of government had both de facto and de jure power, the soldier and the spiritual practitioner might well have been related.

The above parallels show the shared world of the psychic and soldier, and lend understanding to the factors that allow the trained military man to become the trained practitioner of extra-sensory manipulations. Thus the explanation. The question, however, is, *Does it work?*

In this book, it shall be shown that these powers impact on military and intelligence operations. That they are of real tactical and strategic value; psychics are the spies of the future. The answer lies in the supposed successes and failures of the psychic soldier, and an attempt to analyze why what worked, worked, and why what failed, failed.

This analysis required the input of parapsychologists, neuroscientists, the examination of declassified government studies and documents, newspapers and medieval grimoires, the exploration of divinatory methods, and comments from experts in both espionage and ESP. Like the intelligence agent I was, I sifted through all of this material and created a SITREP, or situation report analyzing just what might be going on in this shadow realm of the psychic soldier. Mechanical and electronic devices designed to enhance or inhibit ESP have also been investigated, in a survey of the emerging technologies of the spirit world.

All of this was done in support of the raison d'être of this book—to raise public awareness of the history of the military-occult complex, examine its present status (as far as access to unclassified sources will allow), and consider the future of the use of psychics by the military and intelligence services.

As our material military technologies are constantly being upgraded, so must our spiritual technologies—such as they are, such as they might become. Given modern informational demands on our military, if pyschic soldiers did not exist, we should have to invent them.

This present endeavor is in some ways a further stepping stone in the already existing path of works on psychic warfare. However, it is believed that this work is the first survey and analysis of the entire history of the wizard warrior, from the dawn of man to the eve of the third millennium.

Other works have dealt with specific times and techniques. Herein, all times and techniques are surveyed. And the surveyor encompasses a background not shared by any other who has gone this way before.

The author has served in military intelligence and the National Security Agency in the area of COMINT, communications intelligence. Further, for over twenty years, I have both personally and professionally read and prognosticated from the tarot. I am the legal advisor to a major metropolitan organization of skeptics, and a fellow of the American Society for Psychical Research. Add to that my two decades of working as a civil and criminal litigator and coming up against some rather accomplished liars, I am a rather unusual observer of the psychic soldier scenario.

Research consistently shows that not only does belief in the paranormal persist in spite of increases in education, but that acceptance of the possibility of such phenomena as extrasensory perception, remote viewing (clairvoyance), telekinesis (mind over matter), astral projection (out-of-body experiences), telepathy, all manner of divination techniques, and a host of other paranormal phenomena is greater at the extreme ends of the intelligence scale—that is, among the most intelligent members of society (to whom this work is addressed)—and the less gifted.

The cultural and intellectual middle classes are a new silent majority for the New Age. However, it is hoped that this present volume—with respect to this subject—may shed some light into these darkened crevices of mass culture and belief systems. If completely false, it is at least fascinating and thought provoking, and if even partially true, it represents the greatest revolution in human potential since our exodus from the trees and our standing upon two feet.

Many will question, some incredulously, how those in power and authority throughout history, and especially now, in our microchip, micromanaged age, can spend time, manpower, and money on what may not inaccurately be called witchcraft in modern dress.

This is not an unfair question. It deserves, and shall receive, an answer.

It is not only the tendency, but the duty of the military and the intelligence services to explore every technology, hard or soft, that has potential for effective tactical and strategic use. For it is beyond doubt that the world of wholesale killing, the de facto purpose of the military, and the world of information upon which wholesale killing may occur is not the mundane world of the average man. What works ethically, morally, and practically for the man on Main Street is irrelevant to the CIA (or equivalent) "street man" who must use every vice and virtue to accomplish his aims, which are, in actuality, the aims of his government.

Whether it is a bribe, sexual blackmail, physical intimidation, brainwashing, or even remote viewing, if a technique works, or can be made to work, it goes into the toolbox of the soldier and the spy. And it must. Lives may depend on it. The fate of nations may depend on it. For this arena is not a small one. As in any real arena, death and defeat may be encountered. It is possible that one person can set off Armageddon; and, perhaps, possible that one psychic may prevent it.

Further, to those who might laugh derisively at the concept of warrior-wizards and psychic soldiers, it is respectfully submitted that you look to your churches, your mosques, your synagogues—all age-old institutions built on concepts of the immaterial, which are so fantastic to a rational mind, that remote-viewing and telekinesis pale in comparison.

A man who supposedly rose from the dead two millennia ago gives rise to an institution that in the seventeenth century owned twenty percent of French real estate, and today controls the hearts, minds, and pockets of millions. An Arab nomad founded a faith that is practiced by scores of millions of believers, themselves controlling vast natural

resources of tremendous geopolitical import. A tiny religion which orig-
inated from a volcano spirit, that despite wholesale attempts at its extermination has given rise to some of the greatest scientific and cultural
achievements of man, and whose progeny have created the most effective intelligence organization in the world.

Are all of the above not more fantastic than the idea that the mind
of man may be extended beyond his normal five senses and used for
military and intelligence purposes? Do those who believe in God, yet
scoff at the psychic world, really doubt their own spiritual system, their
own foundations of faith?

These are the subliminal questions one may find one's self asking.
For in a survey of the psychic soldier, we penetrate another dimension,
and challenge conventional wisdom—as if Newton's apple had flown
upward beyond the tree from which it fell and into the ether—into a
pure realm of ideas and images without materiality.

The world stands at the eve of the millennium, witness to a century
where man increased his rate of travel a thousandfold. A century that,
in less than one lifetime, saw a barely airborne, flimsy cloth-and-wire
contraption turn into a vehicle that carried a man to the Moon. We
perform surgery with amplified light, send robots to skip on Martian
sands—and all this we marvel at and accept without reservation, comfortable in the knowledge that this is just man's updating of the lever,
the fulcrum, and the pulley. Merely Newtonian principles modernized.

Yet to cultures where magic is still king, where mythos is the foundation of government and society, these technical achievements become
incredible and wondrous. Our monk in Tibet accepts telepathy without
a second thought (telepathic or otherwise), yet the turning of a metal
faucet to bring forth an unlimited supply of clean water, or a metal
switch to make a glass vacuum ball glow brightly, would have seemed
like the greatest of magic fifty years ago.

Leave behind mechanistic bias, hard-headed support for the hard
sciences, and read what follows. Remember that tens of millions of
dollars were invested in programs dedicated to psychic espionage, and
major scientific research centers have devoted manpower and money
to the study and utilization of parascience. Be mindful that other cultures and other times viewed the paranormal as normal. Some still do.

Men have risked careers, reputations, and even lives in support of
psychic research as it applies to the military and intelligence structures
of our world. There were reasons. There just might be something to it.

It is predicted that the open-minded, after finishing this work, will more willingly consider the possibility of psychic spying and the paranormal abilities of man in general. They will see how the United States government in the early days of modern research, issued a classified report (in 1977) that acknowledged the potential for psychic spying. Yet they will also see that in 1995, for public and political consumption, that same government issued a carefully constructed pile of disinformation that completely misrepresented the real history and utility of modern psychic spying. Perhaps this was done from necessity.

Where there is disinformation, its opposite, truth, is being hidden. What hides, hides because of fear. Fear of discovery, fear of capture, fear of being misused. It is hoped that this work, in some small degree, will expose the truth, freeing it to be nurtured and protected by those who best know how. For the real truth of psychic spying, the revelation that our minds, our selves, are much more than we have been taught and told, will set mankind on the pathway of greater freedom and more rapid evolution. On the other hand, we just might kill each other off more quickly and cheaply.

The above may all sound as just so much science fiction. Taking our metaphor from that genre then, let us submit that Captain Kirk was wrong. It is not space, but mind, that is the final frontier. A frontier we will now explore. And perhaps, during that exploration, we might learn that while Captain Kirk was wrong, Darth Vader was right. The Force does exist—within us.

CHAPTER 2

THE GODS TOOK THEIR SEVERAL SIDES

The Psychic Soldier in Antiquity

Thus spoke Zeus and gave the word for war, whereon the Gods took their several sides and went into battle.
BOOK XX, THE ILIAD

In assessing the psychic battlefield of today, it is important to be familiar with its origins.

The interweaving of martial and magical prowess has been with us since the time man first deemed it in his interest to practice both arts. We shall take a look at this military-occult complex as it manifested in several ancient civilizations, selecting those that had perhaps the largest impact on modern Western society.

Ancient mythologies and religious scriptures had a tremendous material impact on the world of the past, and still manifest their influence on the three-dimensonal world at the dawn of the third millennium. The Vatican speaks, the world listens. The Muslim and the Jew exchange artillery rounds over contested borders, and there are worldwide speculations in the price of oil, of gold, and of strategic metals.

We shall first look to the world as it was in the time of the writings of the Old Testament. A universe where God and men had daily communication. A theater of operations where God was general, where He literally was the Lord of Hosts.

"The Lord is a Man of War, the Lord is His name." (Exod. 15:3)

Throughout the Old Testament, one reads of battle after battle. Miraculous victories of the Israelites against stronger tribes, crushing defeats caused by an angry Yahweh. This god is a jealous god and will lend or withdraw his almighty hand from the armies of his people as he pleases, and as they please or displease him.

Moses, in the story of the Exodus familiar to all, leads his people from the captivity of the Pharaoh. The Egyptians are drowned in the Red Sea, through which the Israelites have passed unharmed. The Lord had forewarned of this outcome in Exodus 14:18, when he revealed, "Then the Egyptians shall know that I am the Lord, when I have gained honor for Myself over Pharaoh, his chariots and his horsemen."

Yahweh commands and cajoles from his volcano. He tells his wandering people, as they move into the mountain territory of the Amorites, "Look, the Lord your God has set the land before you, go up and possess it, as the Lord God of your fathers has spoken to you; do not fear or be discouraged." (Deut. 1:21) "When you go out to battle against your enemies and see horses and chariots and people more numerous than you, do not be afraid of them, for the Lord God is with you . . ." (Deut. 20:1)

The Israelites, in their God-inspired victories, proved themselves a foe of unconscionable brutality and cruelty. Many were the times that the conquered were slaughtered down to the last living soul. "We took all his cities at that time, and we utterly destroyed the men, women and little ones of every city; we left none remaining." (Deut. 2:34)

As one looks at the actions of past armies enmeshed in the military-occult complex, and compares them with the various holocausts and genocides of the modern world, it becomes clear that where there is a Divine Cause—a holy war or jihad,—the primitive destructive urges of man are exalted. Murder is multiplied by mysticism. After all, it is the command of the Almighty.

"But thus shall you deal with them; you shall destroy their altars and break down their sacred pillars, and cut down their wooden images, and burn their carved images with fire." (Deut. 7:5) It appears that Yahweh does not tolerate the competition. He repeatedly demands destruction of the material evidences of other religions. "You shall utterly destroy all the places where nations which you shall dispossess served their gods, on the high mountains and on the hills, and under every green tree." (Deut. 12:2)

There are times in the Old Testament when God isn't satisfied with using his people to annihilate entire nations. There are times he likes to get directly into the act.

The Israelites have routed the Amorites, and they flee in retreat. "And it happened as they fled before Israel, and were on the descent of Beth Horon, that the Lord cast down large hailstones from heaven on them as far as Azekah and they died. There were more who died from the hailstones than the children of Israel killed with the sword." (Josh. 10:11)

The Israelite becomes a military superman when Yahweh is in a good mood. "One man of you shall chase a thousand, for the Lord your God is he who fights for you as he promised you." (Josh. 23:10) "This day I will begin to put the dread and fear of you upon the nations under the whole heaven who shall hear the report of you and shall tremble and be in anguish because of you." (Deut. 2:25)

We of course remember young David defeating the giant Goliath of the Philistines. "You come to me with a sword, with a spear and with a javelin, but I come to you in the name of the Lord of Hosts, the God of the armies of Israel whom you have defied," David tells Goliath in I Samuel 17:45.

This monumental piece of religious scripture, the Old Testament, was one of the pillars upon which the Church of Rome was built. And it was this Church that exercised such tremendous governmental and military power in Europe for many centuries. Thus, we have a document once thought by all to be an actual history of events, wherein the military man is led by his god to victory against those who outnumber him, and can outproduce him; a document that speaks of direct divine intervention in the martial affairs of man. A divine writing that promises him superhuman military prowess when God is on his side, and mandates wholesale slaughter on occasion.

This history, then, was a major wellspring from which poured the makings of what we have herein called the military-occult complex. When we read further in the Old Testament, we see a foreshadowing of the twentieth-century military-occult complex, which was to spend multiple millions of dollars using psychics for military spying.

Yahweh used them in his campaigns; God often employed intermediaries to communicate his wishes to the people of Israel.

But he was rather selective in the messenger he employed. "And to the person who turns to mediums and familiar spirits to prostitute himself with them, I will set my face against that person and cut him off from his people." (Lev. 20:6)

The penalty for being an out-of-favor psychic with Yahweh was death. "But that prophet or that dreamer of dreams shall be put to death because he has spoken in order to turn you away from the Lord your God." (Deut. 13:5) "There shall not be found among you anyone who makes his son or his daughter pass through the fire, or one who practices witchcraft, or a soothsayer, or one who interprets omens, or a sorcerer, or one who conjures spells or a medium or a spiritist, or one who calls up the dead." (Deut. 18:10, 11)

But the word of God wasn't always followed by the people of Israel. Saul was not happy when, during the Philistine War, he could not get the advice and counsel he needed from Yahweh. "I am deeply distressed, for the Philistines make war against me, and God has departed from me and does not answer me anymore, neither by prophets nor by dreams." (I Sam. 28:15) Thus, the famous employment of the witch of En Dor by Saul, who, via necromancy, raises the prophet Samuel to answer his inquiries.

Yahweh also launches an attack on rival prophets of rival gods. "For the nations which you will dispossess listened to soothsayers and diviners, but as for you, the Lord your God has not appointed such for you." (Deut. 18:14) "When a prophet speaks in the name of the Lord, if the thing does not happen or come to pass, that is the thing which the Lord has not spoken, the prophet has spoken it presumptuously, you shall not be afraid of him." (Deut. 18:22) "Therefore look! The Lord has put a lying spirit in the mouth of these prophets of yours, and the Lord has declared disaster against you." (II Chron. 18:22) "And as for the prophet and the priest and the people who say 'The oracle of the Lord' I will even punish that man and his house." (Jer. 23:24)

But, in Daniel, we learn that the officially authorized prophet, ". . . reveals deep and secret things; he knows what is in the darkness and light dwells with him." (Dan. 2:22)

We see contradictory points of view. On the one hand, Yahweh is casting stones at prophets, on the other, he is using selected ones to communicate his commands to his people. Is this what some might call a mystery of faith? Is this merely what occurs when various mythological documents are gathered together in a haphazard manner and made to appear a unified, divinely inspired single work? Partially, probably.

However, if with a skeptic's eye we analyze this Old Testament, this collection of military and mystical history, it becomes abundantly clear that there were great and lasting problems of belief with the Yahweh cult. How often do we read of his people burning incense to other gods in the high places? How often is his anger used to explain the military defeats of the Israelites?

It is the genius of those who compiled the Old Testament to assert that it was God—the only one, by the way—who was responsible for military victory or defeat of his followers. It was the officially sanctioned prophets of God who spoke the truth, who foretold events with accuracy. If they were wrong about the future, well, they just weren't God's employees, and one couldn't complain of God via the doctrine of *respondeat superior* (the legal doctrine that places blame on the boss for the errors and omissions of his underlings).

What better propaganda to prove the reality of Yahweh? When you won wars, it was because Yahweh was fighting alongside. When you lost wars, it was because Yahweh was angry with you for lusting after other gods. When a prophet was accurate about Israelite affairs, he was divinely inspired. When a prophet was wrong (which does on occasion happen in the prophet profession), well, he wasn't a member of God's Prophets, Seers and Soothsayers' Union.

The enemies of Israel used divination and prophecy also. "For the King of Babylon stands at the parting of the road, at the fork of the two roads, to use divination. He shakes the arrows, he consults the images, he looks at the liver." (Ezek. 21:21)

But as the Old Testament tell us, the prognostications of the enemies of Yahweh cannot possibly have any effect or use. We have but to read Yahweh's word on that and what he says is true so long as we stay with the reading of the Bible." (Deut. 18:14)

Before leaving the Israelites, we must examine one of the more "technological" methods of military-oriented divination used by the Hebrews—the breastplate, known as the *Umim-Ve-Thummim.*

In Numbers 27:21, we read of "... Eleazer, the priest who shall inquire for him (the querent) by the judgment of the Urim before the Lord, at this word shall they go out, and at his word they shall come in, both he, and all the children of Israel with him, even the congregation."

The method of divination appears to be the observation of the shining of certain precious stones that spell out the names of the twelve tribes of Israel. A positive or negative answer to the question posed is determined from the shining of the appropriate stones, spelling out the response of God. It was frequently used to determine the time of war, and the outcome of battle.

So it is written in the Talmud in Yoma 73b.

An interesting parallel to the *Umim-Ve-Thummim* method of prognostication occurs in the sixteenth-century divination methods of the English magician John Dee, whom we shall encounter later on. Dee and his associate Edward Kelly used a "shew stone" in which an angelic messenger pointed out certain letters on a magic tablet, spelling out a message from beyond.

Further, the mechanical method of the *Umim* is a forerunner of today's efforts at technological enhancement of psychic powers. The Soviets, who have never been great friends of anything Israeli, were in the forefront of melding the mechanical with the mystical in their science of Psychotronics.

But there are other mythologies, other scriptures, other Gods, and, therefore, other divine sides to the story of the origins and efficacies of the military-occult complex.

The Greeks Had a Word for It

Imagine a deep trench or cleft in the earth, from which wafts upward earth-cooled vapors. Over this yawning ditch, perched on a golden tripod seat, inhaling these fumes of ecstasy, sits the prophetess, who interprets the divine revelations of the god Apollo. This is the Oracle of Delphi. From here the advice and counsel of the sun god was sought and given. The remains of this site still exist, although major destruction was done to it in A.D. 398.[1]

Greek mythology and ancient Greek history are resplendent with governors and generals who consulted the oracles, the seers and the psychics of their time. At times, the advice is amazingly accurate. At other times the advice is disastrously inaccurate.

In Greece, around 480 B.C., the Persian prince Mardonius marched on Athens. The Spartans, ever anxious to do battle, rose to meet him. A third party, the Hellenes, sided with the Persians. Battle appeared imminent.

The soldiers were massed on opposite sides of the River Asopus. Many thousands of combat-experienced, heavily armed soldiers were at the ready to face each other, taunt each other, but did not attack, though they were martially and materially well able to engage the enemy.

The cause of the delay? They were waiting for the word from their seers.

Also present at this battle site of Plataea were three world-class psychics. Wealthy men, powerful men, names to conjure with, if you will.

Present was Hegesistratus, the seer for the Persian forces. He was remarkable for his ability, his cost, and his wooden foot, which replaced the one of flesh he had hacked off himself in order to escape fetters from a time when he was somewhat less popular. (Prophets rarely do well in their own land.)

The Greeks had Tisamenus, who had also competed admirably in the Olympic games. The Hellenes were represented by Hippomachus. This looked to be the heavyweight oracular championship of the ancient world.

Each of these skilled clairvoyants cautioned their respective armies to fight a defensive battle in order to gain victory. The armies listened to this advice for ten days. Outside of a minor skirmish, no swords clashed. But the Persian, Mardonius, grew impatient and attacked, ignoring the advice of the highly paid Hegesistratus.

Having ignored the advice of the seer, Mardonius dies in battle, with plenty of company from his fellow soldiers. In casualty reports of the time (which should be viewed with the same kind of skepticism one employs with casualty reports today), the Persians lost hundreds of thousands of men. The Spartans only lost ninety-one, and the Athenians, fifty-two.[2]

Assuming, for the sake of argument, that the figures have not been fudged, we may conclude from this example that one should listen to one's seer. However, other examples exist that can call this pronouncement into question.

It was 413 B.C. Athenian general Nicias sailed to Sicily to give military aid to the beseiged city of Segesta. His initial successes found him advancing on the city of Syracuse. He did not fare well, and his forces were decimated by the joint efforts of the wily Sicilians . . . and marsh fever. It became evident that retreat was the only solution.

Being a good Greek, Nicias consulted the seers he had on hand. Unfortunately, these were unseasoned replacements for his former highly experienced seer, Stilbides, who died. It was the 27th of August, and a lunar eclipse had occurred. Interested in the meaning of this omen, Nicias queried his psychics.

They advised postponing the retreat for one lunar cycle, or 28 days. Nicias followed their advice. He lost two armies, was himself executed and hanged on the gates of the city of Syracuse. (The fate of the amateur seers is not disclosed by history, although one need not be a seer to suppose that their careers were rather short.)[3]

In another incident involving an eclipse and a Greek general, somewhat later in history, the prognostication of the official seer proved true, and no military disaster occurred.[4]

Man is a creature that can remember his lessons well. The ancient diviners, of necessity, were the more intelligent of their fellows, and we may presume had excellent memories and learning capabilities. As they saw the penalty of an incorrect prognostication, both on the military and their own persons, they learned to couch their pronouncements in equivocal terms. This served as a means of preserving their continued position in society—and the continued presence of their respective heads upon their respective shoulders.

A masterpiece of revelatory equivocation occurred at the Oracle of Delphi in 279 B.C. The power that was Greece was in decline and Celtic hordes had attacked the Greeks. The prophetess of Apollo was consulted. From the fumes of the earth to the voice of the prophetess, the answer came. From the voice of the prophetess to the ears of the expectant Greeks, the answer was that Apollo "would send white maidens to aid the Greeks."

Now this prediction followed safe oracular tradition. It is quite vague, poetic, and capable of numerous interpretations—after the fact.

What did happen was a combination of blizzard and thunderstorm, which caused a huge rock slide. From the cover of the rocks, the Greek archers were able to fire upon the massed Celtic forces and defeat them. The Celts killed their wounded and retreated. Their leader, who was decidedly a poor loser, killed himself.[5]

Was the blizzard a snowstorm? Was the snow the white maidens sent by Apollo? Were the rocks that fell the white maidens?

Again, we deal with the fact that in ancient times and today as well, those who are, or those who pose as psychics and seers, are keen observers, both of their surroundings and their fellows. It takes no leap of faith to presume that the Oracle was well aware of climatic conditions and seasons in Greece. The white maidens might have been a meteorological metaphor that post facto appeared as a divinely inspired prediction. If the region had frequent landslides during the winter, again we have a basis for this prediction, with the white maidens being the falling stones.

Also interesting to note is the use of the phrase "to aid" the Greeks. This is not a prediction of victory, and had there been a defeat, the Oracle could have claimed accuracy nonetheless.

One guess is as good as another, but history chalks this oracular episode up as a success.

When in Rome

It was the first half of March, 44 B.C. Emperor Gaius Julius Caesar, in good ancient tradition, has consulted the haruspices. These were the offical entrail inspectors who prognosticated from the organs of sacrificed animals. A fat bull had been sacrificed for Caesar, and the haruspex examined the remains of the animal. He could not find the heart. He could, however, find the liver, and the condition of the liver, and the apparent absence of the heart, according to traditional interpretations, bore ill tidings. It was indicative of a loss of life.

Caesar, however, was not impressed, and carried on with his business as usual, until on the fifteenth of March, twenty-three daggers were plunged in his flesh, and with a coup de grâce from the sword of Brutus, Caesar was no more. Had he listened to his liver reader, would Caesar have reigned for years to come? Who can say? Spurina Vestricus, the official haruspex, would of course be in favor of obeying the signs of the entrails.[6]

As we have seen in the previous Bible references, heptamancy, inspection of the liver or other body organs, was a common ancient method of predicting the future, and the outcome of military and political events. To the ancient, it was apparent that organic structures, living things, while similar, were yet each distinct. Each liver, each animal (or human) part had its distinct signature. From this fact, they attempted to correlate present and future events with the condition of the anatomical features of the (formerly) living creatures.

In ancient Rome, it was mandatory to consult the official oracles and seers before the undertaking of any important governmental action.

There were the augurs, who interpreted omens. There were the afore-mentioned haruspices who told the future from entrails. The latter were often publicly appointed, with pension benefits to boot. Mostly, they were Etruscans, apparently masters of the art of liver-reading.[7]

As Christianity extended its influence in Rome, divinatory practices fell into official disfavor. In A.D. 319, legislation was passed against the haruspices, which mandated their burning should they cross the threshold of a citizen's house. The citizen who invited him was to be deported.[8]

In A.D. 398, the Temple of Apollo at Delphi was torn down.

The Christian hostility to divinatory practices sprung from its Old Testament origins. Further, the priests of Christendom may not have had the same skills as the pagan seers, and it is often a practical solution to outlaw practices that one is not capable of performing oneself.

Each successive dominant theology appears to need to deny the efficacy of the magical and religious practices of its predecessor. Yet each successor brings its own magic, its own belief system, whether it is couched in the language of mysticism or the mathematics of science.

Throughout the history of mankind, magic has perhaps fallen from favor, but it has never died. Man's searching for divine guidance and inspiration continues, whether he bows before an idol, or an ideology. Rome fell. The temples of its gods went to ruin. New magicians came forth.

Irish Eyes

The Druids gathered. Important questions were to be answered via divination. The means of determining the future? A human victim who was to be back-stabbed. From the movements of his death throes, the future was revealed to the forest magicians.

As it is the practice of modern armies to attempt to destroy the intelligence-gathering capabilities of their enemies, so was it the practice in ancient days. Where magic was the means of intelligence gathering, there the enemy soldier put his torch, swung his sword, wreaked his havoc.

In a Roman attack on a Druid enclave in A.D. 59, the soldiers cut down the sacred oak groves that surrounded the bloodstained altars upon which the sacrificial victims lay. The Celtic magicians, killed by the Romans, no longer ripped open bodies, thereupon to learn from the inner organs their military destiny. *Their* destiny had been determined by the blades of Rome.[9] Frazer, in his classic *The Golden Bough*, spoke often of the magical Law of Homeopathy. This was the doctrine that things that appear similar may affect each other, and that symbolic appearances and similarities might actually be useful in reality.

As the human head is the center for perception and analysis, the sine qua non for intelligence gathering and military strategy, the Celts often cut off the heads of their enemies and mounted them on poles, hung them about their horses' necks, or placed them on their village gates. It was believed that the head contained the spirit and power of the enemy.[10] Ergo, the current possessor of that head would have the same power. It was symbolic logic—of a sort.

It must be remembered that in many of its functions, the brain is an interpreter of symbols. It is a correlating mechanism, looking for patterns, associations, ever with an eye towards survival. Once this is realized, it is not so strange that primitive man might, in search of the hidden future of his tribe, seek the answer in the hidden organs of a man. It is not beyond credibility that, observing the head to be the director of a man's actions, a warrior would seek to possess this head as the situs of sense and cunning of his enemy. It was as if his classified document files had been captured.

But of course, we of the late twentieth century are beyond all of this primitive belief and symbolism, aren't we? Oh yes, our generals have stars on their shoulders, and we have rockets called Jupiter, or Thor, and space programs called Mercury and Apollo, but that's different. And some of our more enthusiastic infantry in Vietnam cut off the ears of the Viet Cong and kept them for trophies, but that is quite another thing from cutting off the heads of your enemies, no?

Have we traveled so far from the ancient ways in our modern wars, or is the military-occult complex still deeply entrenched in our martial societies, along with our fascination for high-tech tools of mass destruction?

Our Druid friends were devoted students. They studied for decades, learning the oral traditions of their societies, their magic, their astrology. In Gaul Caesar, observed many Druid seminaries.[11] These Druids supposedly had the power to render themselves invisible, to cause death via magic spells, and to produce an enchanted sleep.[12] It was an ancient attempt at using what today would be called nonlethal and stealth technologies.

The Druids were the psychic soldiers of their day, often accompanying an army to give aid—via their magical powers—in the destruction of the enemy. Their seers had marched along with the troops in the aforementioned invasion of the Greeks, yet were bested by the Oracle at Delphi.[13]

The psychic exploits of the ancients with respect to their military endeavors are found in scraps, segments of rotting documents and weathered stones. There is not much left of the tales to be told. However, we do have information on their techniques of psychic spying, which may be examined.

The Methods in the Madness

There was divination by dream interpretation—witness Joseph in his many-colored coat, rising to stardom in Egypt. There was divination via necromancy, as performed by Saul via the witch of En Dor, in the raising of the ghost of Samuel to learn of Philistine military intentions.[14]

In Rome during the time of Caesar, there were the sixteen augurs, who in their appointments-for-life would interpret the signs originating from the gods. The movement of birds, the flashes of lightning, were the sky-written messages of the gods to the college of augurs in Rome. Our augur would pitch his tent upon a high hill, and with covered head, ask the gods for a sign. From those flights of birds or from the lightning flashes, advice would come forth. Transmitted by the augur, it would determine the election of Roman magistrates, the times of the movements of armies, and the passing of Roman laws.[15]

Hydromancy,—divination by water,—was used throughout the ancient world, and is similar in practice to crystallomancy, the peering into a crystal ball or other shiny surface.[16]

It has been often determined (whether accurately or not) that hypnotism can bring out extrasensory perception. One of the common methods of inducing hypnotism is eye-fixation or steadily gazing at an object. What happens is that the conscious mind is distracted by this rather boring activity, and the subconscious, which is the seat, as we are told, of the psychic powers of man, has the opportunity to work its magic.

Hypnotism would later be explored by the CIA as an espionage tool, and as a means of conditioning couriers carrying secret documents not to reveal their secrets if caught.

Mice were employed by the ancients to tell the future, in an art called myomancy. The cries of the mice, or the objects that they chomped upon, were indicative of what was to be. Now these mice could roar (at least metaphorically) because we are told that their prognosticatory antics caused the commander of the Roman cavalry, Cassius Flaminus, to resign.[17]

Diverse magical methods with one purpose—intelligence gathering. The ancients had the same lust for victory, the same territorial ambitions that we see evidenced in the world today. What they lacked was the sophisticated technology of a scientifically advanced culture.

What they lacked in science, they made up for in the supernatural, seeking guidance for their military and political dillemmas, seeking what is now, and what was then, the most fleeting, the most valuable commodity in the world—information.

CHAPTER 3

FIGHTING SPIRITS

Astral Advisors to Ancient Armies

In the beginning was the Word, the New Testament tells us. The Old Testament informs us about one of Adam's first actions: naming things. This ancient reverence for the importance of words and names lent its power to the magical world—to the spells used to evoke information-bearing spirits, and the books of magic that instructed mortal man to see beyond the bounds of his mortal senses—often for military and political purposes.

We explore the materials, methods and manuals that were used to contact, or draw power from the fighting spirits of the world beyond. The techniques of occult warfare, the stones of protection, the means of invoking prophetic dreams and the high-ranking phantoms of the military ether shall be explored.

In this exploration, our hands shall lay hold to the studded leather covers of medieval grimoires, or spell-books. Turning the key in the brazen locks and poring over the printed parchments therein reveals dark secrets from these olden tomes of magic, secrets of the realm of psychics and soldiers—a realm that still vibrates today.

Journey back to the deserts of the Black Land, the land of old Khem: Egypt. Great pyramids touch the sky, and processions of shaven-headed priests march to pay homage to Ra, the sun god, to Isis the mother goddess, and their son, Osiris risen. The pharaoh sits in splendor on his throne, holding the crook and flail that symbolize his authority. In a temple chamber, by the flickering oil lamps, the official magicians of Egypt read from the scrolls of Thoth, the Egyptian god of writing and magic. His is the power transcendent over the kingdoms of north and south. His is the knowledge of the world beyond the living, for he is the sorcerer-scribe of the gods.

Our magician, so we are told by the famous Egyptologist, E. A. Wallis Budge, served as messenger and majordomo of the gods. Budge says, "The powers of nature acknowledged his might, and wind and rain, storm and tempest, river and sea and disease and death worked evil and ruin upon his foes, and upon the enemies of those who were provided with the knowledge of the words which he wrested from the gods of heaven and earth and the underworld."[1]

These magical words of power (or *hekau*) were dangerous weapons in the hands of Egypt sorcerers. Budge, in his classic work, *Egyptian Magic*, tells us, "There were many instances on record of Egyptian magicians utterly destroying their enemies by the recital of words possessed of magical power and by performance of some apparently simple ceremony."[2]

There is no doubt that words have tremendous effect on people. Witness today's large propaganda machines—advertising agencies and controlled media worldwide—which all deal with words and images to shape society, and to influence the opinions of those who matter in that society. How much more powerful were words in ancient days, when only the elite could read and write, and there was less of a demarcation between the symbol and the actual thing symbolized.

It is understandable how the Egyptians might believe that the *hekau*, could work magical wonders. Oratory throughout history has driven men to the Crusades, the trenches, the front. Much of magical invocation and evocation is oratorical. The poet, the speaker with charismatic presence, and the skilled actor make for the effective magician; as often do the effective politician and general. The right words can help to establish a ruler, or they may contribute to his downfall.

The coup d'état is not a recent invention. It is as old as man's first organized attempts at controlling the lives and territorial imperatives of his fellow man. The coup was old when Egypt was new. Magic has at times been used to further the attempted overthrow of a ruler; so it was in Egypt.

In Egypt in 1200 B.C. ruled Rameses III, a king, a god; but his reign was not untroubled. A conspiracy was afoot to remove him from the throne, to terminate him with extreme prejudice. The method of assassination was to be magical.

The royal overseer of the royal cattle was a gentleman by the name of Hui. Of course, he was literate, which placed him in the higher strata of Egyptian power. It enabled him not only to account for the numbers of royal cattle, but to understand the dark secrets of Egyptian magic. Those who would overthrow their master must, of necessity, be circumspect in their actions. Secrecy is not only desired, it is of the utmost importance, and there is no method for revolution more secret than the magical. Hui, aware of these political realities, stole into the royal library and, from the vast number of scrolls, selected a work of magic formulae containing the spells necessary to drive terror into the heart of a man and to rob him of his senses.

This was the means by which Rameses III would be defeated, at least according to the intentions of the traitor, Hui.

The ancient spells were performed, the words of power recited by Hui and his conspirators. They magically targeted Rameses III, confident in the power of the magic of the gods. A death resulted, from suicide. A man was driven to terror, robbed of his senses, as promised by the dark writ of the Egyptian spell book.

Had the magic been successful? Had Rameses III been driven from his senses and taken his own life? Well, not quite. Actually, Rameses III learned of the plot—and the conspirators were caught. Hui was ordered to commit suicide. He did.[3]

Now, from a magical point of view, the above may serve as an example that magic *does* work, but it rebounded against the caster of the evil spell. This rebound experience is common among the writers of magical literature. Hui attempted evil sendings, and evil sendings were his undoing.

From a skeptical point of view, the nursery-school morality of the rebound theory may be dispensed with. Power, if it exists, is without morality. Electricity can run a respirator as well as it can electrocute a man. Radiation can shrink a cancerous tumor or fry a city of people. The power exists independently of any morality. Magic, if it works, should likewise be free of moral biases.

But, even given that independence from morality, if we view magic as a de facto force of the natural or supernatural world, it is necessary to subject this force to controls and containment. A biological or chemical weapon out of control can kill the army that used it as well as the army targeted. "Friendly fire" has killed more than its share of soldiers.

Perhaps the magical rites of Hui worked; but, lacking the proper containment, the rites went wrong. From a more skeptical viewpoint, one would look at the Hui incident as the actions of a superstitious fool defeated by superior and mundane tactical intelligence.

Moving forward in ancient time, we encounter another example of magic at work in military affairs.

It was 670 B.C. and the Egyptian King Nut-Amen had a dream. It must be remembered that dreams were viewed as omens, as messages from the gods in a society and culture that had no concept of the subconscious. The dreams of the ruler of the land were of utmost importance, and there was a necessity to have them accurately interpreted.

Nut-Amen dreamed of two serpents. He held one in each hand. Anxious to learn the meaning of his dream, Nut-Amen consulted the royal interpreter of dreams.

"The land of the South is thine, and thou shalt have dominion over the North," said the interpreter of dreams. "The god Amen, the only god, shall be with thee."[4]

Nut-Amen's then-current military campaign proved successful; a significant portion of his war-spoils were dedicated to the service of the god Amen. Magic via prophetic dream had worked. Or had it?

In the previous chapter, it was noted how, in the Old Testament, the Israelites explain their military victories and defeats as by-products of the moods of Yahweh. Of course there is the likelihood that these interpretations were written subsequent to the actual history of the wars.

Now the Egyptians were around a long time before the Israelites became the stars of the desert, and it is also likely, from the skeptic's point of view, that this Nut-Amen dream was carefully manufactured after the fact of his successful military campaign.

From the point of view of the non-skeptic, and from the more modern New Age viewpoint, we might opine that, while Nut-Amen was in a light sleeping state, he was open to messages from the collective unconscious, which symbolically communicated his victory to him in advance of the fact. Unfortunately, as history at the time was solely under the control and direction of the ruler, we will never learn whether the accuracy of the dream was from prognostication or political propaganda.

Let us look at another example of Egyptian wizardry at work in the realm of the psychic soldier. The last native king of Egypt ruled in 358 B.C. Nectanebus reigned, not only as secular lord of Egypt, but as a skilled magician as well. He used the black arts to defeat the enemies of his kingdom.

Foreign armies marched on the land of Khem in an invasion involving naval forces. Nectanebus retired to his ritual chamber and, robed in his wizard's cloak, holding his magic wand, waged a parallel war in the astral world. He had wax figures in a water-filled basin—figures that were the magical proxies of the armies of Egypt and the armies of her foes.

Records from the time indicate that the gods of Egypt animated these figures, and in the basin—in the magical microcosm of the battlefield—the Egyptians were triumphant. Of course, this magic was reflected in the material world, and Egypt remained free of the foreign invaders.

However, the black arts faded a little when a massive alliance of the armies of the east moved against Egypt. Once again, Nectanebus played with his magic toy soldiers in his water basin. But this time, the gods of Egypt let the enemy wax figures win. Armed with this intelligence, Nectanebus, who was no fool, disguised himself as a commoner and made his way to Macedonia to earn his bread as a healer and prophet.[5]

Perhaps actual history. Perhaps after-the-fact politico-psychic propaganda. It must be remembered, however, that the realpolitik level of sophistication of the average Egyptian was at a point that, if he heard these tales, he would believe them to be true. Given his status, if he believed otherwise and did not wish to find out quickly whether the afterlife was real or not, he would keep his mouth shut in any event.

Dream interpretation necessitated a sensitivity to symbolism in the interpreter. Experience in correct dream-reality translation was also a requirement. Over time, a skilled dream interpreter would be able to correlate dream symbols with succeeding actual events, and perhaps be able to make some rudimentary statistical analyses of the symbols that would serve as working aids.

In the modern research that went into remote viewing—the modern psychic spying method of the twentieth century—a similar symbolic analysis and statistical gathering and correlation was performed to make more accurate the predictions and perceptions of the seer. While the modern and ancient methods differed, they were guided by the same necessary principles.

From a papyrus catalogued as number 122 in the British Museum, a method is described for procuring prophetic dreams. "To procure dreams: Take a clean linen bag, and write upon it the names given below. Fold it up and make it into a lamp wick and set it alight, pouring pure oil over it. The words to be written are these: *Arimath, Lailam-chouch, Areseonphrephren, Phtha, Archentechtha.*"⁶

The priestesses of Baal, in ancient Babylon, would lay on beds with sheets of ram-skins to obtain dreams. The ancient Hebrews would sleep near the tombs of their ancient dead.⁷

In Mexico, the *teotecuhili*—official dream interpreters of the Aztecs—used drugs, sleep deprivation, fixing the mind on one subject, tobacco, *maguey*, and coca to obtain prophetic dreams. "They also held that the soul traveled through space and was able to visit those places of which it desired knowledge."⁸

In modern times various intelligence agencies experimented with the use of drugs and the effects they had on the mind. For example, sleep deprivation is an old technique for obtaining visions, and of course, modern sleep studies indicate that insufficient sleep can bring on a whole range of mental abnormalities.

Fixing the mind on one subject, which is another way to describe meditation, is a mainstay of various eastern mystical systems. Ergo, the techniques used by the *teotecuhili* make sense as far as the mind effects they might create. But whether or not these mind effects included the ability to accurately prognosticate in the dream state is another thing altogether.

The concept of soul traveling for informational purposes is an ancient parallel of the modern-day remote-viewing experiments financed by various intelligence and military agencies.

Besides dreams, wax figures and words of powers, the ancients (and many moderns too) were guided by the stars: by the official astrologers who interpreted the celestial messages.

Remember that the mind is a pattern-making device, among its other functions. Ancient man observed that the heavenly bodies had direct effects on his world. The moon controlled the tides of the world's seas; the sun, by its prolonged presence, could mean death to man's crops, and therefore man. Navigators found their way upon the ancient seas by using the stars.

Given his pattern-making function, given his heavy use of and dependence upon symbolism, it is no surprise that ancient man believed that the stars and planets ruled more than tide and growth. He believed the stars ruled his every action. Thus evolved the pseudoscience of astrology.

As this "science" required complicated mathematical computations, those who practiced astrology would of necessity be the more intelligent and more highly educated members of society. As education was primarily had within the province of the priesthood, we can see how astrology could gain such a strong foothold in the ancient cultures that were, without exception, theocracies: theocratic governments in partnership with their military.

As our modern skeptical viewpoint emerges, we ask the questions, "If all of this magic worked, why is it that Babylon no longer exists? Why did Egypt lose a war in six days to the Israeli Army in 1967? Why is it that the artifacts of these magically powerful ancient lands are distributed all over the world in foreign museums?" Our magical point of view might answer, "Well, magic is a subtle force. It is an aid, a catalyst, and not a prime mover of men and events."

The viewpoint in the middle might be neither hostile nor apologetic. Primitive man and his primitive mind sought to control and/or predict external events via processes that could be controlled internally. The microcosm of his mind reflected (supposedly) and affected the macrocosm of the real world. Ergo, the symbolic manipulation of wax soldiers could bring about real-world effects with real armies. The symbols obtained in dreams, or the equivocal pronouncements from oracles, could be heaven-sent messages about what was to happen in three dimensions.

But as internal processes in the minds of men are subject to many variations, many electro-chemical and biological factors, the microcosmic manipulations and prognostications were likewise subject to inaccuracies. Because a system is not perfect, or easily replicable vis-à-vis results, this does not mean that the system is without some value. The official report on the modern seers of the intelligence agencies acknowledges that something is there, but the something isn't accurate enough to warrant continued funding.

When the Roman army buried two Greeks alive at the aftermath of the battle of Cannae (to insure good fortune), we may assume they were sincere in their belief.[9] But from the point of view of the two Greeks, one would expect some skepticism. Whether we choose to believe the stories of the ancient psychic soldiers or scoff at them, it is important to realize that these attempts at magic, or at least the records of these attempts, did exist, and thus influenced the minds of men beyond the times of their occurrences.

Some additional examples are available from our Roman friends, concerning their communications with fighting spirits. The priests of Bellona (the lady goddess who accompanied Mars on the battlefields), in their rituals, would slice their shoulders and sprinkle the resulting blood upon images of Jupiter, to gain his favor in worldly affairs.[10]

Mars, the Roman god of war, was not an easy spirit to shop for. Following the great chariot races, the right-hand horse from the winning team would be sacrificed to Mars (thereby enabling Roman seers to accurately predict the horse's chances at future victories in the races) and the bloody tail given to the ruler.[11]

Besides blood and horses, the gods loved a good show. In Rome, there were colleges of religious dancers, whose spectacular performances were (supposedly) pleasing to the Gods, and useful in currying their favor.[12] But it wasn't spectacles alone that served as a line to the Gods. Stones played a large rôle in the realm of the psychic soldier.

Among the stones of martial and magical use, there was *cactomite*, which made the wearer victorious in battle.[13] *Calundronius*, a truly magical stone (being without form or color) gave advantage over enemies to its wearer.[14] Red coral had the rather handy attribute of stopping bleeding instantly.[15] The diamond (besides being a girl's best friend), when worn on the left arm of a soldier, brought victory.[16] *Draconite,* a shiny black stone, gave its possessor invincible courage.[17] *Garatronicus*, a red-colored stone, made the possessor invincible in battle.[18] Lignite, a glasslike stone, enhanced clairvoyant ability.[19] Lodestone had similar properties.[20] *Mephis* was a stone that, when powdered and mixed with water, caused insensibility to torture.[21] These were just some of the pebbles of power in the rock collection of the psychic soldier. Stones, of course, would be a logical material for making amulets and talismans of protection.

They were portable, durable, and capable of being cut, carved, marked, and stamped. After all, soldiers in ancient times were also portable, durable, and (unfortunately for them) capable of being cut, carved, marked, and stamped in battle. But it took more than stones to make the complete psychic soldier. It took tomes, too.

As the modern military has its field manuals of instruction to impart the arcane wisdom necessary to aim artillery pieces and write performance reports, the military and the magicians of elder times had their own manuals of magic, which enabled them to contact the fighting spirits of the invisible world for assistance. In ancient Babylon, magical writings such as the *Maklu* dealt with the use of magical burning. The *Utokki Limnoti* was a catalog of ancient Babylonian evil spirits, and the *Nis Kati* was a treatise on the powers of gesture magic.[22]

As with scriptures, so is it with books on sorcery. The authorship is either not specified, or is anachronistic and often imaginary. Mostly, these books would be collections of the superstitions and gods of the contemporary users, mixed in and mixed up with gods of the past who had become demonized, and languages of the past that had become bastardized.

Since the only means of reproducing books at the time was by hand copying, and adding to that the fact that the copyist often had no depth of knowledge about the subject (and often the language) that he copied, the spell-books of old are as much a compendium of historical and linguistic errors as they are a collection of effective magical recipes. From the spell-books of ancient Greece, one learned how to commune with the goddess of death and destruction, Hecate. One sacrificed—at the crossing of three roads—a dog, a black lamb, and some honey.[23]

Moving to the great epoch of the grimoires, or magical mystery tour guides, we arrive in the late Middle Ages. In our hands is the rare and valuable *Archidoxes of Magic*, a work by Paracelsus, who was also known by the rather laborious name of Theophrastus Bombastus Von Hoenheim. Physician, sorcerer and chemist, Paracelsus was a genius, although a credulous one. In the crumbling pages therein, the value of imagination for the soldier is revealed.

"Wherefore it becometh him that desireth to be an old soldier or to gain knighthood, or any honor in war, to fix and fasten his minde and imagination firmly upon some excellent stout head and leader of an army . . . and by doing so, if he knows how to use this imagination well, and be of a firm and constant minde, and as if he would attain to and accomplish all the heroic noble acts of such a man, he shall not onely attain to be an old souldier, but shall accomplish his desires in attaining to the like honors."[24]

This advice, in more modern form, is ubiquitous in the self-help books of today. Creative visualization, neuro-linguistic programming, anything by Peale, Hill or Robbins echoes the advice of Paracelsus, and not just for those who wish to be an "old souldier."

In the 1980s, the military of the United States took a page from Paracelsus's book with its human performance enhancement experimentation, code-named Project Jedi. (Which involved the enhancement of pistol shooting skills by mental imagery.) The image-making capability of the mind can perform wonders. There have been reports of hypnotically accelerated healing, the effect of mental stress on biological systems, and in the success stories of our athletes, actors, and acquisitive business types; and we are often told of the powers of mental rehearsal. These same skills are used in military training and operations. We hear of airborne units named Screaming Eagles, and operations like Phoenix.

In another of the famous grimoires, the *Sworn Book of Honorius*, we learn the names of the Angels of Mars, the plenipotentiaries of the God of War: *Satyhel, Ylurahyhel,* and *Amabyhel.* "Their nature is to cause war, murder and destruction, and the death both of people and all earthly things. Their bodies are of a mean stature, dry and lean and colored red. Their region is in the South."[25] Red, of course, is the traditional martial color, for its obvious association with blood. The dry and lean nature of the bodies is a visual parallel with the dry and lean nature of the traditional image of death. It must be remembered that Honorius didn't just name names in the ether, he gave specific instructions on the tools and the times necessary to contact, communicate, and command these entities. One of the tools was suffumigation, or censing. The proper recipe in *Honorius* to make the incense necessary to commune with martial spirits requires red, white and black sandalwood, "and all sweet woods such as lygnum aloes, cypress, balsam . . ."[26]

To contact the spirit of Mars, we must cook up a magic stew of "euphorbium bedelium, gum ammoniac, roots of both hellebore, myrrh, powdered lodestone, and a little sulphur, mix with human blood, the blood of a black cat, and the brain of a raven."[27]

Now the skeptic might opine that the foregoing recipe is rather bird-brained in concept and contents, but a somewhat more neutral observer, in analyzing the above, may see items that actually make sense in the real world. It must be remembered that, in medieval times, there was knowledge of the powers of certain herbs; not just the magical powers, but the medicinal ones as well. We must further take notice that the world of the Middle Ages was heavily symbolic—and symbols are the lingua franca for the world of magic.

Hellebore, besides being useful to wage war against caterpillars and lice, (in its American White variety), contains *helleborein*, which our chemist friends refer to as $C_{37}H_{56}O_{18}$, and is a heart stimulant. Gum ammoniac was used to treat bronchitis; myrrh was an ingredient in incense. Sulphur, of course, is a constituent of gunpowder, and blood is obviously symbolic in a martial stew. The raven is a carrion feeder, and wars produce plenty of carrion. Thus, there is sense in all of this symbolism.

A close analysis of some of the ingredients and instructions of medieval grimoires brings to light some items that might have a logical reason for being included. It is not surprising that, limited in scientific knowledge and filled with religious dogma, the people of the ancient world and Middle Ages would mix practical knowledge (herbal medicine, limited chemistry) with the other worldly knowledge in which they had been instructed practically from birth.

These martial spirits also had the power to raise armies. The southern demons of *Honorius* could raise a thousand soldiers.[28] In other works, different spirits could raise even more soldiers. Thus, not only could the psychic realm inspire soldiers, forewarn them, protect them, but—according to the grimoires—could actually supply them with more soldiers.

In another famous grimoire, *The Fourth Book of Occult Philosophy*, supposedly (albeit doubtfully) written by Henry Cornelius Agrippa, is another description of the appearance of the fighting spirits of the magic world. "They appear in a tall body, cholerick, a filthy countenance, of colour brown, swarthy, or red, having horns like hart's horns, and griphin's claws, bellowing like wild bulls. Their motion is like fire burning, their signe thunder and lightning about the [magic] circle."[29]

Again, let us analyze this in a tolerant light. Once again there are beings colored red, for the obvious blood symbolism; and the horns and claws are excellent symbols for martial spirits, as flesh is torn and ripped in battle. The bellowing was common to the psychological warfare of primitive armies, and in an age like the Middle Ages, where gunpowder-based weapons were in use, the symbolism of the thunder and lightning is obvious.

Agrippa tells us these martial spirits can appear as an armed king riding upon a wolf, an armed man, a woman holding a buckler on her thigh, a he-goat, a horse, a stag, a red garment, wool, a cheeslip.[30] These appearances make sense also, for the most part. Agrippa, like any good author of a grimoire, not only tells us the players, but gives us their magical "phone numbers" by providing the ritual means of calling them. In order to receive oracles from those spooks that can assist the planners of military campaigns, Agrippa says: "Let the man that is to receive any oracle from the good spirits be chaste, pure and confess'd. Let him begin to walk about in a circuit within the said circle from the East to the West until he is wearied with a dizziness of the brain."[31] First, we pare away the part about "chaste, pure and confess'd" as being mere surplusage by Agrippa to help him avoid being excommunicated, executed, and burned on the Inquisition's stakes.

But in the meat of these instructions is an old and effective means of achieving an alternate brain state. Circumambulation to the point of exhaustion is an old shamanic technique to achieve visions. The whirling dervishes of the mysterious east weren't just jitterbugging to the latest song by Abdul and the Camel Drivers. They were moving in intentional ways to affect brain chemistry—although maybe they weren't aware of the technical details behind what they were doing. This alternate state was conducive to visions and messages from beyond.

Thus, someone following Agrippa's oracle recipe may indeed achieve a state of mind where visions occur and messages are received whether they are generated due to changes in brain chemistry or sent from some spirit in the ether. In reviewing the training methods of the modern psychic soldiers of the last part of the twentieth century, we learn how important these alternate brain states are to enhance the perception of psychically obtained intelligence data. Apparently, extraordinary perceptive methods require extraordinary mental states.

Peter de Abano is the author of the *Heptameron*, yet another medieval grimoire. His martial spirits can raise double the soldiers of the *Sworn Book of Honorius*, providing the armchair general-sorcerer with two thousand soldiers![32] In *The Arbatel of Magic*, we learn therein the "third lesser secret," which should be learned by every aspiring psychic-soldier. This secret is ". . . to excel in military affairs and happily to achieve great things and to be head of the head of kings and princes."[33]

Now, one who is even mildly observant in the world of corporations and countries would think that the third lesser secret would actually be the prime mover in human affairs. It would appear to be the number-one secret devoutly to be wished. What, therefore, are the first and second lesser secrets? What, for that matter, are the great secrets of the *Arbatel*? Well, this author shall not reveal them here. However, as a compensation to the reader, I will supply the wisdom of the 49th aphorism in the *Arbatel*: "Courteous reader apply thy eyes and minde to the sacred and profane histories, and to those things which thou seest daily to be done in the world and thou shalt finde all things full of magick."[34]

Enter Remote Viewing

One of the major areas of endeavor of the modern psychic soldier sponsored initially by the CIA, is "remote viewing." This is the pseudo-technical term for what has for ages been called clairvoyance. The old grimoires gave the historic psychic soldier various techniques to accomplish clairvoyance. In the magical manual entitled *The Six and Seventh Books of Moses*, we are told, "Contempt of the world, and pride in his own worthiness and knowledge characterize the magical seer."[35]

In the book *The Enochian Invocation of Dr. John Dee*, author Geoffrey James tells us, "One standard test for the presence of the supernatural is precognition of future events."[36] (Of course precognition would have to be related to future events, wouldn't it?) Combining the messages in these two quotes gives us a pretty good picture of the garden-variety psychic in today's media and today's military. The world of the supernatural, as it manifests in the world of man, creates incredibly large egos, incredibly inflated claims, and bitch fights between the real psychics and the pretenders.

It was no different "back when." Dee was a mathematician, astronomer, astrologer, secret agent, and seer to Elizabeth I. He claimed, with his cohort, Edward Kelly, to be in touch with angels who communicated secrets of the psychic world via a "shew stone." (In effect, crystal gazing.) The angel supposedly pointed to letters arrayed on a table, and after reversing the letters, messages were transmitted in the magical Enochian language. Some of these messages, according to James, were precognitive, and related to military and political events. This "took place at least twice during the Dee-Kelly workings, the spirits predicted the Spanish Armada and the execution of Mary, Queen of Scots, well before these events could have been known." Dee was deeply concerned with matters of state security . . . and possessed an extensive knowledge of coding and decoding messages."[37] Therefore, Dee could be termed the first director of the CIA—the Celestial Intelligence Agency.

Was this just an after-the-fact bit of psychic propaganda? Perhaps, but the later in history, usually the better the record keeping (especially before the invention of the shredder). The more we learn of psychically obtained military and political intelligence as it occurs later in time, the more possible, if not probable is that there is some grain of truth to the event.

We see simple technologies being used towards the same goals as our modern military psychics shared. The stone, the crystal, the magic spell, all used to gain insight and foresight into developing military and political events. Without a knowledge of brain function and chemistry, the old-time seers did the best they could to "scry into the aether" and learn what was to be. They were the early pioneers of the final frontier, which is mind.

Beyond the techniques of psychic contact, the manuals of magic, and the rituals performed for victory or intelligence, there was another important historical building block in the formation of the military-occult complex. It was the real actions of real people. Gilles de Laval, aka Gilles de Rais aka Bluebeard, was a marshal of France in the fifteenth century. He served under the famous Jeanne d'Arc. Besides his early loyal service to king and cross, Gilles endeavored to find the Philosopher's Stone, and not only spent a large fortune in the fruitless search therefor, but managed to murder hundreds of the local peasantry for fun and profit.[38] A military leader, an alchemist, a man who tried to raise the devil. A living fifteenth-century embodiment of the psychic soldier. His fearless leader, Jeanne d'Arc, was another hero who saw visions, was accused of sorcery, and burned at the stake. This, after she had led a 6,000-man army against the English. Her dying word was "Jesus."[39] Jeanne d'Arc was also reported to have a clairvoyant vision of a sword in the church at Fierbois, "seeing" it hidden behind an altar.[40] One observer of the psychic scene has said: "May not her mission and her doings have been the outcome of merely subjective hallucinations . . . ?" The army, being ignorant and superstitious, would readily believe in the supernatural nature of her mission; great energy and valor would result—for a man fights well when he feels that Providence is on his side."[41]

Of course this burned-at-the-stake unpleasantness might not have occurred had Jeanne been carrying the Sixth Pentacle of Mars, a great talisman described in *The Greater Key of Solomon*. This grimoire describes the use of the pentacle: "It hath so great a virtue that being armed therewith if thou art attacked by anyone thou shalt neither be injured nor wounded."[42] This is what the Sixth Pentacle of Mars looks like: "Around the eight parts of the radii of the pentacle are the words Elohim qeber' elohim hath covered or protected, written in the secret alphabet of malachim, or the writing of the angels."[43]

Perhaps Jeanne should have carried the Tabula Martis or the Table of Mars. This is a five-by-five square containing 25 Hebrew letters. Hebrew letters, like Roman letters and Greek letters, have numerical equivalents. The 25 Hebrew letters of the Table of Mars total 65 in any direction. We are told in *A Treatise on Angel Magic*, edited by Adam Mclean, "This table engraven on an iron lamen or sword makes him that bears it valiant in war and terrible to his adversaries and shall conquer his enemies."[44]

Thus Jeanne d'Arc's cross proved an insufficient talisman with respect to her victory and protection. Of course, had she been caught with the aforesaid pentacle or table, her own side would have burned her at the stake, so what is a poor psychic-soldier girl to do? Who did one contact in the days of the grimoires, when good old Jesus just wouldn't serve to protect your martial interests and exploits? There was Forcalor, a great duke "who comes forth as a man with wings like a griffin. He killeth men and drowneth them in the waters and overturneth ships of war. He hath three legions."[45]

Gamigin was a great marquis and is seen in the form of a little horse "who bringeth to pass that the souls which are drowned in the sea shall take airy bodies and evidently appear and answer to interrogations at the magician's commandment. He hath many legions."[46] Now the creative magician could use these two spooks in tandem for intelligence gathering. First you use Forcalor to kill your enemy's naval forces, and then use Gamigin to call them up with questions. Whether this dynamic duo was ever used in this fashion is unrecorded. Marchosias was another great marquis who "showeth himself in the shape of a cruel she-

wolf with griffin's wings and a serpent's tail. When he is a man's shape
he is an excellent fighter, answereth all questions truly, and has thirty
legions."[47]

Leraje was a marquis who appeared as an archer clad in green,
carrying a bow and quiver. "He causeth all great battles and contests,
and has thirty legions."[48] Eligos was a duke who appeared as a knight
carrying an ensign and a serpent. "He knows of wars and how soldiers
shall meet. He commands sixty legions."[49] Malthus was an earl who
appears in the unlikely guise of a dove. "He builds up towers and
furnishes them with ammunition and weapons."[50] Vepar was a duke
"who appeared as a mermaid. He guided ships of war."[51] Sasnock was
a marquis who "appeared as an armed soldier with a lion's head, riding
a pale horse. He was a castle builder and an armourer."[52] (Obviously
a competitor with Vepar.)

In trying to make sense of the array of ancient technologies used to
contact and control the fighting spirits of the magical plane, the fact
that such magical experiments occurred and were performed in good
faith, at least by some, is indisputable. We can accept that certain rituals
and rites were performed, and certain events occurred thereafter. What
we need not accept, and what we cannot accept without the kind of
proof that does not exist, is that the performance of the ritual was the
reason behind the outcome of the subsequent event. We are lacking,
as we lawyers say, proximate cause. We need proof of a causative relationship between the method and the result.

I am at the same time a lawyer, a skeptic, and a Fellow of the
American Society of Psychical Research; I can make the argument that
proximate cause is irrelevant to the world of magic. It is the old saw
that "he who has the *how* is careless of the *why*." If, in a certain number
of rituals, a certain amount of sought-after results occurred, at some
point there exists a statistically significant relationship. Our ancient and
medieval friends didn't know statistics from fiddlesticks, but our modern military mystics do understand, and use statistics to analyze the
abilities of psychic soldiers, as we shall later see. Thus, if there is a
significant correlation between ritual and result, we may begin to infer
proximate causation, even if we haven't the faintest idea how that causative relationship could logically exist. To proffer the opinion that all
of this ancient and medieval mumbo-jumbo was merely psychological
warfare, disinformation, or a manipulative technique to be used upon

the ignorant armies of the time, is perhaps to credit the generals of old with a level of sophistication they probably did not have.

Given the fact that the monopoly on learning and knowledge was with the politicians and priests of early days, and that learning and knowledge often came tightly wrapped in religious dogma (from which deviation meant death), it is more likely than not that the practitioners of magic for martial purposes believed in what they were doing. Seeing a desired result spring shortly after the performance of an intended ritual would reaffirm the power of the magic to the practitioner. Seeing an undesirable result occur would easily be explained by some malfunction of the method, or some displeasure existing in the spirit contacted.

But the realm of the psychic soldier is not only involved with the seeking of outside knowledge and power from "third-party providers." It is also heavily influenced by the attempts of the individual soldier, and his trainers, to create a super warrior, a man whose abilities would be far beyond those of mortal men. It is with this subject that our next chapter deals.

CHAPTER 4

THE SOLDIER AS SUPERMAN

Martial Training Techniques of Various Times and Places

Training is key to a soldier's performance, and always has been. The Roman foot soldiers in Gaul and the American infantrymen in the Gulf were products of their training as well as their times. Ever in search of better training methods, the armies of the world have on occasion turned to techniques of the supernatural, to turn their soldiers into supermen—or at least, make the attempt.

Now when we speak of supernatural training methods, we focus on the psychological and psycho-physical techniques used to enhance human warrior performance. Visualization, hypnosis, and gesture magic have been used both by ancient soldiers and the military men of today.

In the search to "supersize" the effectiveness of the fighting man, the present century is witness to the emerging nonlethal technologies that use the "hard science" of physics to accomplish what would have, in earlier days, been called the supernatural. These developments demonstrate the new threats in military encounters, and suggest ways that the soldiers of the third millennium may be trained to effectively deal with these threats. Some of these suggested methods employ the very techniques used to alter consciousness common to yogis, shamans, and sorcerers.

While we may fully expect to see, in the twenty-first century, guerilla tactics and brush-fire wars—common in the last several centuries—our technologies and our communication hardware and software shall cause some radical changes in the wars of the future, and our soldiers must be trained in some radically different ways to adapt to these changes.

Our evolving knowledge of exercise physiology, nutrition, and mind-body interaction have already begun to change the training of the modern soldier. As we continue to progress in our understanding of these areas, including our understanding of parapsychology, we are going to see more changes in military training regimens. We must, to remain combat-effective.

"Military operational requirements can demand a broad range of intensities of physical exertion from prolonged low intensity to short bursts of maximal intensity. The focus of our research is on identifying and understanding muscle fatigue and limiting physiological factors, predicting the capacity to sustain work performance and improve physical training methods."[1]

The above quote comes from the website of the Defence and Civil Institute of Environmental Medicine, a Canadian think tank for defense research and human performance studies. Some of the techniques that might help "identify and understand muscle fatigue and limiting physiological factors" might be the psychological and psycho-physical techniques that were used by the psychic soldiers of old. Prior to the days of advanced medicine and developed exercise physiology theories, the soldier of the past turned to more magical methods of enhancing his performance. Ancient armies wore stones of protection, invoked martial gods and spirits, and contacted supernatural intelligences for battlefield advice and counsel. In the present century, the magic of science has been drafted to create our military superman.

One of the age-old techniques of enhancing physical performance was through controlled breathing and visualization exercises. The ancient yogi promised "He who can fully master the five pranas or hold them in their respective centers will gain the following merits: His body will become sturdy . . . and he will be full of energy at all times; even a thick high wall can not impede him."[2] *Pranayama* is the ancient yogic art of breath control and manipulation. *Prana* is the yogi's version of Ch'i; or if we are fans of Star Wars, "The Force." (All being an invisible, intangible energy form that nevertheless can cause physical and psychic effects.)

For anybody who has ever run a military obstacle course, this breathing art could definitely come in handy when climbing over those thick high walls that we fondly remember.

Among the other benefits promised to those who could "bring the prana mind and the pure essence of the five elements into their central channel," were the abilities to "walk on water, without sinking, enter fire without being burned, travel to far distant cosmos in a few seconds, and fly in the sky and walk through rocks and mountains."[3]

But getting beyond the exaggerations, we can see how visualization techniques combined with certain methods of rhythmic (and arrhythmic) breathing could have a performance-enhancing effect on the warrior.

Breathing involves the exchange of gases within and without the blood, body, and brain. It is no great leap of logic (or faith) to conclude that changes in normal breathing patterns can have other than normal effects in blood, body, and brain chemistry. Combine these physical changes with the quasi-hypnotic effects of visualization exercises and we see—or may see—enhanced physical and mental performance. Just as emotions affect physiology, physiology affects emotions, and emotional control and content can enhance martial skills.

For several years I was a full-time martial arts instructor. Anyone engaged in this profession who has experience and intelligence knows that different people respond to different types of physical and mental training. Using the "cookie cutter" grunt-and-sweat approach to martial arts training (and what else is military training but a variety of different martial arts lessons?) is ineffective when it comes to turning out enhanced physical performances from individuals with different body types and mental makeups.

Using visualization techniques, however, on an individualized training basis, both enhanced the performance level of the martial arts student and reduced the training time necessary for him to acquire the necessary technical skills. In teaching a new technique, prior to any physical instruction, I told the students *not* to expect gruelling difficulty and awkwardness in acquiring the new flying kick, or spinning backfist.

After demonstrating the correct method of performance, I instead instructed them to visualize already being capable of the successful execution of the technique; to experience in advance the feeling of *effectiveness* that would be their reward in its successful execution. Marrying this visualization with certain breathing techniques, and then breaking the technique down into a series of easily accomplished interim steps, proved highly effective in reducing student injuries, training time, and frustration in learning martial arts. Ergo, non-physical techniques enhanced physical performance. Little did I realize, while teaching kempo in the late 1970s, that the U.S. Army would be using a very similar experimental enhanced performance technique for martial arts instruction in 1983.

The World of the Ninja

Some of the greatest warriors of history, the best spies and assassins, were the Japanese ninja. Some of the greatest psycho-physical techniques for martial arts performance enhancement came from the ninja, and of these, the art of *kuji-kiri* is the most "supernatural."

Kuji-kiri, which means, more or less, nine cuts, is a form of psycho-physical discipline wherein certain finger positions, visualizations, and breathing methods are combined to achieve altered states of consciousness. In more mystical terms, it is a form of gesture magic.

Gesture magic is a method of embodiment and achievement of a desired mental or physical state, via a movement or knitting of the fingers or hands. It is a "shorthand" form of meditation and/or magic. By repetitive use of hand positions while meditating or visualizing on a certain desired state, eventually the practitioner will quickly and effectively come to that state using the hand position alone. It is merely the anchoring of a desired psychological condition with a physical posture. (Much of Yoga in its psycho-physical exercise "Hatha" form might be likewise described.) Some of the *kuji-kiri* techniques are reported to imbue the practitioner with the power to kill and restore life, and enable the ninja to perform telepathy and the mastery of time and space.[4] Once again, we have hyperbole in action, but it is indisputable that ninja techniques did make for a very effective killer elite.

In more modern times in the West, the world has seen a form of gesture magic at work in the military. The American salute, the Nazi "heil Hitler" arm movement—all were useful in generating certain psychological states conducive to obedience and aggression.

The Chinese, originators of many of the Far Eastern martial arts, also had techniques of magic for their martial artists. In 1900, the *I-*

Ho-Chuan, or Society of Righteous Fists, engaged in a massacre of Chinese Christians and missionaries. These "Boxers," so called because they were practitioners of martial arts, were the force behind the "Boxer Rebellion."

Martial arts legend tells us the Chinese had mastered certain techniques in their training that enabled them to be immune to foreign bullets. "One of the principles of the Boxers was the belief that if they were armed with their faith, followed the prescribed rules and fought against the Christians, they could not be killed in battle. They believed that bullets would turn away from their Holy Bodies as they marched forward."[5] Faith is wonderful. However, facts have often served as a corrective device to faith that was pure fantasy.

In Beijing, the Boxers discovered they were wrong. Yes, Christian bullets would kill them—many Boxers died from Christian bullets turning into them instead of away from them as advertised. Further, the erroneous belief did not evidence any greatly enhanced martial prowess, although it did serve to increase needless casualties suffered in ill-advised maneuvers. More modern armies use techniques similar to the ninjas' and Boxers', but with more realistic expectations. Autosuggestion and hypnotic techniques are among the supernatural elements in some military and espionage training regimens.

Hypnosis as a Weapon

During World War II, experiments were conducted with hypnotically trained couriers. Hypnosis was used to split their personalities. One persona would deliver a message. The other would not remember the message, the recipient, or the assignment. G. H. Estabrooks, one of the hypnotists who trained couriers for military intelligence duties, believed, "The potential for military intelligence has been nightmarish. During World War II, I worked this (split personality) technique with a vulnerable Marine Lieutenant I'll call Jones. . . . I split his personality into Jones A and Jones B. Jones, once a normal working Marine, became entirely different. He talked communist doctrine and meant it. He was welcomed enthusiastically by communist cells, was deliberately given a dishonorable discharge by the Corps (which was in on the plot) and became a card-carrying member."[6] Jones A was the loyal American who spied on the subversive activities of Jones B.

Another use of hypnosis was for enhanced physical endurance and insensitivity to pain. "Trained in autosuggestion or self hypnosis," says Estabrooks, "he can control the rate of his heartbeat, anesthetize himself to a degree against pain of electric shock or torture."[7] These are decidedly handy skills for a soldier or a spy. The CIA engaged in mind control experiments in the 1950s, which were part of a "systematic program to create and manipulate alternate personalities as the foundation for programmed couriers resistant to torture . . ."[8]

On the other hand, a declassified study by the CIA on *Hypnosis in Interrogation* by Edward F. DeShere states, "Providing by hypnotic suggestion for amnesia upon capture is an intriguing idea, but here again we encounter technical problems . . . a general suggestion such as blanket amnesia has unpredictable effects on very good subjects. . . . Only a relatively small number of individuals will enter a sufficiently deep somnambulistic state to produce profound analgesia."[9]

Whether or not hypnotically trained spies are more pain resistant and less likely to spill the beans on capture is questionable. But the fact remains that the training was undertaken, the techniques tried, and these attempts at using the "magic" power of hypnosis in seeking a soldier-superman are another foundation stone in the building of the military-occult complex.

Some of the modern methods in creating the super-soldier were more brutal than hypnotic suggestion. In training members of the Nazi SS, a variety of schools used rather original techniques in creating the soldiers of the "Master Race." "In each of these schools, men stripped to the waist and without any defensive weapons were taught to become hard by such ordeals as fighting off for twelve minutes attack dogs that were unleashed and incited to kill. If the candidates took flight, they were shot."[10]

This kind of training parallels the rites of passage of certain primitive tribes. Unfortunately, these exercises also have a tendency to deplete the physical resources of a soldier (blood, flesh, bone) rather than to enhance them. But the psychological effects would be of immense value. A soldier brave enough to fight off an enraged attack dog without any weapons or protective gear might show superior courage against men when he was in possession of weapons and armor.

It should be remembered that the ordeal and physical torture were often parts of the shamanic heritage. The Indians of North America were devoted practitioners of various ordeals. The Sun Dance Ritual was enacted by Richard Harris, hanging from hooks, in the movie, *A Man Called Horse.*

The fakirs of the East also ritually demonstrate their supernatural tolerance to pain. When I visited Singapore, I witnessed the Hindu festival of Thaipusam, where the faithful parade around with a variety of complicated patterns of spikes in their flesh—for the purpose of showing their devotion, and the ability to withstand pain inherent with that faith.

Then there were the National Socialist *Übermenschen* in the SS. "The SS functioned as a kind of elite corps of pure blooded Aryan Supermen."[11] The SS, a military elite of "supermen" developed by Heinrich Himmler, added myth to its military might. Seeking pure-blooded specimens of Aryan stock, SS candidates had to prove racial purity prior to admission, and were given large doses of master-race mythology to go along with their more conventional training. Did it work? The SS often performed exceptionally well on the battlefield.

Boxer magic failed. SS mythology came up short. We have seen a debate about the effectiveness of hypnotically trained spies. With all of this historical failure and dissent, why has the military continually sought out occult techniques of performance enhancement for its soldiers? Because sometimes they work.

Performance Enhancement

Colonel John Alexander, U.S. Army (ret.), was involved in many Army performance-enhancement studies, some of which used methods that might be termed mystical. "When shorn of spiritualism and trained by scientific method, the shaman of the past becomes the techno-shaman of today. A psychic warrior capable of using the tools of science to reveal the secrets hidden within the human mind," says Alexander.[12]

One of the projects in which Alexander participated that was apparently successful was the 1983 U.S. Army Jedi Project. Named after the *Star Wars* Jedi Knight, this project used visualization and suggestion methods to improve soldier performance in shooting the .45 pistol, the standard service sidearm. According to Alexander in his book, *The Warrior's Edge*, even soldiers who had no experience with the pistol learned better and more quickly when visualization, suggestion, and positive reinforcement techniques were used. It was the psychological enhancement of physical training techniques. Alexander says, "Human willpower and human concentration affect performance more than any other single factor."[13]

Jedi was an early attempt at using new discoveries in neuro-linguistic programming and other performance-enhancement techniques to shorten training time for soldiers. The Jedi Project was a landmark experiment that evidenced the modern volunteer army embracing the New Age. Alexander, in and out of uniform, was instrumental in wedding the military and what might be deemed the magical. It was a bold undertaking featuring motivational guru Anthony Robbins as the primary instructor. (He makes mention of the experience in his "Unlimited Power" tapes, but doesn't refer to the project's name.)

One of the more bizarre psychic soldier superman projects of the U.S. Army was the concept of the First Earth Battalion. This idea by Army Lieutenant Colonel James Channon for an army think tank—Task Force Delta—was spawned after Channon toured over 130 California New Age groups. "Channon's ideal warrior monk would be proficient at every level of force. At the monastery, the plan of the day will begin with yoga stretching. A primal scream to 'feel their power' will replace the traditional military bugle reveille. The monks will breakfast on Belgian waffles, protein sponges that digest for hours, ginseng tea for emotional balance, and amphetamines for pep."[14] This was a far cry from situps and chipped beef on toast. What will these supersoldiers do for our country? "Warrior monks will clear landing sites for UFOs and prepare to communicate with extraterrestrials."[15]

When not doing the above, we can find them "inside new age tanks, [with] headphones (not needed for radio communications because warrior monks use ESP) [that] will play something like the sound of a one hundred ten piece black high school band when they are really jiving . . ."[16] And some people accuse the government of wasting money on frivolous projects!

The purposes behind using the supernatural to train superior soldiers are valid enough. Traditional strategists were cognizant of the need for superior individual soldiers. Sun Tzu, in his *Art of War*, said "Anciently the skillful warriors first made themselves invincible, and awaited the enemy's moment of vulnerability." (Chapter IV, verse 1.)

But when it comes to the supernatural, especially in its use for intelligence-gathering purposes, Master Sun proves himself a skeptic. "What is called foreknowledge cannot be elicited from spirits, nor from gods, nor by analogy with past events, nor from calculations. It must be obtained from men who know the enemy situation." (Chapter XIII, verse 4.)

But perhaps Master Sun's advice has been eclipsed by modern intelligence techniques and modern military training orientations. After all, the United States government spent over $20 million on remote-viewing projects in the 1970s through the 1990s. To spend money on a project for over two decades that, if publicly revealed, would spell political disaster, indicates that the program really worked. And it demonstrated that, despite the opinion of Master Sun, foreknowledge could be psychically obtained by military men.

The world of war is changing radically. Fewer soldiers are being used to cover the same square of ground. High-technology weapons have made pinpoint bombing accuracy a reality. (The American public will remember the video-game-like technology guiding smart bombs into ventilation systems during the Gulf War television coverage.)

Communication technology and informational volume has increased exponentially. Officers and men engaged in battle command and control are literally bombarded with data via phone, radio, computer and facsimile. There is a changing perception of what war is, how it should be fought, and how costly in terms of human life it should be. (Witness the super-low U.S. casualty rate in the Gulf War and Kosovo.)

With these changes, the sensory and mental capabilities of military leaders must be enhanced and maximized to their fullest potential. From where will the training come? It will come, and has come, from a variety of existing human-potential movements, and the organizations that perform the research, both for private and government clients.

Whether their conclusions are proven or not, it is certain that the fields of psychology and parapsychology are on the front lines of the human-potential movement. It is perhaps fitting that representatives and organizations involved with this research area participate in training the modern intelligence and military service personnel.

It is not only fitting, it is being done.

When the CIA wished to explore the possibilities of using clairvoyants as spies (in what was called remote viewing), it turned to the Stanford Research Institute. Once affiliated with Stanford University but now autonomous, SRI operated many government-funded projects. One of those, conducted in the 1970s, was involved with developing and analyzing training methods to create psychic-soldier remote viewers. If this seems incredible to the reader, in the light of modern weapons development, it shouldn't. The hard science technologies that are being exploited for wars of the future make remote viewing look as avant garde as tunafish for lunch.

Already developed are combat lasers, which can blind infantry and optical instruments at significant distances. The Americans have, and the Chinese are rapidly developing, lasers that can "kill" satellites from earth-based beam weapons. There is a bioengineered Central American fungus that turns the plastic material of computer chips into a green goo. Research is being conducted in the field of high-powered micro-wave generators with anti-machine and anti-personnel applications. In-frasonic weaponry has been tested successfully, and radio-frequency weapons to jam the nervous systems of soldiers is far beyond the drawing-board state.[17] Our men must catch up with the machines de-signed to help them kill each other.

"Technology is easy, training is hard. This is why there are so many well equipped troops in the world who don't know how to use their weapons very well," says James F. Dunnigan, the author of *Digital Soldiers*, a work that deals with the technology of future war.

In that spirit, there must be significant changes in the mental and psychological orientation of the human beings that man our weapons; and of those who tell them where the weapons should be placed and fired.

"Successful warriors tend to be brighter people, as well as being stronger and more aggressive."[18] It is submitted that the more intelli-gent person will be more receptive to the innovative training techniques that are being slowly introduced into today's military and intelligence organizations.

We read opinions that "the future of warfare is robots,"[19] and that the "one thing that is agreed on is that new forms of warfare will be highly dependent on computers, lots of different kinds of computers."[20]

"New technology not only makes the fighting troops more deadly, but also makes them a lot faster . . . everything moves a lot faster and combat goes on around the clock."[21]

These statements are true. One of the first attacks of the Gulf War by our military forces was aimed at the communication and control computers of the Iraqi forces. Their computers were decimated before their forces were destroyed. Smart bombs have been used to wreak pinpoint destruction on the enemy without destroying politically sensitive targets of no military value. Individual laser weapons for the foot soldier will be a reality in the very near future. How then will the spy and soldier deal with the man-machine interactions, more efficient killing, and faster decision-making requisites of future war? There are psychological, spiritual, and mental efficiency considerations involved. Won't the training of the future soldier be heavily involved with psychological, spiritual and mental exercises and protocols?

In around-the-clock combat, biological clocks must be considered when dealing with enhancing the performance of soldiers. Nutrition and biofeedback methods must be incorporated in the training regimen. (The military has already performed a study of the use of carbohydrate-electrolyte solutions to enhance physical performance.)[22] New forms of mental toughening and training are required in a military world filled with infra-sound generators and nano-tech weapons. Advanced infra-sound weaponry, which emit ELF (Extremely Low Frequency) sound waves, has already been tested in France, as well as in other nations. These weapons can affect both the physical and mental capabilities of humans.[23] Nano-machines, mechanical devices operating on molecular levels, will, when sufficiently developed, be able to destroy both men and machinery on a molecular level.[24]

Psycho-physical exercises have been useful in the mental toughening of martial artists. Meditation has been determined to have an effect on brain waves. These supernatural training techniques might afford some protection or at least forewarning to soldiers fighting in the world of third-millennium, science-fiction weaponry. "This vision of every soldier a superman . . . is taken seriously enough for a group of researchers to have formed around the concept at the U.S. Army's Human Engineering Laboratory in Aberdeen, Maryland."[25]

In a published announcement from the National Research Council, released August 26, 1997, there was a discussion of advanced technologies that can aid future naval forces. We quote from the opening: "The U.S. Navy and Marine Corps are facing a daunting task: how to protect national interests and respond to international crises in an increasingly technological world. Emerging regional powers and possibly old foes in new guises will present unexpected challenges to the nation."[26] Given the above, these forces need superior and innovative training. If the government is, as it has in the past, going to continue to fund psychic research for military purposes, the information and experience gained from this research should be utilized in military and intelligence training. For example, in the announcement by the National Research Council dealing in part with military operations in populated areas, it was stated, "Novel weapons systems and techniques should be used to fight in populated areas against organized military forces, terrorists and criminals, and other hostile groups."[27]

This military situation is tailor-made for psychically trained soldiers. Being able to determine, via remote viewing, the location of hostile troops in building interiors inaccessible to other technical means of surveillance would be of great help in directing forces and saving lives. If psychokinesis is a reality, at least on what is called the "micro-PK" level, then psychic interference with electrical and phone systems of a building housing enemy forces could be of obvious tactical benefit.

Now, all of this may seem fantastic at this point, but from the research already performed vis-à-vis the use of remote viewing and psychokinesis as tools of potential military and intelligence value, there are—or might be—soldiers who can sense electromagnetic radiation and extreme-low-frequency sound generators. These will be of immense reconnaissance value in a twenty-first-century battlefield with weapons like ultrasound guns (already capable of causing animal death at fifty meters)[28] and ELF weaponry used for behavior control purposes.[29] Instead of wasting valuable hours in practicing such useless skills as close-order drill, perhaps the military trainers of the future will devote time to meditation and biofeedback techniques to enhance the energy level of soldiers and enable them to have greater control over such bodily functions as heart rate, blood pressure, and blood-clotting. On a more mundane level, but in concert with "supernatural" training techniques, the still horrible fat-laden army diet should be improved in light of modern nutritional knowledge. The effect of diet on the mental and psychological factors of military men should be continually studied to determine the best diet for the mental, physiological, and psychological requisites of the modern soldier. Yogic breathing techniques may be incorporated with traditional aerobic exercises to increase soldier endurance and lung capacity. Hypnosis may be used to extend the mental and physical capabilities of the soldier to their maximum. Such "inner" styles of martial arts as *tai ch'i chuan* and *pa kua* may be incorporated into the hand-to-hand combat training of the infantryman.

We should be open-minded about the incorporation of any training technique and technology that might enhance the effectiveness of our military fighting man, whether it is obviously physically oriented, or seems to come from the realm of the supernatural. New stresses and new technologies are realities in modern war. It may serve the new soldier to use some of the old techniques of meditation, hypnosis, and other psycho-physical methods in preparing for the battles of the third millennium. In war, after all, it isn't whether you win or lose, it is whether you win.

While our technological wonder-weapons are developing at ever-increasing rates and costs, our researchers are discovering cheaper, more efficient ways of killing and destroying. Electromagnetic pulse weapons to devastate electronics, computers, and communication, and bioengineered bugs to kill and disable, exist now, with more horrific versions due in the future.

If we can develop the minds and perceptions of our modern warriors via paranormal research and human performance enhancement, we might evolve communication and control systems independent of electronics and radio waves. We might develop human biosensors, acting like canaries in a cave, to sense invisible chemical and biological agents before they have the opportunity to do their devastation. Low-technology methods and low-cost techniques of human performance enhancement in concert with the expensive high-tech military toys, may make all the difference in the wars of the next millennium.

CHAPTER 5

SHAMANIC INFLUENCES ON THE PSYCHIC SOLDIER

Alternate Realities and Alternate States in the Military-Occult Complex

One of the important magical/mystical traditions that had a great influence on the present-day psychic soldier is the shamanic tradition. We will see that many of the accomplishments of the shaman are shared by the modern military magician. Many of his ancient techniques and theories parallel modern government remote-viewing and "remote influence" endeavors.

From the time of the cave dwellers, and continuing throughout history, the shaman has served as the intermediary between the mundane world and the magical realm beyond. He has been the intercessor with the gods for the tribe, the thaumaturgic guarantor of a successful hunt, and the receptionist for divinely inspired messages.

"Shamans are specialists in ecstasy, a state of grace that allows them to move freely beyond the ordinary world," says David Friedel in *Maya Cosmos*, a book dealing with the traditions of Mexico and Central America. "Beyond death itself—to deal directly with gods, demons, ancestors and other unseen but potent beings."[1] "It began thousands of years ago when human beings first conceived of a place beyond death inhabited by ancestors, spirits and gods-the place between worlds."[2] "We of the modern world come from a society in which mystical

knowledge is sometimes admired and honored, but is more often regarded as lunatic and irrational."[3]

Psychotherapist Bradford Keeney tells us in *Shaking out the Spirits*,
his book detailing his shamanic journey, "Every one of us exists in two
worlds at once. There is another earth existing side-by-side with this
earth."[4] "In spiritual work," says Keeney, "one needs to focus on becoming a clean empty tube for the spirits to come through . . . But
preparation of the tube is only half the story. The rest involves getting
self out of the way and letting one's empty clean tube be used."[5] However poetic, the protocols used and conclusions made by the government's remote viewers echo this advice, although it is expressed in
government language. Shamanism was alive for a time at the Stanford
Research Institute.

Harold Puthoff and Russell Targ, two of the major brains behind
the 1970s remote-viewing studies at Stanford Research Institute, in
writing about their conclusions of the studies, state, "From these experiments we conclude that:

1. A channel exists whereby information about a remote location
   can be obtained by means of an as-yet-unidentified perceptual
   modality.
2. As with all biological systems, the information channel appears to be imperfect."

Might it be that the channel which these scientists refer to is the
same channel to which shamans are tuned? The "noise along with the
signal," is the ego—and analytical tendencies of the remote viewer. By
becoming the empty tube, by eliminating left-brain analysis and the
personality of the remote viewer, the channel becomes clearer: more
information comes through. (At least this is the theory shared by some
researchers.)

In examining and investigating the world of the psychic soldier, I
have been both the skeptic and the seer. As an experienced attorney,
a member of a major skeptic organization, and a card-carrying member
of the Association of Former Intelligence Officers, I have also experienced the unexplainable in my efforts at tarot-card reading and in on-
line remote-viewing experiments from major parapsychological institutions. This is mentioned in support of the above submission. There

have been times during the hundreds of readings I have performed when I was able to access specific data about the persons being read—many times. I have told querents the specific diseases from which their relatives suffered. On one occasion, I was able not only to accurately describe the type of work performed by a querent, but also named the company for which he worked. I had no way of obtaining this information beforehand, as these readings occurred at psychic fairs where I had no previous knowledge of whom I would be reading.

It was during the times that I did not involve my ego in search of specific "hits," a "lust for result," that my readings were most specific. It was the times that the desire to impress was turned off, and the mind was blank and open, that I obtained the most specific and accurate descriptions of the querent's present and past histories.

While it is realized that the personal experience of the author is not statistically significant, it does confirm the concepts of both shamans and parapsychologists. The ego is a hurdle in the pathway of what is now called "anomalous cognition" by government researchers. It was the shamanic technique, via song, dance, drugs, ordeal and ritual, to transcend this ego, to turn off the left brain, so as to be able to access a clear channel to the realm beyond.

We are advised by Keeney in his aforementioned work, "Having dreams of ecstasy does not make one spiritual if it fills one with pride and blindness to the needs of others. It is a curse."[7] Some former government remote viewers occasionally forgot this lesson, exuding pride and blowing their own spiritual horns about how they were the real force behind the program. These shamans of the CIA seem rather stuck on themselves. (The best ones, however, did not exhibit this tendency. Mel Riley is a humble man. Joseph McMoneagle, perhaps the most highly skilled of the military remote viewers, is extremely down-to-earth and accessible.)

Keeney warns us, "The temptation of all spiritual walks is to leave this center point and become infatuated with any particular side, good or evil, light or dark. To do so is to inflate one's self."[8]

In an analysis of the claims of the recent remote viewers, we will see some egos so inflated that they could pass for dirigibles. We will see others who exhibit the Zen-like calm and quiet of true masters of an art and discipline.

"Wisdom does not come from any particular source," says Keeney. "Wisdom is the result of how we transform and utilize all sources. Since all living things are related, any part is capable of speaking or listening for the whole."[9] This idea parrots animism, and the animist tradition is one of the major sources for the shamanic practices. The surprising thing about animistic shamans is the widespread respect they receive from traditions wherein animism is anathema.

A South Dakota shaman was, among other fellow Native Americans flown to Libya to receive a "peace prize" from none other than super-Muslim Moammar Khadaffi. He received the royal treatment. "Whatever they wanted they received with excessive generosity. . . . Feasts were given and they were taken into the mountains to be welcomed by secret forces." (Military, not spiritual forces).[10] This Libyan entertainment of a practitioner of shamanic arts is somewhat ironic, for later military remote viewers targeted Khadaffi for the American bombers sent to put a dent in his tent. Perhaps in the spirit of animism, the project was called Bluebird.

"More and more investigations are focusing on the power of shamans in primitive societies," Dr. Richard S. Broughton, director of research at the Parapsychological Institute points out in his 1991 classic work, *Parapsychology: The Controversial Science*:[11] Were the Libyans interested in shamanic techniques for military purposes? A good question that presently lacks an answer—at least an unclassified answer. However, from my conversations with remote viewer Joseph McMoneagle, it appears that terrorist organizations take the paranormal seriously. (Not surprising, given the religious background most of them come from.)

No matter how ancient their belief-system, shamans are still trying to influence politics today. Lynn F. Monahan, an Associated Press writer, in her January 6, 1997 article in *The Washington Post*, tells of Peruvian shamans (who) prayed . . . "for a peaceful end to the hostage crisis" then taking place in the Japanese embassy in Lima.

"Circled by cameramen, photographers and reporters, the shamans carried out a ritual that included chants and prayers and the customary practice of *singear*, a blessing of herbal water that is spit out of the shaman's mouth in spray."[12] One of the shamans explained, "It is a purification to nature and man so that he has peace, calming his spirit." It was a nice try by the shamans, but they failed to have their deeds live up to their intentions, as a shoving match broke out between the shamans and a woman who "held a portable tape recorder over the shaman's heads and played Christian music."[13] How often is it painfully obvious that mystics can be just as troubled by egocentric tendencies as mere mortals?

Shamanic methods developed in cultures that were technologically challenged. Yet the principles behind the techniques are similar to modern methods of achieving the altered state of consciousness, which appears to be a sine qua non for paranormal functioning. The shamans used psychotropic drugs, as did the CIA in its MK-ULTRA human-use experiments of the 1950s and '60s. The shamans used visualization methods, as did the soldiers involved with Project Jedi in the 1980s. The ordeals of ancient shamans are mirrored (although less painfully) in the sensory-deprivation techniques used to enhance paranormal functioning in modern psychic warrior endeavors (dim lighting, sound-proofed chambers, neutral environments, etc).

The influences of ancient magic and the techniques of sorcerers and shamans were the precursors of modern military experiments in the black arts. Now our vision turns to those medieval desert sands where once trod the Christian psychic soldiers known as the Knights Templar, as we examine the mystic traditions of the Soldiers of Christ, and then of their enemies, who followed in the way of Allah.

CHAPTER 6

CROSS, CRESCENT, AND THE CRUSADES

Military Use of the Supernatural in the Middle Ages

Despite its historical predilection for turning sorcerers into barbecue, the medieval Church itself was—in rhetoric, ritual, and reverence for Holy Relics—a rather magical religion. Rome took a significant role in the furtherance of the military-occult complex. "Like the loaves and fishes of the master, prayers and Biblical lessons were multiplied in rich profusion and then adorned with incense, organ, and chant . . ."[1]

The magical language of the liturgy—Latin—vibrated in the hearts and (somewhat primitive) minds of the illiterate, whether poor or rich. "Denied even the rudimentary education of most of the clergy, aristocracy and peasantry alike were quick to suppose that the miracle of the sacraments depended in no small measure on the magical qualities of the language in which they were performed."[2] A language that few, beyond the upper clergy, understood.

A megalith of mystery, thes church of Rome was, at the end of the first millennium a witches' brew of superstition. As an example, at the terminus of the ninth century, the Church had exhumed one of its former popes, Formosus, and placed him again on the throne of Peter—to be charged and convicted of heresy. His judges then mutilated his corpse, dragging its extremely-naked skeleton through the streets of Rome. Formosus, enduring this treatment without complaint, wound up being thrown in the Tiber. A rather ignoble second baptism for one who, in life, was deemed to be infallible.

This church, when not engaged in such ghoulish actions, when not joyously torturing and burning those who dared to deviate from its dogma, spent its time coveting the gold and glory of others. (*Magna gloria Dei*, of course). This marriage of faith and fortune-seeking was to spawn the holy wars of the Crusades; a military-magical marriage in itself.

The Crusades, undertaken for reasons of spoil as well as spiritual duty, gave rise to a series of military religious orders. The warrior-monks of the Knights Hospitalers, the Teutonic Knights, and the Templars came into existence to protect the pilgrim on his way to the holy land; and to battle the Saracen hordes for control of the most religious real estate in the world.

In A.D. 1095, Pope Urban II stood in front of a multitude of the faithful, in search of recruits to battle the Saracens who had taken Jerusalem. Addressing the masses in search of gold and glory, the Pope issued the following proclamation, "Wherefore, I exhort with earnest prayer, not I, but God, that as heralds of Christ, you urge men by frequent exhortation, men of all ranks, knights as well as foot-soldiers, rich as well as poor, to hasten to exterminate this vile race from the lands of your brethren, and to aid the Christians in time. . . . Oh! what a disgrace if a race so despised, base, and the instruments of demons, should so overcome a people endowed with faith in the all-powerful God, and resplendent with the name of Christ."[3]

In short, the Pope was not a big fan of the Islamic usurpers of the Holy Land. Therefore, in good religious tradition, he demonized the trespassers and ordered their extinction. The Saracens at the time were rather tolerant of competing religions, but the Crusades were to change that attitude. Even today, those faithful in the ways of Mohammed the Prophet refer to some infidels as the "Great Shaitan," demonizing the West, as a cry to the faithful to take up their own holy war, or jihad.

The cry to war was heeded by those in search of glory and gain. In 1097, the Crusaders marched towards Jerusalem to occupy Antioch. There, by some coincidence, mysterious or Machiavellian, the "holy lance" that pierced Christ's side at his crucifixion was "discovered." This relic inspired the Christian knights to victory.[4]

Relics were the remnants of the Church's saints, or even of Christ—either human remains, or objects associated with the holy men of old. "It was an age of relics. Men prized and cherished relics of the saints as well as wonder-working images."⁵ The hand of John the Baptist, or what was supposedly his hand, in its reliquary resplendent with precious stones, inspired the Knights Hospitalers to many acts of battlefield bravery.⁶

Thus, another stone in the foundation of the military-occult complex had been laid. These wars, which were not only to see the wholesale slaughter of soldiers and innocent noncombatants, but would bear witness to a revival of lost learning and arts. As the northern European Christians absorbed the more advanced culture and knowledge of the East, such knowledge proved of immense impact in the development of western Europe.

The Cult of the Knights Templars

Wars of faith, inspired by the words of the princes of the Catholic Church, the Islamic leaders, and the superstitions of both concerned parties, gave proof once again of the bond between the military and the magical. This bond formed the Knights Templars. In 1118, Hugh De Payens and eight other knights took vows of poverty, chastity, and obedience. They pledged themselves and their swords to the protection of the Christian pilgrim on the route to the Holy Land. From these original nine would spring a military-religious army that was to prove itself neither poor, chaste, nor obedient.⁷ The Templars originally gained the favor of Rome, and were deemed answerable to none but the Pope. They obtained farms, factories, and wealth. They became the bankers of Europe and the creditors of the secular rulers. But this overnight success story did not have a happy ending.

By 1291, the Templars had lost their Holy Land holdings to the Saracens. In another fifteen years, they witnessed themselves under arrest and accused of heresy, among other allegations. It was, perhaps, no coincidence that Philip the Fair who ruled then in France—was heavily indebted to the Templars organization: and that heresy was the only charge for which conviction would result in forfeiture of the Templars' property.

Tortured to obtain confessions, burned to death on the stakes of

Rome, the Templars were, by and large, destroyed by the very organization that had given them the ability to become wealthy and powerful. When one's avenging angels prove inconvenient, they become sinners and devils.

An interesting "magical" event in the destruction of the Templars is found in the dying curse of the last Grand Master, Jacques De Molay. Prior to being incinerated, he offered the prediction that King Philip and Pope Clement would join him within a year. In what was apparently a rather cooperative turn of two minds, Clement died within a month, Philip within a half year of Clement's death.[8]

Whether true or not, it was tales like the above that put the imprimatur of the supernatural over the political and military actions of man. The Templars were formed as holy warriors, monks in armor. They died as heretics, unholy enemies of the Church. While they prospered as good members of the military-occult complex, they structured their rituals to mix faith with force.

At the initiation of the neophyte Knight, he was asked if he believed in an immortal god. He was asked if he was an excommunicate. He swore his allegiance on the Holy Bible. He was required to pray in the Templar chapel for courage in the service of the Order.[9] All supernatural elements. From the initiation followed the favoring of the organization by the princes of the Church. The Order was sanctioned as The Defenders of the Faith by papal bull pronounced in 1139 by Pope Innocent II. Knights Templars were exempt from tithing and taxation and allowed to keep the spoils of their battles against the Saracen. They were made answerable to the Pope alone. In 1145, Pope Lucius III allowed them to build their own churches.[10]

In the daily life of the Templar Knight, religious obligations were amazingly burdensome. In the morning they recited twenty-eight paternosters. This was repeated up to four times a day, depending on their engagements in battle. At their first meal, taken at midday, they recited an additional sixty paternosters. Their beards, which were mandatory, were styled in what they believed to be the mode of Christ.[11] Ergo, we see a complete immersion in religious practice of what is essentially a military organization. "They become the militant arm of the Catholic faith, fighting and dying not for their own glory, but for God, the Christian god—it was a revolutionary concept and one that the church was eager to promote."[12]

This military elite organization was also to indulge in archaeological exploration in the Holy Land, excavating what was supposed to be Solomon's Temple. The accepted reason for this endeavor was their search for the alleged Ark of the Covenant. This exploration did occur in fact, for the remains weapons of the Knights Templars were found in 1894 by a British expedition to the site.[13]

Expeditions for religious or other dogmatic reasons were not the sole province of the Templar or of his historical period. In our own century, the National Socialist SS *Ahnenerbe* undertook an expedition to Tibet to search, justify, and reaffirm the superman theories that served their faith in the Führer and his racist fantasies. The Templars, in fact, had a significant rôle model utility for the *Übermenschen* of the Third Reich.

The activities of the Templars gave birth to some rather bizarre legends. One rather necrophilic one is that of the Skull of Sidon. The Templars being chaste, were forbidden to even kiss a woman. However, humanity being what it was, this rule was sometimes violated. It appears that a knight became enamored of a lady of Maraclea, who then died. Not being of a mind to forget her, it seems our knight exhumed the corpse and engaged in intercourse with it.

Nine months later, he returned to the site, pursuant to some inspiration, and upon examining the remains, found a skull over the thigh bones of his beloved. This skull became "his protecting genius and he was able to defeat his enemies by merely showing them the magic head. In due course it passed to the possession of the order."[14]

It is not uncommon in martial traditions for relics to be a rallying point for aggression, as well as a supposed repository of power. The French Foreign Legion has, for example, a relic consisting of a prosthetic arm used by one of its heros. Soldiers of every age have carried their amulets and talismans to protect them from the weapons of their enemy. Even if they are ineffective de facto, they do serve as powerful symbols for the generation of that esprit de corps that is essential to the effectiveness of any fighting unit.

Steeped in religious dogma and practice, brimming with supernatural legends, it is no wonder that when the Templars turned from triumph to target, they would be accused of all sorts of evil magical practices and anti-religious activities. We shall examine in detail some of the accusations lodged against the Knights of the Temple by their Papal inquisitors, for this shall serve as an example of the military-occult complex at its worst.

The allegations made against the Knights Templars consisted of 127 articles, drawn up by William de Nogaret, the main advisor to Philip IV. "These are the articles on which inquiry should be made against the Order of the Knighthood of the Temple. Firstly, that although they declared that the Order had been solemnly established and approved by the Apostolic See, nevertheless in the reception of the brothers of said Order, and at some time after, there were preserved and performed by the brothers, those things which follow: Namely, that each in his reception, or at some time after, or as soon as a fit occasion could be found for the reception, denied Christ, and sometimes Christ Crucified, sometimes Jesus, and sometimes God, and sometimes the Holy Virgin, and sometimes all the saints of God, led and advised by those who received him."[15]

Well done, de Nogaret! In the first salvo of superstitious nonsense, the Church created the legal reasons to deprive the Templars, when convicted, of their property. Philip IV was now off the hook with respect to his heavy indebtedness to the Knights of the Order.

This was also an excellent technique of psychological warfare, especially considering the fact that the government that sponsored the military was empowered by the Church. King and pope both ruled by divine right. Since military and occult powers are heavily dependent on authorities and authority figures (whether they are temporal, spiritual, or traditional in origin), by demonstrating a rebellious attitude towards that authority, religious deviation became equal to defiance of the temporal power, and the heretic became the traitor, deserving of death and deprivation of property. This is more specifically demonstrated by those accusations wherein the Templars are alleged to have denied the divine power and authority of Jesus Christ.

Now, even if we would allow that Templar contact with the East would have exposed them to various Islamic theological ideas, it is unlikely that this would cause them to denounce Christ as a false prophet: in the Koran, Jesus is acknowledged as a veritable prophet, but not the son of God. Here we see heresy being amplified and exemplified beyond any doubt, so that the triers of fact and law against the Templars must surely convict. To have done otherwise would have placed the inquisitors themselves under suspicion.

An attack on the symbols of its authority, especially in the time of the medieval Church, would have been viewed as tantamount to an actual attack on the Church. Thus, it was again an excellent psychological warfare ploy of de Nogaret to lodge the following accusation against the Knights Templars. "Item, that they made those whom they received spit on a cross, or on a representation or sculpture of the cross and an image of Christ, although sometimes those who were received spat next to it."[16]

In the above we see echos of the Black Mass, when the rites of the church are mocked by a parody, and by scatological practices. What a marvelous touch to inflame popular and political opinion against the Order.

Here is heresy at its most scatological. It is a recurring theme throughout the inquisitions of the Church to mix the sexual acts and excretory functions of the heretics with the symbols of the True Faith. It is abundantly evident from what mindset the inquisitors themselves sprang. Supposedly chaste, supposedly pure, they tortured the supposed heretic, and sought not only evidence of heretical acts, but evidence of the most vulgar and revolting kind.

The propaganda purposes of these accusations is clear, but it was also a fact that in the magic of the times, and in the past, body excreta were often important ingredients in spells, and in countering the magical or religious power of one's enemies. Sexual irregularities likewise had their place in magic, and in the demonizing of one's enemy.

"Item, that in the reception of the brothers of the said Order, or at about that time, sometimes the receptor and sometimes the received were kissed on the mouth, on the navel, or on the bare stomach and on the buttocks or the base of the spine."[17] This act, known as the *osculum infame*, was often described in other confessions by witches and sorcerers. It is again indicative of the mindset of the inquisitors. "Item, that in each province they had idols, namely heads, of which some had three faces, and some [had] one, and others had a human skull. Item, that they adored these idols or that idol, and especially in their great chapters and assemblies. Item, that they venerated them. Item, that they venerated them as God. Item, that they venerated them as their saviour. Item, that they said the head could save them. Item, that it could make riches. Item, that it gave them all the riches of the Order."

Once again we see the justification of plundering the rich Templars by demonstrating that their gains were indeed ill-gotten. To ruin a church, to loot a country, it is often useful to show those thus employed that they are right in doing so, for the gains of the enemy have been obtained from improper or illegal methods. The Church was master of the technique.

In our own century, the National Socialists spread their poison about the Jews, and many cartoons were created, showing the Jew as a manipulator of the people, grown fat by illicit means, while the "people" suffered. The accusations of the Nazis were well timed in a Germany devastated by inflation and unemployment.

The allegations against the Templars made by de Nogaret were clearly levied with this propaganda principle in mind. "Item, that they did not reckon it a sin in the said Order to acquire properties belonging to another by legal or illegal means." (This from the Church!) "Item, that it was authorized by them that they should procure increase and profit to the said Order in whatever way they could by legal or illegal means."[18]

Thus, by and large, allegations of magical practices and accusations of antireligious activities were used to strip the military order of the Templars of their power and their wealth. Tactics that, while not originating with the Church, were certainly perfected by them. Tactics that would be used throughout the history of the military-occult complex to condemn the enemies of the established state and demonize the foreign enemies of that ruling power.

The Muslim Magical Mystery Tour

But the Church was not the only power during the times of the Crusades to merge magic and martial doctrines. The great leaders of the Saracens were masters in using the mysterious to further military aims, creating an Eastern tradition that still lives in the actions of the terrorists of Islam. "Those who are slain in Allah's way are not dead, but alive." These words from the Koran (3:169) have been used from the time of the first jihad to the present to inflame the blood lust of the faithful as they battle the infidel. The Saracen had lost the Holy Land in 1099, and the Cross threw its shadow over Jerusalem. The few Islamic leaders who could afford it were ransomed, thus saving their heads. The rest had their last taste of Christian charity when the crusaders' swords sent them in Allah's way.

The loss of Jerusalem was unacceptable to the Saracen, and as usually occurs in history, when the military champion is needed, he appears. Salah-ad-Din (Saladin) came to power. A devout Muslim, Saladin led the Saracens to victory over the Christians in the battle of Hattin in 1187. The majority of the Church's soldiers of Christ came to learn about heaven first-hand, thanks to the swords of the followers of Allah. Then Saladin marched on and captured the Holy City. Jerusalem was once again in the hands of the Saracen.[19]

It was at the battle of Hattin that an important Christian relic was taken—a piece of the True Cross.[20] Of course, there were enough pieces of the True Cross floating around Christendom to have made a nice "True" log cabin, but history tells us, via Ermoul the Frank, "The anger of God was so great against the Christian host, because of their sins, Saladin vanguished them quickly . . . the Holy Cross was lost."[21]

Symbols and relics are often the rallying point for religious and military campaigns; fighting for the Holy Land continued for centuries. The Christian reign over Jerusalem was short-lived and perhaps served as an omen for the gradual decline of Rome in the future, for Martin Luther was soon to appear to rend the church in twain.

The armies of Islam engaged in a variety of magical and shamanic practices designed to improve the effectiveness of the man wielding the scimitar. One of the most magically oriented Muslim military leaders was the notorious Hassan Sabah, also known as the Old Man of the Mountains. From Sabah came the expression, "Nothing is true, everything is permitted."

Despite this cynical opinion, Sabah was a believer in the use of ritual and intoxicants as the recipe for creating a super soldier. Hashish was used by the followers of Sabah, and from this Arabic word, the *hashishin*, or assassins, arose. Intoxicated by the drug, and taken to what was for them a "garden of earthly delights," the strong-arm killers of Sabah were there to sample the joys that awaited them in heaven, after dying in battle.[22]

Through the various degrees of initiation into the assassins, the followers were force-fed dogma, until they reached the ninth degree of initiation, where they learned that the prior teachings were false. "Prophets and teacher, heaven and hell were all nothing, future bliss and misery were idle dreams."[23] Small wonder that the majority of the actual killers of the assassins were those who themselves had never undergone initiation.

The Church and Islam spread promises of glory and gold to its respective soldiers. The fear of death, ever present in the combat soldier who wishes to become old, was assuaged by visions of heavenly pleasures without end. The Christian would be near his Savior, and the Muslim would enjoy the more sensual pleasures of Paradise, with wine-bearing, dark-eyed houri to serve his whims and will.

History must bestow its respect on Hassan Sabah for being perhaps the only religious and military leader with the guts to call a scam a scam. Sabah admitted that religion was a racket, but only to the most advanced initiates of his group. He was wise enough to keep the truth that "Nothing is true" from those of his followers who were doing the actual wet work.

Such is the use of superstition to prop up an army. There were times, however, when the occult beliefs of the military man detracted from his martial effectiveness. In 1486, at the siege of Rhodes, the Turks fought the Christians for control of the island. The Bashi-Bazouks, fierce Turks, were undone when they saw the Christian armored knights and the waving banners of Christendom. To their superstitious minds, these banners became "terrifying djinns, devils from the abyss."[24] The Turks cut and ran, preferring life to the promises of Paradise.

Whether they bore cross or crescent, those who fought for control of the Holy Land had one armored foot in the blood of combat and the other in the clouds of the heaven promised to those who died in defense of their faith. The shades of the Crusaders are permanent residents in the realm of the military-occult complex.

CHAPTER 7

JOHN DEE

Patron Saint of the Military-Occult Complex; Dawning of the Modern Sorcerer-Spy

The Saracens eventually triumphed in the Holy Land, but the Christian knights who survived and returned did not come back empty-handed. The learning and culture of the East accompanied them and new ideas and ideologies entered Western Europe. This light of the East brought change to the medieval Western mind. Doubt began to creep into dogma.

The influences of the Middle Eastern enlightenment were overshadowed by the heat of the Middle Ages Reformation. Weary of the materialism and immorality of Rome, disgusted by the sale of indulgences, the gluttony and lechery of the priesthood, the Protestant movement violently raged throughout Christendom in the northern countries. Into this milieu came the man who was to become the embodiment of the military-occult complex: Doctor John Dee of Mortlake, England. A brilliant sixteenth-century scholar, Dee entered Cambridge at fifteen[1] and by his early twenties was a well-known lecturer in mathematics. His intellectual pursuits encompassed astronomy, mechanics, mathematics, military strategy, and, of course, the occult.

This embodiment (in one person) of the methodical scientist and the credulous magician made Dee one of the earliest patron saints of the modern military-occult complex. It also made him rather useful to his monarch of that time, the Virgin Queen, Elizabeth I.

In 1564, Dee was appointed Royal Advisor in Mystic Secrets and received frequent visits from Elizabeth at his library-laboratory house at Mortlake on the River Thames.[2] The Virgin Queen believed in astrology, alchemy, and magical doctrines. One of these doctrines was that of magical correspondence, which in essence claims that the use of psychic force on a seemingly unrelated material part of the universe may have an effect on another seemingly unrelated part. It was a doctrine of the magical relationship that anything in the universe had with everything else in the universe.[3]

When in her late thirties, the bloom of youth fading fast, Elizabeth I engaged the services of a Dutch alchemist, one Cornelius Lannoy, who claimed to have created an elixir to restore the Queen to her former youthful self. Many experiments resulted in many failures. Finally, Elizabeth realized that the only magic Lannoy was performing was transforming her gold into his—so she imprisoned the Dutchman for fraud.[4]

Dee, at the request of Elizabeth, had cast her horoscope to determine the most auspicious date for her coronation. His choice must have been correct, for the Virgin Queen reigned long in England.[5] It should be noted that in Elizabethan times, fortune telling among the nobility was a popular pastime.[6] Dee was also to use astrology to advise Elizabeth against a marriage with the duke of Anjou.[7]

Royal courts bring royal intrigue; Elizabeth was concerned with the possibilities of assassination, whether by conventional or supernatural methods. Even though she had been assured by no less a personage than the Archbishop of Canterbury that as long as her birth sign, Virgo, was in the ascendant, she would be safe from harm,[8] she shuddered when the discovery was made that a Catholic priest had been found with a wax image of her royal person, which (according to his confession) was to be used as an effigy for magical assassination of the Virgin Queen.[9] (One of the more ironic phenomena of the military-occult complex in these times was the credence in and employment of magic by those institutional forces that tortured and burned magicians as a matter of public policy and private profit.)

Elizabeth ruled an England where spiritual struggles spilled out upon and spilled blood throughout the secular world. It was a time of Protestant forces intercepting shiploads of Catholic contraband containing religious items and "holy" relic remnants of saints.[10] It was a time where recusant priests (those who failed to observe the 1559 Act of Supremacy declaring Elizabeth as supreme governor of the church) were hanged, disemboweled, and quartered. The faithful and the profit-minded sought to catch bits and pieces of martyred blood and flesh for later use (and sale).[11]

In this clash of Christian ideologies, the ruler of Protestant England kept a wary eye on the Catholic countries of the south, particularly Spain. Elizabeth had many spies throughout Europe and Spain: spies who were not only intelligence agents, but believers and practitioners in occult matters.

In 1583, astrologers had predicted great calamity and the end of the world.[12] This is not surprising, given the historical tendency of sooth-sayers to offer doom and gloom in lieu of a peaceful and benevolent future. The tendency made some sense. As magicians and astrologers were normally attached to the ruling classes, and the ruling classes of warring nobles and ambitious politicos were more experienced with strife and struggle than cooperation and kindness, those who divined the future spoke in the lingua franca of those who employed them as prognosticators. Wise soothsayers usually predicted doom and gloom for the enemies of their patrons.

The founder of the British Secret Service, Sir Francis Walsingham, believed that "the prosperity or adversity of kingdoms dependeth on God's goodness."[13] Walsingham certainly had textual support from his Bible for this opinion, as God was the Lord of Hosts. When Jehovah was upset with His people, they had a tendency to lose military engagements. (Napoleon, centuries later, would put a more ballistic spin on this viewpoint, finding God on the side with the heavier artillery.) In order to better determine God's goodness, Walsingham had set up a wide-ranging network of informants. He also engaged Dr. John Dee for his valuable insights.

Dee, who was a close associate of Walsingham, and bore the title "Queen's Intelligencer," used both his logical and magical powers in the defense and expansion of the realm. He believed that England was destined to empire and the overthrow of Spain. In 1577, Dee wrote *A Treatise on Naval Defence* which provided for a fleet "which would rule the waves and form the bodyguard for a future British Empire."[14] With and without Walsingham, Dee took an active role in British military and diplomatic affairs.[15]

Now, of necessity, intelligence-gathering and subversive activities are clandestine endeavors. In such endeavors it is useful to have a structured and disciplined underground organization. To this end, it was rumored that Elizabeth's premier spy, Walsingham, was using witch covens as intelligence agents.[16] Whether actually true or not, the rumor made for good spycraft, and therefore made good sense.

Besides his astrological predictions, Dee entered into one of the more bizarre regions of the occult world, experimenting with angelic communications, or what we might call channeling today. His first efforts met with insignificant results. However. Fate delivered to Dee one Edward Talbot, later known as Edward Kelly, who was to enable Dee to communicate with the spiritual realm of the angels quite frequently and easily.

Kelly was a convicted counterfeiter, and had lost his ears as punishment. This physical evidence of his criminal record was kept concealed under a cap. But when it came to making pronouncements supposedly obtained from the angelic spheres, Kelly did not hide his light under a bushel. In 1581, Kelly and Dee claimed to have achieved contact with the Angel Uriel. Later, other celestial celebrities would join this psychic party line, giving Dee, in 1582, the keys to what was called the Enochian or "angelic" language. This was obtained by Kelly's having gazed into his magic "shew stone" or crystal.

The angel would instruct Kelly to point to specific letters of this Enochian language—which had been arranged on a table—and by reversing these letters, messages would be obtained. The letters of this language look something like Cyrillic put in a blender at low speed, and the words themselves sounded like Hebrew poorly transliterated into English syntax.

The following sample of this doggerel is instructive: "*Amidan gah lesco van gedon amchib ax or mandol cramsa ne dah vadye legsamph af mara panosch aschedh or samhampore asco pacadbaah.*" (Note the Hebrew-like sounds, and the striking similarity between a word like *samhampore* and the Hebrew word for the seventy-two names of God, *Shemhamphorash.*)

There was speculation that this spiritual speech was in reality a code used by Dee for intelligence purposes.[17] Again, whether or not this was actually true, it would make good sense from a spycraft point of view. This could have been some simple letter-substitution code instead of messages from magical mouthpieces.

The angelic communications of Dee and Kelly were to provide much information of a political and military nature, foreshadowing similar workings that we shall read about taking place in the late twentieth century. A Polish nobleman, Laski, was informed by the team that he would be instrumental in the reconstruction of Europe. (Kelly was quite instrumental in the deconstruction of the nobleman's purse).[18] King Stephen of Poland was told that the Emperor Rudolf of Germany would be assassinated, and the Pole would ascend to the throne.[19] The Spanish Armada was foretold, along with the execution of Mary, Queen of Scots.[20]

For all their esoteric ability, for all of their magical insight, Dee and Kelly were sometimes reduced to petty fortune-telling to earn their bread, and neither of them exactly lounged in the lap of luxury. Kelly died trying to escape from prison; Dee died in poverty at his house in Mortlake.[21] Were the Dee-Kelly workings actually angelic communications?

It is easy to reach the conclusion that Dee was Kelly's willing dupe. The fact that it was only Kelly who saw and heard the angels while Dee acted as mere scribe gives credence to the theory that the messages of Kelly were as counterfeit as the coins he passed.

Lewis Spence, in his *Encyclopedia of Occultism*, put it this way: "A clever rogue was Kelly. Gifted with a fertile fancy and prolific invention, he never gazed into the great crystalline globe without making some wondrous discoveries, and by his pretended enthusiasm, gained the entire confidence of the credulous Dee."[22]

In examining the military-political pronouncements that supposedly came forth from the Dee-Kelly angelic communications, it is well to remember that Dee and Walsingham, the seer and the spy, were close associates—and Walsingham had an excellent informant network in place.

The Spanish Armada prediction of Dee might well have sprung not, from angels in heaven, but from agents in place on terra firma. The prediction of the execution of Mary, Queen of Scots might have logically been determined upon realizing that a Catholic queen might have her neckline significantly altered in a land where the Protestant Reformation ran rampant.

Again, quoting Spence in his *Encyclopedia of Occultism*, "On a careful perusal of Dee's diary, it is impossible to come to any other conclusion than that he was imposed upon by Kelly, and accepted his revelations as the actual utterances of the spirits."[23] With all due respect to Mr. Spence, it might not be impossible to form another conclusion. Having done our skeptic skip through this phenomenon of the military-occult complex, we shall now, like the dervish, whirl about into a more sympathetic view of the Dee-Kelly workings.

Whether one is a skeptic or a believer, it is obvious that Kelly was intelligent and imaginative. Being a counterfeiter, one may opine, without undue criticism, that he probably had a good visual sense. This is a good combination for a psychic. (In fact, one common denominator of those who participated in twentieth-century psychic spying for the CIA was their artistic ability and visual sensitivity.) Having the mental ability required, Kelly, by his gazing into the "shew stone," might have intentionally or unintentionally hypnotized himself, as eye fixation is a common method of doing so.

If Kelly were operating in a hypnotic altered state, this could affect his perception of reality to a degree where visual and aural hallucinations could occur; it is common in hypnotism. Now, given this scenario, it is understandable and credible that an entranced Kelly could believe he heard discarnate voices. Whether they were actually independent entities or merely verbalizations originating in Kelly's brain is another question, but we can at least see how the raw materials of the Dee-Kelly workings might not have been spawned by fraudulent intent. Since Kelly was operating in a time where angels and demons were a matter of faith, under a normal mental state he would be operating in a milieu conducive to the possibility of angelic communications. In an altered state, this possibility might have been perceived as a reality.

Given the political and military information to which Dee and Kelly might have been exposed, it is not incredible that in their legitimate belief that they were in communication with actual angelic beings, that they accessed data that had been normally obtained in an other-than-normal way, they concluded that they had achieved communication with the spirit world. Unfortunately, many of the predictions of Dee and Kelly were flat-out wrong. Others were of a nature so vague as to be amenable to a wide variety of post facto interpretations.

Historically, it is important that the Dee-Kelly angelic communications took place, whether or not they were what they were purported to be. These channeling efforts are an important milestone in the history of the military-occult complex, foreshadowing the psychic soldier's endeavors of three hundred years in the future.

It is a matter of historical fact that the business of secrets and the business of psychics shared many qualities. Occult means "hidden." Both the efforts of spies and seers are often hidden, therefore occult. The mentality that is attracted to secret service is usually of an intelligent and elitist nature. The mentality that was traditionally attracted to ceremonial magic (as opposed to the more rustic witchcraft) was also intelligent and elitist, for the average peasant would not be conversant with Latin, Hebrew, and Greek, which were the linguistic building blocks of magical literature. Nor would the peasant have had the materials to work magic. Both of these endeavors—carried out by those of superior intelligence and elitist leanings—would point to the practitioners as being members of the upper classes, the landed nobility.

Therefore, the Dee-Kelly workings make sense for the times in which they took place, and for the participants thereof. It was a time of the establishment of the British Secret Service, and a battle in the ether and the earth between great religious institutions. A time when geography often indicated theology, and science was emerging as a co-pilot with religion. Thousands of years after the theocracy of the Egyptians, and the workings of its magicians, Europe was still a de facto and de jure theocracy—or—a conglomerate of competing theocracies.

In this ambience of religious turbulence and emerging geopolitics, strong undercurrents of power were forming: They would grow in power and influence. Men would band together in underground associations to work in the shadows and behind the scenes in their quest for power.

The subsequent history of the world would lend evidence to this fact, formed in the *athanor* of the military-occult complex.

CHAPTER 8

BROTHERS IN ARMS

Secret Societies and the Military-Occult Complex

It has long been the experience of the military and espionage establishments that a small cadre of dedicated, highly trained men, with a solid esprit de corps, can prove highly effective vis-à-vis combat and intelligence operations. Witness the special forces of today's militaries—they are taught to wage war or gather information in small groups, well-drilled in operational security, and from their specialized training, the risks they take, and the interdependence among them, enjoy a strong esprit de corps.

The above qualities, at least in part, may also be found in the realm of secret societies. By definition, these are occult organizations. Their members are usually well-drilled in security matters, forewarned of extreme penalties for breaches of confidentiality, and taught to use secret signs and code words in their dealings. Having endured common rituals, shared common secrets, they too, often have a strong unit identity and loyalty to the organization.

Therefore, it is not surprising that occult secret societies have often played a rôle in the military and political arenas of the world, achieving status as permanent residents in the realm of the military-occult complex.

A secret cabal with indigenous contacts, untraceable funding, and a built-in chain of command is just what the revolutionary or the espionage organization ordered. The history of revolution and intelligence provides us with examples of how secret societies have participated in geopolitical struggles, and how occult symbolism and ritual have been found alongside the bayonets and bombs that have changed governments and established—or overthrown—tyranny.

Masons and the Military

In the history of its existence, the organization known as the Freemasons, or Free and Accepted Masons, proudly speaks of its participation in revolution. Masons are told the "fact" that fifty of the fifty-six signatories to the document of the American Revolution—the Declaration of Independence—were Masons. These facts, however, are not beyond dispute. The Freemasons are today well-known for their charitable works, contributing millions of dollars on a daily basis to burn-victim hospitals, cardiac research centers, and other beneficial purposes. The Shriners, who are all Thirty-Second-Degree Masons, are remembered for their clown costumes and their tiny cars as they horse around raising money for all sorts of good works.

There has been another side to the organization throughout history, however. During the American Revolution, members of the Freemasons were allegedly significantly involved in the rebellion. Benjamin Franklin, a Mason (and member of a feasting and fornicating society known as the Hell Fire Club of Sir Francis Dashwood), used his Masonic connections in Paris to raise funds for the Revolution and buy arms.[1]

Washington was a Mason, as were at least some of the signatories to the Declaration of Independence.[2] This means that certain of the political names to conjure with were members of the same secret society, shared the same ritual background, and experienced the same initiations. But how important was the role of Freemasonry in the American Revolution? How significant was the involvement of the membership of this occult society in the birth of the United States?

It is true, George Washington was a Mason. However, Washington has been quoted as saying to a correspondent, "To correct an error you have run into, of my presiding over the English Lodges in this country. . . . The fact is I preside over none, nor have I been in one more than once or twice in the last thirty years."[3] This was written in

1798, and therefore shows little real Masonic participation by Washington since well before the Revolutionary War.

Jefferson, Paine, Adams and Patrick Henry were not Masons, yet these names are in the Hall of Fame of revolutionary American history. Another well known name in early American history was also a Mason. Benedict Arnold.[4]

Regardless of the degree of Masonic participation in revolutions in the eighteenth century, it is not disputed that members of the organization were involved in the process, nor can it be disputed that Freemasonry is a secret society making significant use of occult symbolism.

What is the occult nature of this organization? I have been an officer in two Masonic lodges, one English speaking, one conducting rituals in German. My mother Lodge raised President Theodore Roosevelt. All Masonic lodges share common rituals and certain common beliefs. A candidate for initiation must profess his belief in God, and credence in the doctrine of immortality of the soul. Without these beliefs, he does not become a Mason.

While relaying herein the specific details of the degree work of a lodge would be a violation of the oath your author took, it can be related that many occult symbols are used in the various rituals of masonry. The coffin, the skull and crossbones, the Seal of Solomon, and other religious and occult symbols are important ritual component parts in Masonry. Secret signs, grips and words are the means of Masonic recognition between lodge brothers.

This organization then, where occult symbols and spiritual doctrines are in abundance, has taken an active part in political movements; and in wars. Besides the aforementioned Masonic influence during the Revolutionary War, the American Civil War also saw significant Masonic participation. At the Battle of Gettysburg 18,000 Masons were engaged in the fighting.[5]

Take a dollar bill from your pocket and look at the obverse side. You will see one of the more important Masonic symbols, the Eye in the Triangle, or the All-Seeing Eye. Take the train to the station at Alexandria, Virginia, and look at the Egyptian-looking obelisk there. It is from the Masonic Temple.

The point is, many of the participants in American politics, many American symbols, have come from the society of Free and Accepted Masons. It has been and still is an occult organization of much political and military influence. This becomes evident as one travels farther south in this country.

While journeying to Virginia to meet with a modern psychic spy-master, I received several acknowledgments and inquiries regarding Masonry, as I bore its symbol on my finger. The reaction of those who were also members was that of a co-conspirator recognizing a fellow traveler. Those who were not members regarded the symbol with re-spect and some suspicion.

Today, Masonry is no longer in the forefront of revolution, and is not striving for one-world government, despite the ravings of conspiracy-obsessed authors. It consists of men who are "free born, of lawful age and well recommended," who seek to aid their brother Ma-sons, and the community as a whole. Today's Mason is more likely to be seen hoisting a beer glass than a bomb; or making a martini instead of a Molotov cocktail.

However, not all secret societies were involved with charity. Some concentrated on revolution and criminal activities.

The Illuminati

It was the first of May 1776, the year of the American Revolution, but the country is Germany. May first, the day that follows the high holiday of witchcraft and satanism, *Walpurgisnacht*. A professor of canon law at the University of Ingoldstadt, Adam Weishaupt, has just created the Society of Perfectibilists, soon to be known as the Bavarian Illuminati.

Weishaupt was Jesuit-educated, but also studied the Greek myster-ies and other pagan practices. He believed that man could be perfected by a return to the occult pagan practices of earlier days. He and his organization were dedicated to European revolutionary politics.

In 1784, the Bavarian Illuminati attempted to overthrow the Haps-burgs. Five years later, they were at the forefront of the French Revo-lution.[6] One of their more prominent members, the Comte de Saint Germain, was a paid agent of the French Revolution, involved with the ouster of Peter the Great in Russia, and a key player in the achievement of the Franco-Prussian alliance.[7] Our Comte was also a practitioner of tantric magic, earning him permanent resident status in the military-occult complex. He had other illustrious company among the Illuminati. Comte Cagliostro, or as he was more accurately known, Giuseppe Balsamo, was an accomplished Sicilian confidence man (at least), and perhaps something more. His revolutionary activities were accompanied by his occult activities, for in his Paris apartment, besides many statues of Egyptian deities, there was an altar upon which sat a human skull.

Thus we have an influential secret organization (the Illuminati had contacts in the highest realms of European power) striving for revolution, made up of some key players who practiced magic, believed in the pagan mysteries, and shared living quarters with human bones. This is the essence of the military-occult complex.

This indeed was an age of revolution. Governments were being challenged by ideas of individual liberty that had not so flowered since the days of Athens. The institution of the church was being assaulted by the progress of science and growing historical scholarship. The old guard was in trouble; often, the voices of contrary religious opinions and antiestablishment sentiments issued from the same mouth. As the occultist and magician found himself in revolt against established Christianity, his new political leanings placed him opposite his government.

As both such oppositions could land a revolutionary in jail—or the grave—he voiced his ideas and met with fellow travelers in secret—at first. Thus, in the Age of Reason, the dwellers of the military-occult complex met in secret to insure their survival until the time came when they had sufficient power and numbers to be overt in their challenges to religious and secular authority.

It was not only in the western hemisphere that occult practitioners and politicians gathered. In the Far East, in what its citizens called *Chung Kuo*, or Central Kingdom, the monks of Buddha were to become the martial forces behind revolution.

The Triads

Through low-budget Chinese films and cliché television shows, many have heard of the fighting monks of the Shaolin Temple. Visions of meditating saffron-robed, peaceful martial artists have been fed us by the media, but like many visions, they deviate from objective reality.

It was the Shaolin Temple monks who were responsible for starting one of the most powerful political, social, and criminal Chinese secret societies—the Triads. Originally formed to overthrow the Ching dynasty and restore the Mings to power, the Triads participated in many military struggles, and both Chinese and foreigners confronted members of this secret organization.

During the Boxer Rebellion, the White Lotus, Big Sword, and Red Fist Triads battled Christian guns—and found out the hard way that their magic spells to ward off European bullets were somewhat ineffective.

The Communists, prior to the Maoist takeover, found themselves against the Green Tang Triads, and the Triad motivation towards armed conflict with governments in power did not necessarily spring from an Age of Reason love of liberty, fraternity, and equality. The Triads were involved with some high-profit criminal activity, drug running, prostitution and extortion; they were somewhat resentful of government interference in these endeavors.

The rituals and customs of the Triads demonstrate the tendencies of secret societies everywhere towards occult trappings and symbols. One of their symbols was the Magic Sword of the Great Bear, which was used to exorcize evil spirits. The Triads would also cast huge quantities of paper (funny) money at funerals, for use by their fallen comrades in the next world.[8]

Like the Masons, the Triads had their secret signs and words for recognition among members of the society when outside in the world. For example, if a man being robbed was a Triad member, he would extend his thumb as a symbol. If the robber was a Triad, he would extend his pinkie, and go off and rob someone else (thus, via the use of his short finger, avoiding potential run-ins with the long arm of the law).

It is not only the fact that secret societies are (of course) practiced in keeping secrets, and that their members are not unfamiliar with coded words and symbols that makes them useful for military and intelligence purposes. Many members of the Triads, the Masons, and other secret organizations have access to economic, social, and political human intelligence sources that are of tremendous value for espionage purposes, and possibly of great value for military strategic and tactical purposes.

It might be interesting for the reader to note that, insofar as the Freemasons are concerned, discussions of religion and politics are strictly verboten in the lodge. That does not mean that these involvements and discussions do not occur outside of the lodge. Patriotism abounds in Masonry, and all Masons must be believers in deity and immortality.

The Triads, besides being mutual-benefit societies for their members, are still involved with criminal activities; they may have a member or two involved in the Golden Triangle drug operations and, hand-in-hand with that, political influence. It is meet and just that they are, for survival is the primary goal for any living entity, whether it is an individual, or an aggregate of like-minded individuals. Political influence and free access to those in power aid in that survival.

The secret societies are a microcosm of the blending of occult beliefs and territorial ambitions, which are the building blocks of the military-occult complex. From another secret society sprang a Siberian peasant, who, in saving a prince, was to rule a king and queen.

CHAPTER 9

THE MAD MONK

How a Siberian Peasant Ruled an Empire

Throughout history, there seems to have been a tendency for those in positions of political power to consult with and sometimes excessively depend on the advice of those with supposed psychic powers. The most casual reader of newspapers in the last fifteen years is familiar with White House first families consulting with astrologers and psychic advisors. In modern history astrologers played a rôle in the Nazi Third Reich, and in the escape of Rudolf Hess to England in 1941.

We shall herein focus on one of the most amazing political-psychic connections in the history of the military-occult complex, that of the last of the czars and a Siberian peasant named Grigori. He is more widely known as Rasputin.

Untutored, unkempt, unclean, certainly uninhibited, yet undoubtedly one of the most powerful personages in the reign of Czar Nicholas II, Rasputin once claimed, "Between these fingers, I hold the Russian Empire." It wasn't all brag and boast—there was much truth in the statement.[1]

The son of a carter from Pokrovskoe, Siberia, Rasputin rose to a position of being the right-hand man to the Romanovs, Nicholas and Alexandra. The Holy Devil (as he had sometimes been called) was a prime example of how an air of mystery and a reputation for other-worldly powers can cause a virtual nobody to rapidly rise to become a political name to conjure with. Even as an infant, Rasputin demonstrated a predilection for matters religious and spiritual. [2]

A chance meeting with a monk while Rasputin was working as a carter found him, at thirty, in a Siberian monastery. This hermitage, while maintaining the trappings and suits of Orthodox Christianity, was in reality a refuge for the Khlysty—a sect of mystically minded believers who supposedly could perform miracles, heal the sick, raise the dead, and enact such other wonders as caused men to offer their prayers, their money, and their power. Willingly. After the monastery, Rasputin became one of the *stranniki*, or wandering Siberian holy men prevalent at the time. In his wanderings, Rasputin participated in the religious rites of the Khlysty, which, to say the least, were rather lively compared to the traditional mass.

Chanting, singing, wild dancing, flagellation of the faithful, and as a finale, the Khlysty believers would engage in an orgy. "In sinful encounter the people of god roll on the ground and copulate regardless of age and relationship."[3] In time, Rasputin's reputation as a wonderworker and healer grew. Tales were told of how he could control the weather—having once cursed a village with a three-week-long drought.[4] His healing skills were to elevate him to a position of power and control in the house of the Romanovs—powers that still seem incredible for an uneducated peasant to have achieved.

It was the son of the Czar, Alexei, who suffered from what had been called "The Royal Disease," hemophilia. One injurious incident left the czarevich in great pain, and near death. His royal parents, who had long dabbled in spiritualism and occult matters,[5] sought the aid of their "Doctor of Tibetan Medicine," one Badmaev. Possessed of supposedly great mystical powers, Badmaev had a reputation as a powerful healer.[6] But when it came to curing the suffering Alexei, Badmaev proved not to be good enough. Then came Rasputin.

The boy was hemorrhaging internally and in great pain. Desperate, Alexandra, the boy's mother, who had heard of the exploits of Rasputin, sent for him. The wait was a long, nervous one. Finally, the Siberian mystic appeared at the house of the Czar. He entered Alexei's room and knelt in prayer by the icons in the corner of the bedroom. Over the head of the czarevich, Rasputin made the sign of the cross, and told the boy, "Look Alesha, look, I have driven all your horrid pains away. Nothing will hurt you anymore, and tomorrow you will be well again."[7] And it was so. Rasputin turned to the tear-filled Alexandra and said, "Believe in the power of my prayers and your son will live."[8] The hypnotic power of the peasant had effected a cure, or at least an improvement in the condition of the boy. To say that the royal parents were grateful would be an understatement.

The relationship between czar and psychic had begun, and was not to end until the assassination of Rasputin in 1916. It was a relationship that saw this "Holy Devil," despite his constant debaucheries and drunken bouts, advising the czar on political and military strategy.

In the history of the Romanovs, this political-psychic alliance was no aberration. They were a dynasty of which it has been said, "Modern diplomacy joined hands with necromancy, the supreme business of state with magic spells. . . . The policy of all the Russias was jointly decided by ministers and magicians."[9]

Czar Alexander I had been a recipient of military counsel from a psychic, Madame von Kruderer. She was his spiritual guide. She had divined that it was the destiny of this czar to defeat Napoleon. This medium with a military message was established in a hotel in Russian-occupied Paris in 1815 and was consulted by the czar on a daily basis.

Von Kruderer must have liked the accommodations, for she revealed that a message from beyond had been given her that the czar was the reincarnation of Jesus Christ. In this case, flattery did not get the psychic everywhere. It was the start of her falling out of favor with the czar. Alexander changed psychics. He now took up with one Koshelav, who was involved with the rather interesting Skotpsi sect. This particular religious group practiced castration as a religious rite. (Often man's sexuality is viewed as the enemy of his spirituality. This in turn leads to an excess of carnal desire, which then must be repressed as a sacrifice to the ethereal.) One of the female devotees of this sect, Catherine Tatarinova (who in her position was fortunately exempt from castration), was paid an annual salary of six thousand rubles by Czar Alexander. In return, she instructed him in the esoteric meanings hidden in the Bible.[10]

Moving forward in Romanov history, Czar Alexander II was a devoted spiritualist. Séances were regularly held at the Imperial Palace, and the famous nineteenth-century medium, Daniel Dunglas Hume, was a guest at the royal home. The library of the czar had thousands of occult books.

Later, we find Czar Nicholas II again holding séances, one of which saw the appearance of Czar Alexander III, who gave political advice from beyond the grave to his living son. The Romanov involvement with the occult was so great that the French magician, Dr. Gerard Encausse, whose magical name was "Papus," was to opine that the czar depended too much on advice from the beyond and was too reluctant to listen to his earthly advisors.[11]

Given its historical involvements with the mystical, it was no mystery that Rasputin could enchant the Romanov family. The Siberian peasant type of the early twentieth century had been called "narrow-minded, conservative, with a deep and often less than orthodox religious faith, and was frequently profoundly superstitious."[12] The description seemed to fit some of the aristocracy of Russia as well.

It was the peasant soldier of Siberia who, when encountering German airplanes in World War I, was to believe it proof that God was fighting on the side of the enemy.[13] But magical beliefs did not serve only to delude the peasant class. For the Prince of Peasants, Rasputin, was to proclaim, "The fools don't understand who I am. A sorcerer perhaps, a sorcerer maybe."[14] This sorcerer witnessed his power expand in the Imperial Court from spiritual advisor to political and military consultant. "Not only did Rasputin enjoy the reputation of possessing unlimited power, he was regarded as a holy man who had extraordinary mystic faculties."[15] These faculties were put at the disposal of the Czar for mundane use as well as mystical. On the recommendation of Rasputin, Grand Duke Nikolai Nikolaevich was removed as commander-in-chief of the Russian military and sent to the Caucasus front in World War I.[16]

This peasant, although extremely opposed to war, gave advice and counsel on military matters that was sometimes useful, sometimes ridiculous. "Our aristocrats are always howling about war to a victorious end," said Rasputin, "But they walk about Moscow and Petrograd, while out there the peasants are shedding their blood."[17] He warned the Czar against an offensive in 1915 in Galicia (which did prove to be a disaster),[18] supposedly controlled the weather in battles,[19] prayed for battlefield success,[20] and, on a more mundane level, advised that it was pointless to sacrifice thousands of men in an assault on a few yards of dirt.[21]

Healing, weather control, hypnotic ability. What was the source of Rasputin's power? What made this peasant commander-in-chief of the military-occult complex? According to Rasputin, he offered two types of counsel. There was his "advice" and there were "things seen in the night." Advice was peasant good common sense. Things seen in the night were probably obtained while Rasputin was in some trance or altered mental state.[22]

It is well known that altered states of mind can either produce or allow to come forth certain mental and physical abilities that can operate at enhanced performance levels. Hypnotically induced insensitivity to pain is frequently demonstrated, along with what purports to be age regression and even past life regression while in the hypnotic state. Mental rehearsal is frequently touted by motivational gurus as a technique to enhance physical performance, and alternate healing methods of mind and body interaction are constantly being championed.

When speaking of altered states of consciousness, often (but not always) we are dealing in a realm that is right-brain dominant. It is in the right hemisphere of the brain that our imagination, our creativity, our non-linear cognition occurs. It might be called the hemisphere of magic. The fact that Rasputin had not been the beneficiary of formal education—and the left-brain dominant training this demanded— might also have been a contributory factor to his ability as a "sorcerer." In other words, Rasputin could avoid taking the raw data of psychic output and arranging it in some conclusory fashion; in a logical, albeit incorrect manner. (Even in modern psychic spying, logical conclusions about extrasensory input, analytic overlay as it is now called, is a thing devoutly not to be wished. It easily ruins perceptual accuracy.)

As Rasputin was devoid of education, and from a deeply religious and superstitious background, we, in our rôles as sympathetic believers, can see how the information he received from higher sources would not be as likely to be tainted by left brain-analysis. It would be of greater purity. Thus goes the argument in the affirmative. It was an argument that would be readily accepted by the czarina, Alexandra, who urged Nicholas to always keep the photograph of Rasputin nearby, in order for him to benefit from its power. Regarding the clairvoyant ability of Rasputin, the czarina said, "He sees far ahead and therefore his judgment can be relied on."[23]

In accordance with her faith in the peasant psychic, Alexandra would continue to seek his advice on battlefield strategy in World War I.[24] Rasputin and his rise to power might also be viewed in a somewhat less favorable light. Perhaps it was via a fortunate coincidence; Rasputin happened to be at the czarevich's bedside just when the boy's condition was about to improve by itself. The peasant received the benefit of this coincidence, experienced by a Romanov royal family that for centuries had believed in and consulted with supposedly supernatural forces.

The timing was right, the "mark" was right, and so the Siberian seer becomes a royal advisor.

But when the chips are really down, when the use of his supposed psychic ability is most needed (by the seer himself), it fails—fatally. Reason? The powers never existed in the first place, and the pose was insufficient to save the poseur.

Then there is the question of the intelligence level of the czar and czarina. You have an uneducated *muzhik* giving military and political advice to the family that ruled the Russias for three hundred years. He is blatantly antiwar. Yet he is consulted on battle strategy—a peasant whose military experience is zero. Brilliant. Not surprising, however, for this was a czar and czarina who, on the day it happened, did not know that they were about to be lined up and shot.

The Romanovs, who "took a great interest in spiritualism, the occult, and table turning," never seemed very interested in political reality.[25] They were warned by Rasputin's enemies, who blamed his advice for Russia's military failures, but this was ignored. In fact, criticism of the "Holy Devil" was usually a one-way ticket out of the Czar's inner circle.[26]

Whether we take a favorable or skeptical view of Rasputin and his abilities, for the purposes of a historical analysis of what is herein called the military-occult complex, the story of this peasant and his royal dupes serves as a classic example of how the appearance of extrasensory ability can cause one's fortunes to rise in the realm of the ruling class.

Rasputin, who regularly dined with Prince Andronnikov to advise on affairs of state, with fish dinners paid for by the Russian secret police,[27] this "Holy Devil" who approves candidates for Prime Minister, has alliances with officials of the Ministry of the Interior, and is a player in diplomatic and espionage circles, has dirty fingernails, gets falling-down drunk, and sleeps with whatever doesn't run away.[28] (In certain respects he seems to be a combination of Charles Manson and Bill Clinton.) This is history, not fantasy. This rise to power of Rasputin happened, and had political and military effects on an international scale.

The net result of the Rasputin-Romanov connection was a decimated Russia, a drowned Rasputin, and a bullet-riddled czar and czarina. Did he see some of it coming? "His clearsightedness was so great that he once proclaimed with the mien of the prophet that the blood shed in this war (World War I) would take a frightful revenge not only on the generals and the diplomats, but even on the Czar himself."[29] Was this clearsightedness, or clairvoyance, if we like our French lessons? Or was it merely a mystical version of what should have been obvious in a Russia where soldiers had no bullets and civilians had no bread.

The Rasputin story took place in the first two decades of the twentieth century. It was a ripe era for spiritualism, for belief in the hereafter tends to increase when large numbers of the populace are getting massacred in war. It was a time where, in other lands, the cauldrons of psychic and political stews were bubbling, which would lead to a second world conflict and an almost successful attempt at the extermination of the Jewish people.

Rasputin had been one of the key players of the time in the military-occult complex. Was he only a cunning peasant who took advantage of a gullible ruler, or was he truly a gifted psychic? Against his being gifted, we submit in evidence his total failure to predict the circumstances of his own murder. Against his being a mere charlatan, we submit his curing of the czarevich.

But whether he was a psychic or a pseudo-seer, he was not the only one in his generation. In the early part of the twentiety century we meet some other remarkable men who played the two dangerous games of sorcery and espionage. Most of these had significantly more formal education than Rasputin, but were not hampered by the fact. Yet none of them were to attain the political power of Grigori Rasputin.

CHAPTER 10

SORCERER-SPIES OF THE EARLY TWENTIETH CENTURY

In the military-occult complex, it seems that the same characteristics and motivations that turn one to the potential power of the occult also direct that person to the arena of espionage. Perhaps we should not be surprised at this phenomenon. After all, both sorcery and spying are, by nature and necessity, clandestine. Both involve the ability to exhibit and exploit multiple personalities, or at least different facets of one's psychological makeup. Both endeavors also have an elitist appeal to them. The average man is obvious, simple, and not very good at anything; he is, well, average. But the sorcerer is a man (or woman) who seeks to become a superman. He strives to obtain powers far beyond those of mortal men.

The spy, with his secret work, with his lifestyle of dutiful deception and professional pretext, is also above the realm of the ordinary man. His aims are usually national or international in scope, and the arena he strives in is often in the center of the corridors of established political and military power. Therefore, it should come as no great surprise that at times our sorcerer and our spy come home to roost in one and the same individual.

Georgy Ivanovich Gurdjieff

Born sometime around 1872 (it is difficult to be sure), Gurdjieff entered the material world in Alexandropol in the Caucasus. Originally studying to be a priest, he abandoned the road to Rome for the more mysterious highways of the East. It is believed he spent some time in Tibet as an advisor to the Dalai Lama, according to a British intelligence agent who saw him there. Gurdjieff did the obligatory wanderings in the wilderness of Asia, and studied various means of psychic development. Supposedly, he could telepathically communicate with his students, and had boundless physical energy even into old age. His scientific knowledge and sophistication was remarkable to the British Intelligence types who knew him.

In 1910, in Moscow, Gurdjieff founded the Institute for the Harmonious Development of Man; after the Russian Revolution, he moved its headquarters to Paris. It is believed that Gurdjieff had worked for the Russian secret service against British interests in India and Afghanistan. Other incidents of his sub rosa political activities include his interaction with the German occultist Karl Haushofer, who had been the German military attaché to Tokyo prior to the first World War.[1] What is known for certain is that the highly psychic Gurdjieff had meetings with high-level military and intelligence personnel, was often in possession of abundant funds, and widely traveled throughout Europe and Asia. If he wasn't an intelligence agent, he certainly showed all the symptoms.[2] This sorcerer-spy of the early twentieth century military-occult complex is also memorable for having said one of the more unusual exit lines of any psychic. His last words on earth were "Now we can have a cup of coffee."[3] He died in 1949. His philosophy and works survive.

Karl Germer

A German who fought in World War I and was awarded the Iron Cross,[4] Germer was a long-time student of the occult and a prolonged financial supporter of the infamous Aleister Crowley.[5] He was also a devoted astrologer.[6] This psychic soldier was convinced that Crowley had been magically responsible for Hitler's destruction, although he was unclear as to how he determined this "fact."[7] More conservative historians have not sufficiently explored this rather curious conclusion to offer competent comment. Germer was also a member of a German secret organization called the OTO, or *Ordo Templi Orientis*, which means Order of the Eastern Temple (or Templars). He was later to succeed Crowley as the head of this order.

When Germer lived in New York, he attracted the attention of the FBI and J. Edgar Hoover for his World War II efforts to bring Crowley into the United States.[8] The FBI believed Germer was an intelligence agent for the Germans during the Second World War.[9]

Whatever the truth is, he was a soldier, he was a devoted student of the occult, and he was the head of an organization whose main mission was magic. These are the facts that make him one of the luminaries of the military-occult complex in the early twentieth century.

Germer studied a form of magic that dealt with the use of sex as a means of transcendence and magical evocation. Whether he succeeded in achieving new and more powerful levels of reality is open to question. However, his sex/magic career was terminated by his death from testicular cancer in 1962, showing that the military-occult complex has an ironic sense of humor in the method by which it disposes of its denizens.[10]

Karl Haushofer

A general in the Kaiser's army and military attaché in the Far East, Haushofer could speak fluent Japanese, was a professor of geopolitical theory at the University of Munich, and was the developer of the Nazi Lebensraum ("living room" territorial expansionist) doctrine. He was also a student of the occult. His son, Albrecht was an astrologer and a Nostradamus fan. In Tibet, he had met with Gurdjieff and together they are credited with being the force behind the founding of the German Order (Germanen Order). Haushofer was to become one of Hitler's top advisors until the astrologically timed flight to England of Hess in 1941, when Haushofer fell from grace. His participation in the 1944 assassination attempt on Hitler found him in Dachau, which he survived. His survival in the death camp was a short-term triumph, however, as Haushofer committed suicide by arsenic poisoning while being questioned by Nuremberg tribunal investigators. His son Albrecht had been executed on the streets.[11] Another military mystic in the realm of the psychic soldier, Haushofer died as do many in the military-occult complex—unnaturally.[12]

Dennis Wheatley

Hack horror writer Dennis Wheatley was perhaps best known to the public for his book, *The Devil Rides Out*, which later became a Hammer Film in the 1960s. The book dealt with an Aleister Crowley–like magician who led a cult of devil-worshipers. Wheatley was writing from experience. He had several times dined with the "Great Beast" Crowley, and claimed to have been working with Churchill's joint planning staff in World War II. Wheatley was to hobnob with various MI5 (British Military Intelligence) types during the war, and had helped Maxwell Knight of British Intelligence get his book published in the 1930s. Knight was the real-world rôle model for "M" of Ian Fleming's James Bond novels. It was Wheatley who had introduced Knight to Crowley while they were involved with the psychic side of getting Hess, the Nazi astrology fanatic, to fly to England. Wheatley's wife was also an employee of MI5.[13] Espionage was a family affair at the Wheatleys, and even his stepson worked for—guess who—MI5.[14]

Another interesting phenomenon in this era of the military-occult complex was the propensity of sorcerer-spies to have literary ambitions—many of which were successfully fulfilled. Wheatley, a writer of horror fiction, Fleming, who created the world-famous super-spy James Bond, and Aleister Crowley, who created brilliant psychic and intellectual detective Simon Iff. Perhaps they doubted their abilities to achieve immortality through their magic, and sought it via the efforts of their pens. Crowley, discussed next, was perhaps the most prolific—and least successful writer of the group.

Aleister Crowley

One of the most famous, or infamous, citizens of psychicland during the first half of the twentieth century was Aleister Crowley. Born in 1875 to a father who had made his fortune in the ale business, Crowley was to drink deep of the intoxicating waters of the occult, and become known as the "Wickedest Man in the World," and the self-titled "Great Beast." So much ink has been spilled about Crowley since his death at the age of 72 in 1947 that the reader will be spared the usual biographical irrelevancies, and we will focus on his participation in the military-occult complex.

Crowley was a mixed bag. Mountaineer, poet, sorcerer, and mystic, he had an encyclopedic knowledge of magical lore—and a heroin habit that could kill a horse. Despite all of his bad press, bad poetry, and his bad boy black-magician image, Crowley was not unknown to or unused by British Intelligence in the course of his long and bizarre life. During the World War I years, Crowley, having been rejected for service in the military, made his way to New York, where he cast spells, whored around, and nearly starved. A fortunate meeting with an Irishman on a public conveyance led to his becoming a staff writer for a pro-German publication, *The Fatherland*. This propaganda rag supported Crowley for a time and earned him the title of small-time traitor from a high-ranking member of British Intelligence.[15]

Crowley had also become a member of the previously mentioned OTO, and later became its head—although not without significant protest from certain factions of the organization. He claimed his efforts for *The Fatherland* were actually in the service of British interests, as the pro-German propaganda articles he penned were so ludicrous as to be obviously tongue in loyal British cheek. British Intelligence denied that he was working for them, which of course could be true, or could be false, and the denial would be standard operating intelligence procedure. As an interesting aside, the OTO that Crowley joined and later ruled was started by an agent of the German secret service. This organization, at which we shall take a close look in the following chapter, was a veritable nest of sorcerer-spies. So we have a Crowley who in 1912 joins a German secret society started by a German spy. He writes pro-German articles during World War I, and claims he does it all for the interests of "that realm, that England." Was the claim valid, or was it disinformation?

On the one hand, Crowley was such a monumental liar and poseur that one has the tendency to take any claim of his with a large Siberian salt mine. On the other hand, several sources relate to Crowley's World War II participation in the Hess escape for British Intelligence, and that during the '20s and '30s Crowley worked for MI6, providing information on European communist activities, and the relationship between the Nazi movement and various occult organizations.[16] Using Crowley as an intelligence operative in some ways would be nonsensical, and in some ways would make sense. Notoriety is not a thing devoutly to be wished in a secret agent. Crowley was known and disliked throughout Europe, and was as much a self-publicist as Oscar Wilde, but with less literary skill.

Further, Crowley had demonstrated a cavalier attitude towards what was intended to be confidential information. He had exposed many supposedly secret occult rituals, and shifted loyalties on the whims of his gigantic ego. A dedicated (at first) member of the Golden Dawn in 1898, which was an occult organization of spurious Germanic origin, Crowley was responsible for the creation of splinter groups that helped to decimate the membership of that organization.

On the positive side for using Crowley for espionage purposes, he had extensive contacts in European magical lodges and secret societies. He belonged to the OTO, which provided many German contacts until Hitler outlawed secret societies, and had widely traveled the continent. His knowledge of the lore of magic and his astrological expertise (such as it was) could be put to good use against the occult-ridden Nazi command. Therefore, a Crowley might be useful in psychological warfare, but a definite dud as a clandestine operative in the field. How a bisexual heroin addict could hope to get a top security clearance is a great mystery in itself, but then again, we are talking British Intelligence, with Kim Philby, Guy Burgess, and other colorful alumni.

How could people entrusted with the conduct of war, and the gathering of information upon which wars must be fought, seriously use individuals who were openly and notoriously proclaiming their psychic and magical powers? The answer is that, in the world of intelligence and in the world of the military, you sometimes get to lie down with strange bedfellows, just like politics. The key in war is to win, no matter how. The key in intelligence is to get accurate and useful timely information, no matter how. If you need to use a heroin-addicted third-rate poet and poseur to get a high-ranking Nazi to fly to England, you do it. If you need to use a literary hack to set up a meeting between your intelligence head and said heroin addict, you do it. You don't have to like it, but you do it anyway.

The reader has no doubt seen exposés alleging that the CIA and the Mafia have worked together, that in Laos, our government supplied transport to drug-dealing Asian warlords, and that spies use sexual blackmail to gather information. All's fair in espionage and war.

The use of psychics, sorcerers, magicians and wizards is within the rules of the military-occult complex, and there are times they can prove quite useful. Clandestine agents and magicians alike, to be effective, must be comfortable in the use of alternate personalities—alternate realities, if you will. The spy must appear to be his cover, he must believe he is whatever he has been instructed to appear to be, so that he may hopefully obtain his information unfettered by undue interest by others. The sorcerer must, during his ritual work, become an alternate personality in an alternate reality of spirits and disembodied intelligences. The mental prerequisites for success in both fields are similar.

One organization combined a significant amount of occult activities and espionage endeavors: the cauldron of spies and psychics known as the *Ordo Templi Orientis*—an organization still working its magical influence today.

CHAPTER 11

MARCHING ORDERS

The Military-Occult Marriage in the OTO

During the end of the nineteenth and the early part of the twentieth century, a variety of magical "orders" were created that were populated by men who, besides their spiritual endeavors, were deeply involved with military and intelligence matters. These were times of great conflict, of a defeated Germany, and of economic chaos. These factors would turn the minds of certain men to the mythological times of old, when all was glory and power. The orders formed would give renewed strength and hope to those who had no practical right to either condition. Of these magical orders, perhaps the best known example was the *Ordo Templi Orientis*, the OTO, or the Order of the Eastern Templars.

Founded around the turn of the century, one of its co-founders was a former agent of the Prussian secret police. The OTO became a haven for psychics who would be spies and soldiers—those seeking magical power to triumph over the material devastation that surrounded their lives. Such luminaries as Crowley and Germer, whom we met in the previous chapter, were joined in the OTO by such (literal) rocket scientists as Jack Parsons. These were men who straddled the dual pillars upon which the military-occult complex was founded.

The co-founder of the OTO, Theodor Reuss, also known by his magical moniker of Frater Merlin, had spied on German socialist expatriates in England,[1] including the family of Karl Marx,[2] and was an undercover agent in the Socialist League until he was found out, then thrown out.[3] Reuss, after having made the acquaintance of Aleister Crowley, and impressed by his magical knowledge, brought Crowley into the fold of the OTO and appointed him "Outer Head" of the Order (OHO) for all of Great Britain. Crowley, as we already have seen, operated not only on the fringe of reality, but also on the fringe of British Intelligence.

With his large and deviant sexual appetite, Crowley was tailor-made for the OTO, as this organization of magicians practiced the various arts of sex-magic. Depending on the degree of initiation in the OTO, one practiced heterosexual, homosexual, or autoerotic magic. As sex and magic were Crowley's two favorite hobbies, it is not surprising that he would be a long-term member of the OTO, benefiting both sexually and financially from his association with it until his death in 1947.

The theory behind sexual magic is ably stated in a book about an OTO organizational offshoot, the *Fraternitas Saturni*, or Brotherhood of Saturn. S. Edred Flowers, in *Fire and Ice*, explains:

"In traditional historical sex magic, as it has been filtered into the Western Magical Tradition, there seems to have been the common belief in the notion that the sexual fluids contain/are a power which can be manipulated by the will of the magician. . . . From a pragmatic viewpoint the central fact surrounding sexual magic is that it works on the basis of sexual energy or arousal. The higher the level of sexual excitement, the higher the level of energy available to the magician.[4]

Did sex magic really work? Crowley, a bisexual and master masturbator, was kind enough to history to record many of his sex-magic rituals in his diaries. Some examples follow.

On November 23, 1914, Crowley rents the services of a black prostitute, one Grace Harris, and proceeds to engage in such activity as one traditionally engages in with a prostitute. His goal, besides the obvious one, is to obtain "immediate money." The result: in his diary two weeks later, Crowley writes, "$15.00 between me and the workhouse and I owe $200."[5] In another sex-magic experiment, on February 7, 1915, Crowley engages in an act of magical masturbation, seeking to obtain the princely sum of $20,000.[6] No money was forthcoming from this hands-on working. Crowley was always long on sexual partners and short on funds.[7]

During his stay in New York during World War I (having been found unfit by England for military service), Crowley was to obtain employment of a sort, although whether this was related to his sexual sorcery or not is open to question. In any event, he met up with a publisher of a pro-German propaganda rag, *The Fatherland*. Crowley was hired as its editor, filling the pages with his magical theories and other bizarre ideas. Yet, in the post–World War I years, up until the early years of World War II, Crowley did in some capacity or other serve the needs of British Intelligence, working for MI5. (In the previous chapter we heard of his involvement with the flight of Hess in 1941 from Germany to England.) Given the political fallout that would have resulted in making this involvement public, it should be no surprise that there is a paucity of documentation concerning Crowley's intelligence efforts. (Any witnesses have long since died, and since then, they have not been heard from.)

Crowley was to appoint Karl Germer as his successor in the OTO. Germer had served with the German Army in World War I and was said to have worked for German Intelligence.[8] Eventually Germer arrived in the United States after a brief period in a concentration camp. When Germer, who had been investigated by the FBI, died in 1962, there was a controversy over who was entitled to be the next Outer Head of the Order.

One pretender to the throne was a Brazilian homosexual writer named Marcello Motta. Motta had ably described himself as a mixture of paranoia and megalomania, and was convinced he was a target and mind-control victim of the FBI, the CIA, Shin Beth, and Brazilian Intelligence.[9] Motta found himself at odds with one of the magical practices of the OTO, that is, with the physical practice of masturbation. He referred to this form of sexual self-help as "One of the most insidious and vicious of practices."[10]

When not practicing sex magic, or being controlled by various intelligence agencies, Motta sought to defend his title as OHO of the OTO. He failed. Grady McMurty, another who claimed the right to the title from Germer, officially gained the prize after a determination by the United States federal court. Motta was to blame the spy agencies for his defeat.

When he joined the OTO, Grady McMurty was also a lieutenant in the U.S. Army, therefore having excellent credentials for membership in the military-occult complex, being both sorcerer and soldier.[11] After his military service, McMurty worked for the government as an analyst and taught political science at George Washington University.[12]

The man who brought McMurty into the OTO was Jack Parsons, one of the most bizarre characters to inhabit the realm of the magical military mystery tour. Parsons, bizarre enough to believe in the efficacy of sexual magic, was a rocket scientist. He had shown an early aptitude for chemistry and physics, and was affiliated with Cal-Tech and the Jet Propulsion Laboratory. In 1939, Parsons joined the OTO.

During World War II, the Americans were in a race with the Nazis in the development of rocketry. The good guys of Pasadena versus the bad guys at Peenemunde. The V-1 and V-2 were already raining destruction on England, and the Americans were anxious to develop a solid rocket propellant. It was Parsons who succeeded in this, and his research and development was put to practical use by the Navy at the end of World War II. In honor of his achievement, Parsons had a lunar crater named after him, which was appropriately located on the dark side of the moon.

Parsons became the OHO for the OTO "Agape" Lodge in California. A rocket scientist working for the war effort, he was also leading a group of sexual magicians trying to contact and exploit other-worldly powers—the very essence of the military-occult complex at work and play. But despite his brilliance as a scientist, his discretion as a participant in secret government work was somewhat lacking. In 1940, one of Parson's comrades in the OTO wrote of him, "Twenty-six years of age, six feet two, vital, potentially bisexual at the very least, University of California and Cal Tech, now engaged at Cal Tech Chemical Laboratories developing bigger and better explosives for Uncle Sam. Travels under sealed orders from the government."[13]

The above is a little too much information for a sex magician to have without a clearance and a need to know. This breach of operational security, however, could be expected from a man who six years later would be referring to himself as the Antichrist, and in 1952 would blow himself up by his rather careless handling of fulminate of mercury.

It is a common phenomenon in the realm of the military-occult complex for the possessors of magical and military secrets to be rather loose about security. After all, what is the use of being privy to deep, dark secrets, whether martial or mystical, unless you can impress your friends with all the really neat stuff you know, but can't tell them about?

Both magic and intelligence work are by their nature elitist. Not everybody gets to learn or use the secret spells, not everybody gets to know who is working on classified rocket projects, etc. Not everybody should know. The premature exposure of military or intelligence secrets can cause death, destruction, or derisive laughter. (The exposure of magical secrets usually just causes the last event.) Unfortunately, it often appears that the type of person who engages in magic or spying is possessed of a rather substantial ego and wants public recognition of how really important he is. The frustration comes when this spy or this sorcerer cannot spill the beans, magical or otherwise, and these types usually don't handle frustration well (or for long), and if they can't blow something or somebody up, either by explosives or spirits—guess what. They will violate their oaths of secrecy.

Crowley had violated magical oaths by revealing the secret rituals of the Golden Dawn, a magical organization he joined in 1898. Parsons violated security by talking about his rocket work—otherwise how could his fellow OTOer know about it? Both were possessed of enormous egos, Crowley warming up to his rôle as wickedest man in the world, and Parsons deeming himself to be the Antichrist. Both were unstable personalities.

In 1940, Parsons, working in concert with a "Frater H," performed a sex-magic ritual to contact the Goddess "Babalon." This has been referred to as the Babalon Working, the resulting communication from this nonexistent spiritual entity taken down in the form of 77 verses. "Frater H" was none other than L. Ron Hubbard. Crowley learned of Parson's later misfortunes, and in typical Crowleyan sympathy, wrote "I have no further interest in Jack and his adventures; he is just a weak-minded fool, and must go to the Devil in his own way." (Parsons went to the Devil in one hell of an explosion six years after Crowley's pronouncement.)

Despite his loss of love and money, Parsons continued. He continued to lose. He was bounced from his leadership of the OTO and in 1948 lost his security clearance due to his "membership in a religious cult believed to advocate sexual perversion."[14] Still pressing on, Parsons lost his job at Hughes Aircraft in 1950 for being in possession of classified material without authorization. In 1952, Parsons performed his experiments in determining whether there really was life after death by dropping a vial of fulminate of mercury. To date, Parsons has not been forthcoming with the results of that experiment.

In this survey of the *Ordo Templi Orientis,* we have seen a heroin-addicted bisexual magician working for British Intelligence (Crowley); a rocket scientist–sorcerer developing solid fuel while working sex magic (Parsons); and a writer of science fiction (Hubbard).

How can it be that such insanity and nonsense can occupy the minds of those who are also involved in one degree or another in espionage or military work? Yet remember: this is a work of nonfiction, these people existed, these organizations were founded, and the events described took place.

The purpose of this work is to illuminate a dark corner of the history of the military and intelligence establishments. The corner where the practical soldier or spy meets the otherworldly occult devotee—what has been herein often called the military-occult complex. It has been so-called to parallel the phrase military-industrial complex, which we all heard so much about in the 1960s and 1970s via the media. That was a symbiotic relationship between the Pentagon and corporate America. It still exists.

The Thule Society

We examine the relationship between the armies and spy agencies of the world and those who claim to be possessors of supernormal powers and spirit communications. This military-occult complex was best exemplified in the early part of the twentieth century by the OTO. The OTO still exists in various chapters but is a ghostly shadow of its former self.

However, there were other organizations of soldiers-spies-psychics, some of which had a direct effect on the development of the greatest horror of the twentieth century—the Nazis. In most of the works that deal with the occult influences on the Nazi movement, one organization is named as a leading contributor, *Thule Gesellshaft,* or the Thule Society. This order was named after an imaginary *wunderland* that paralleled Atlantis in its advancement and the development of its people. It also shared with Atlantis the quality of never having existed in reality. But that didn't stop its members from asserting Thule as a golden age paradise. Undaunted by the mythological origins of their name, Thule members practiced yoga, gesture magic, pan-Germanism, and a traditional favorite pastime of the prewar German race, anti-Semitism. They also became involved in military action, hoarding weapons and pummeling suspected communists.

Thule was founded in 1918 by one Rudolf Blauer, a skilled laborer, who in good occult tradition had aristocratic pretensions and dubbed himself Baron Rudolf von Sebottendorf. His father was a "noble" railway worker, and Rudolf himself was engaged in the aristocratic art of working on a steamship. (The pretensions of occultists, who are usually collectors of titles and honors toward aristocracy, is common. Crowley often called himself Prince Chioa Kahn, or Count Svareff, or some other such creation. Samuel Mathers, one of the co-founders, or better said, co-frauders of the Golden Dawn, pretended to be to the manner born, although he was a penniless clerk.) In any event, Sebottendorf went to Turkey and Egypt in his travels. His meetings with Sufi masters and Cairo conjurers led him to formulate the practices that would be used by the Thule Society. Sebottendorf, a wounded veteran of the Balkan War of 1912, became the Grand Master of Thule. He would soon add mayhem to the magic.

It was a Thule member who designed the final version of the Nazi flag, and it was another Thule member, Dietrich Eckhart, who trained Adolf Hitler in oratory and introduced him around in Munich society. Sebottendorf himself was a supposed authority on astrology, alchemy, dowsing, and rune symbolism.[15] He killed himself after Germany's defeat in World War II. Thule deserves its own special place in the hall of shame of the military-occult complex. Its official and active life lasted somewhere around two years, and its most influential members were executed by a firing squad. This was not very strong tangible evidence for the magical powers of this mythologically oriented order. The aristocracy of blood did not endure. Yet Thule was partially responsible for the meteoric career rise of a certain failed Austrian artist from whom the world was to hear much for a time. Hitler, who adopted the occult symbolism of the swastika, whose elite SS funded excursions to magical Tibet, established a thousand-year Reich that fell quite short of its durational goal. Germany, the fatherland of the master race, once again mastered the art of coming in second in world military conflicts. Were they out-magicked as well as out-manufactured?

Another of the German occultists who deserves recognition in the pre-Nazi era is Adolf Lanz, who also became an overnight aristocrat, calling himself Lanz von Liebenfels. He was an astrologer who knew Hitler in 1909. In 1894, Lanz had formed the *Ordo Novi Templi*, the ONT, or the New Templar Order.

In 1907, from ONT temple headquarters, the swastika flapped on a flag in the wind. Lanz believed the swastika symbolized "an abandonment of Christianity, an embracing of neo-paganism, a desire to become or create the superman, and an affirmation of Aryan racial superiority."[16] This is a lot of mileage for a little cross with bent ends, especially when one considers that this blond-haired Aryan race of supermen had absolutely no historical existence, thereby making its superiority most difficult to affirm. Lanz, when not waving swastikas or waxing eloquent about races that never existed, published an occult rag known as *Ostara*. It was read on a regular basis by Hitler, who even went to the trouble of obtaining back issues.

These organizations, which, to some degree or another, played a part in the rise of the National Socialist German Workers Party, soon became victims of the organization they elevated. When Adolf Hitler came to power in 1933, secret societies were verboten. (Totalitarian governments are never fond of organized cabals operating in their borders under oaths of secrecy.) Many members of secret societies were sent to concentration camps; many died there. Yet, when these occultists were needed for the Reich's purposes, they were freed to enable the Nazis to use their extrasensory powers. It has been rumored that German occultists (some who came from the camps), engaged in map dowsing to find Mussolini when he had been kidnapped by the Allies.

It seems that in the West at least, the more benign the secret society, the longer it will endure. Thule, with its magic, hate-mongering, and gun running, lasted only a few years. The ONT vanished. The OTO still exists.

Freemasonry, which was outlawed by the Nazis and considered to be part of the international Jewish conspiracy for world domination (another myth-based theory) not only exists today, but thrives. The Mason, unlike the Thulist, does not hoard weapons. He no longer plans armed revolution, and he preaches brotherly love, not racial hate. Freemasonry sponsors medical research, free burn-victim hospitals, and other charitable works, yet still maintains various occult and mystical trappings and doctrines.

When secret societies like Thule and ONT are violence-oriented and hatred-based, they attract the disenfranchised, the untutored, the unemployed, boosting their spirits with myths and theories that have little or no basis in reality. In return they obtain numbers for their secret armies, blood to spill in the name of glory and sacrifice. A breed of supermen who bleed just like regular folks, and are only following orders—magical orders.

The OTO and ONT with their Templar pretensions as new crusaders are now irrelevant or ancient dust; their conflicts, their temporary triumphs, now merely a tale to be told. Growing like a fungus in the post–World War I devastation of Deutschland, these magical-military fraternities helped to create a movement that was to be responsible for the slaughter of scores of millions of human beings. Yet now they either don't exist or have no de facto power.

Perhaps this particular lesson from the military-occult complex teaches that while mythology (as well as manufacturing capability) can temporarily cause tremendous destruction to occur, in the final analysis, myths of hate or myths of bogus racial superiority will not survive, and will become as the spurious "truths" upon which they were created-nonexistent.

Our primitive symbol- and pattern-making brains seem to require guideposts and glyphs for our beliefs and prejudices. We can murder under a cross, we can murder under a swastika. These same brains require or at least request external and extraordinary justifications for what really is nothing more than territorial instinct, like the dog that urinates on a tree to mark its territory or the crow that cackles from a branch to claim its stake; even the German who cries for *Lebensraum* while depriving others of their territory and their lives. The dog is programmed to so act, the crow has no other behavior to choose. But man can choose. Man can be the generator of genocide or the *parakletos* (the comforter) who brings peace and tolerance. He can be both.

The myths he uses give him the justification he must have for his primitive urges. The magic he exploits gives him, in theory at least, the means to become superman, or in other words, to triumph over his enemies. These myths and this magic have blended together with his military might throughout the ages to form the military-occult complex.

CHAPTER 12

THE MAGIC OF THE "MASTER RACE"

Aryan Astrology and Nazi Necromancy

Perhaps to the observant eye, there had been a foreshadowing of events in the chiaroscuro of the German expressionist films of the 1920s. Witness the hypnotic control exercised over the somnambulist, Cesare, in the 1919 classic *The Cabinet of Dr. Caligari,* the semitic caricature of the Vampire, Count Orloff, defeated by pure German womanhood in the 1921 film *Nosferatu,* and the creation of a robot human in the 1926 Fritz Lang classic *Metropolis.* To see these films, even today, gives one a disturbing image of what Nazi Germany was to become. The hypnotism of Caligari was reflected in the hypnotic control Hitler had over his massed audience. The destruction of a blood-sucking, hook-nosed vampire by a pure-blooded German heroine paralleled the racial hygiene and *Lebensborn* sentiments of the National Socialists. The mechanization of man in *Metropolis* predicted the human robots that were to become the members of the SS.

These films, with their occult overtones and undertones, were a celluloid rendering of the occult influences that were to mold the National Socialist German Workers Party—the Nazis. This exploration of the metaphysical madness and mysticism that helped create Hitler, Himmler, and Hess is the most horrific chapter in the history of the

105

military-occult complex. While German occultism existed for centuries, it was the influences of the occult groups of the nineteenth- and early twentieth-century movements that helped form the Third Reich.

Kaiser Wilhelm was an adherent of spiritualism and often attended séances. When exiled in Holland in 1918, he took advantage of his enforced leisure to study occult subjects. The supreme leader of Germany undertook an investigation into the supernatural, setting the stage.

In Germany, it was the Thule Society that is often given credit for being the foundation of the fantasy that fueled the Führer. Thule mixed fascism and fable to the delight and delusion of some 1,500 highly placed members of German society. (It is a common phenomenon in occult circles for practitioners to ascend to false aristocratic pedestals—and real aristocrats to seek such power as occult societies might offer.)

Membership of Thule included the minister of justice of Bavaria, Franz Gurter, the commissioner of the Munich police, and others. Officials and professionals, they nevertheless believed the pronouncements of a peasant seer who proclaimed that there would be a German messiah who would lead the country to victory and worldwide domination.[1] Of course, said seer was engaging in political correctness (or psychic inaccuracy) in calling the murdering Hitler a messiah. This failed artist with a Chaplinesque mustache was to lead Germany into destruction and depravity, not world domination. (This was one medium who certainly missed the message.)

There was no Thule like an old Thule, and this organization of mystics took their name from the ancient mythical land of the frozen north, supposedly located between Greenland and Scandinavia. Thule participants practiced spiritualism, and the deceased members of the Thule Society were often "contacted," regularly "appearing" in séances. Even the shade of the Bavarian Prince von Thurn and Taxis appeared in the dimly lit rooms where the German living communed with their honored dead.[2]

Wishing to hold more than seances, the Thulists were to accumulate a vast store of weapons and organize a terrorist network, thus becoming full-fledged members of the military-occult complex. It was the membership of Thule that gave birth to the German Worker's Party, soon afterwards to become NSDAP, the Nazis.[3] The emblem for Thule was none other than the swastika. Everyone knows what the emblem and symbol for the Nazi Party was. The painting of the swastika on a wall, even today, is viewed as more of an act of vandalism than a political statement. Yet for many centuries, it was a religious symbol.

The SS

Thus, from an organization of misty-eyed mystics with a taste for terrorism sprung the Nazi movement, which was to give new dimension to the words "mass murder." It is this mysticism and magic that colored the entire Third Reich. When one envisions marching Nazi troops, the mechanical Golem-like goose step comes immediately to mind. The Darth Vader–like black uniforms of the SS set them apart from the rest of the German war machine, along with their *Totenkopf* (death's head) insignia.

It was these SS men, originally formed as the bodyguard for Hitler, who were to become the modern satanists of the Reich. Applicants to the SS had to prove their racial purity ("Aryan" ancestry) back to 1750. They had to meet stringent physical requirements, as they were to formulate the core master-race *Übermenschen* of the new Aryan superman, fathering their blue-eyed, blond-haired bastards in the breeding camps of the *Lebensborn* movement.

They were to abandon the Christianity of their native land, and study a mish-mash paganism, where Christmas was replaced by the age-old Yule celebration, and the runes of old were again studied for their symbolic meanings. The very SS designation was made up of a rune; the men of the *Schutzstaffel* became the new Knights Templar, defending the Nazi "faithful."

Paradoxically, the leader of this organization of blond, blue-eyed supermen was a former chicken farmer who had a weak chin, glasses, and was somewhat less than heroic in his physical proportions. His name was Heinrich Himmler.

Himmler, deserving of special mention in the history of the military-occult complex, shall herein obtain his due. He was not the first SS officer; his official number was 168.[4] In 1929, when he was 29, he was appointed *Reichsführer SS*. It was also the same year in which Himmler saw the birth of his daughter, Gudrun.[5]

Himmler set up a Race and Settlement Office, which became involved, among other things, with the mythos of an Aryan race; a people of pure Aryan blood (whatever that was supposed to mean). Eugenics programs were established, along with the strict SS marriage code that forbade marriage to those women who could not prove their blood purity back to 1750.

Besides being Aryan, the SS wives had to be fertile, to be able to contribute junior supermen to the thousand-year Reich (which lasted a dozen years). Pregnancy in and out of wedlock was promoted by the Nazis, who gave special economic incentives to those it wished to engage in breeding, while they freely offered sterilization and abortion to those who should not continue to reproduce their own "inferior" subspecies. This was a journey back in time, to fertility cults, "blood is the life" nonsense, and other occult trappings.

The SS opposition to the established church caused much anticlerical propaganda to be disseminated. The doctrines of Christ did not dovetail with the Nazi "religion." You can't have the meek inheriting the earth while you are promoting a mythical race of fair-haired supermen. Turning the other cheek does not exactly go hand in hand with dreams of world domination, and the ways of Jesus were discouraged in the darkness of Hitler's dominion. The Nazi movement was perhaps the strongest example in the twentieth century of how what was essentially a military and political enterprise created its own occult mythos and actively opposed established religion.

Himmler, the SS leader, had some strange individual beliefs. Fascinated by the history of King Henry the Fowler, a tenth-century German despot, Himmler claimed to be in communication with the Fowler's spirit. He purchased, and at great expense renovated, the dilapidated Wewelsburg castle in the Westphalia region of Germany, holding rituals in the cellars paralleling pagan ceremonies.

One of the more interesting episodes of Himmler's endeavors in the history of the military-occult complex was his attempt at what would now be called remote influence. It was during the trial of a Nazi general named Fritsch, when Himmler, with a dirty dozen of his handpicked SS henchmen, sat in an adjoining room, attempting to mentally force Fritsch to tell the truth.[6]

One presumes that while these SS men were concentrating on Fritsch, they wore their SS rings with the runes, swastika, and a human skull boldly emblazoned thereupon.[7] Thus this would have been a full-blown magical ritual working, in its suits and trappings, and in its purpose.

Besides the magical mystery tour that was Himmler's, there was Rudolf Hess, Hitler's right hand man, who was a devotee of the occult in general, and astrology in particular. Hitler was somewhat less than pleased when, in May of 1941, Hess took off to England, wearing his special Tibetan magical charm, to sue for peace with Great Britain. This was the same Hess who consulted card readers and star gazers regarding the proper timing to obtain offspring.[8]

Astrology Goes to War

We know that Germany was defeated by the superior war machine of the Allies, especially that of the United States. But it wasn't just rockets and bullets that were used against the Nazis. The Allies used their own astrologers to obtain intelligence about what Hitler's horoscope pundits were saying to him. The British hired well-known astrologer Louis de Wohl, who joined their Psychological Warfare department for this purpose.

Allied planes dropped bogus German publications containing negative astrological predictions of the outcome of the war, and the prophecies of Nostradamus (a converted Jew) were used by both sides to prove that the stars were on their side.[9]

The British even had their own remote viewer who, sitting in her London flat, could send her spirit out into the ether and listen in on the German high command as it plotted strategy, and "read" classified Nazi documents. Her name was Anne, and whether she could do all that, or this was just a propaganda ploy is not yet beyond the realm of debate.[10] Many psychics at the time claimed that it was their magical powers that averted the Nazi invasion of England. The paranormal is much stronger post facto, of course.

The use of horoscopes and prophecies was old hat in the military-occult complex and, of course, it wouldn't end with World War II. (We shall see how the full-dress uniforms of the supernatural were used in Vietnam, the Philippines, and the Congo.) Ever since warriors wore animal skins and horned helmets, the paranormal has been used, not only as an intelligence collection tool, but as a means of psychological warfare.

Assuming the British Anne was real, then this might be the first modern instance of a remote-viewing mission being carried out in times when radio communications were well established. This is significant. In the times of conflict wherein the paranormal was used predating the radio age, there was nothing "in the air." There were no man-made electromagnetic radiations in the ether. Therefore, any psychic functioning that might have occurred could not be impeded by electromagnetic effects. There are some indications that electromagnetic radiation may have an effect on extrasensory perception.

If, as appears to be the case, remote viewing can successfully occur in an atmosphere that is superabundant with electromagnetic transmissions of widely varying frequencies, this might indicate that electromagnetics might not be useful as a psychic spying countermeasure. (The jury is not in on this one yet, as frequency range might be significant, but the fact is worth remembering.) From the modern remote-viewing experiments that we shall soon learn about, it is possible that an "Anne" could have informed British Intelligence about Nazi plans. Possible, but not necessarily likely, for the methods and protocols of modern remote viewing did not then exist.

It is important for the reader to realize that, as far as the actual influence of the occult on the Nazi movement goes, there has been much confusion, misinformation, outright fabrication, and hyperbole. There has also been some truth. That Himmler and Hess were *okultniks* has never been disputed. How much influence the occult had on Hitler is a topic of hot debate. (Remember, it was Hitler who outlawed secret societies and put many mystics in concentration camps.) There were magical voices that influenced the philosophy of NSDAP, like Alfred Rosenberg who, in his book *Myth of the Twentieth Century*, wrote, "The calm of the Nordic man is self-reflection before action, is mysticism and life simultaneously."[11]

Regardless of the actual utility of the occult to the Nazi war machine, we cannot dispute that a prefabricated mythos, backed by rituals and mass gatherings, amplified by the powerful symbols of the runes, the death's head, and the swastika, all combined and congealed to help create a force of terror, genocide, and near-Armageddon that the world had never seen before.

Now, it is the theme of this work that all world military and intelligence services throughout history have had some involvement with the occult. One of the unique aspects of the Nazi movement, however, was the blending of the magical and quasi-scientific to create a nonsense alternative pseudoscience. This took place in a Germany that—in the years after World War I—had more astrologers per square kilometer than anywhere else in the world.[12]

Nazi Pseudoscience

One of the more interesting byproducts of Nazi "science" was the *Welteis*, or World Ice theory. This was a theory of a universe made of ice crystals, and of a Nordic man as a "creature of the ice fields and the natural ancestor of the human race."[13] This Nordic man was most fit to reign in an icy universe, which of course had been borne out by the old fairy tales of Ultima Thule, where life supposedly began. The World Ice theory was to be extremely useful in weather predictions, so they said, and of course, weather predictions in wartime are of rather significant importance. (War being somewhat of an outdoor activity.) Unfortunately, the World Ice scientists predicted a mild Russian winter when the Germans invaded. The eastern front Nazis were in summer uniforms in freezing Russia. More than a million died there, and more from freezing than bullets. Apparently the World Ice theory was, in reality, all wet.[14]

Nordic man, as Rosenberg the mystical philosopher saw him, "believes deeply in the eternal law of nature: he knows that he is manifestly linked to it. He does not despise nature, but accepts it as the allegory of something supernatural."[15] Maybe so, but on the eastern front, Nordic Man had icicles hanging off of his Nordic Nose, and it is not a wild leap of faith to assume that not every Nazi on the eastern front was a big fan of the World Ice theory.

Despite the failure of Nazi pseudoscience, it is an important lesson in the history of the military-occult complex: how a myth, a fairy tale, a bunch of high-sounding lies that some theorist made up can be used to cause definite effects (useful or harmful) in the real world of military and intelligence endeavors. Remission of sin helped fuel the Crusaders (along with greed and bloodlust), and the Christ concept has helped the Catholic church become one of the biggest holders of land in history. Nazi myths helped to formulate the SS, led to archaeological expeditions as far as Tibet, and caused the death of millions of Jews, Gypsies, and other social "undesirables."

Those on the other side of the eastern front had their magical techniques for war also, and while God was dead in post-revolutionary Russia, the paranormal was alive and well.

CHAPTER 13

SOVIET SOCIALIST SORCERERS

Psychic Spying in the Eastern Bloc

A specter is haunting Europe . . .
—KARL MARX AND
FRIEDRICH ENGELS

That the Eastern Bloc would become a haven for psychic research in the twentieth century was in some ways surprising and in others, predictable. The atheism of communism (one of the only potentially liberating and empowering aspects of that otherwise stifling philosophy) would sometimes impede Soviet psychic research, as the paranormal could be viewed as antithetical to Marxist doctrine.

It would be the tendency of our Soviet Socialist sorcerer friends to take a mechanistic approach to psychic research, seeking physical explanations and enhancements for phenomena that were elsewhere viewed as metaphysical and supernatural. For a long time, Soviet encyclopedia definitions of the paranormal were derisive, and negated the possibility of such a thing existing. Yet this was not always the case.

Precommunist Russia under the Romanovs romanced the paranormal for three hundred years, climaxing in the relationship between the peasant prophet Rasputin and Czar Nicholas II, in the first two decades of the twentieth century.

With the Russian Revolution came sweeping reform, but no Bolshevik broom could brush away the mystical nature that lay deep in the soul of the Russian. The emergence of the Soviet Union would make Eastern Europe look to electronic and radio phenomena as its source for paranormal explanations, analogies, and augmentation. God in Russia may have been officially dead, but the magic and superstition that long inhabited the land before any communist ever set foot on the Red earth, survived.

Telepathy

Siberia was known for its shamans: men who could supposedly wield the powers of telepathy, clairvoyance, and psychokinesis. These same powers—to be generated not by shaman drugs, dance, and drums, but by the power of physics and electronics—were searched for and experimented with by the Soviets. The paranormal, when properly harnessed in the bonds of science and acceptable doctrine, were to be employed in the service of the Russian state—in other words, militarily, and for espionage purposes. Russian experiments centered around three paranormal abilities with obvious military and intelligence applications: clairvoyance (remote viewing), psychokinesis (mind over matter), and telepathic projection, or remote influencing. Soviets claimed that in 1924, a Russian psychologist, Dr. Platonov, was capable of causing a telepathic knockout, putting a female subject to sleep at his command—remotely. This occurred at a meeting of the All Russian Congress of Psychoneurologists, and supposedly was repeatedly performed.[1] Repetition of results is a sine qua non for the traditional scientist, whose mind is closed to the possibility of the existence of phenomena that do not occur regularly under the same or similar conditions.

Shortly thereafter, another Russian psychologist, Dr. Kotkov, was to succeed thirty times out of thirty in putting a female student to sleep, not by the normal academic method of lecturing, but by remote influence, by the power of his mind alone, and at a distance.[2] Or so Russian science claimed. It is important for the student of the history of the military-occult complex to take any Russian paranormal claims during its Soviet period with a grain of salt.

In 1932, a Dr. Vasilev, who was to reign long as the Soviet champion of psychic phenomena, was ordered by Joseph Stalin to investigate telepathy and develop a physical explanation of telepathic phenomena, one in line with Soviet doctrine. In his research, Vasilev did much to prove that electromagnetic waves did *not* serve as a carrier for telepathic transmissions.[3] The doctor's findings were at odds with the doctrine's wishes, thus the electromagnetic approach to psychic phenomena was to be continually studied by the Russians and their Eastern European satellite countries. The experimentation still continues; only the doctrine has become somewhat outmoded.

The Supernatural Submarine

One of the catalysts that helped spur Soviet psychic research in the Cold War years was an article that appeared in 1959 in the French periodical *Constellation*, entitled, "Thought Transmission—Weapon of War." This told of supposed telepathic experiments the United States was conducting with the nuclear submarine *Nautilus*. The Soviets had already been made aware of military funding of psychic research by the government in America when the Office of Naval Research gave financial support to the parapsychology lab at Duke University in 1952. But now the article spoke of American ability to communicate mind-to-mind with sailors aboard a submerged submarine.

The U.S. Navy denied the existence of the experiments; this aided the Russians in swallowing this piece of American disinformation, hook, line, and periscope. Once again, Dr. Vasilev, the prime Soviet Socialist sorcerer, some twenty years older than his telepathy research for Stalin days, came to the rescue of Russian psychic spies.

A laboratory was set up at Leningrad University. The paranormal research was not so remotely influenced by communist dogma, and the Soviets again sought the secrets of telepathy in the realm of ELF or extremely low frequency waves. The mechanistic approach to the metaphysical continued. As Vaughan Purvis stated in his work, *The CIA and the Battle for Reality,* "Thus Soviet telepathy research was almost immediately taken out of the hands of psychologists and redefined as a problem of radio engineering, hard applied science that readily attracted funds and military interest."[4]

Extremely low frequency waves are the medium for the message to submarines, and they can carry limited information. Whether telepathic communication experiments were ever carried out aboard the USS *Nautilus* is a topic that generates much doubt and dispute among paranormal enthusiasts. In analyzing the arguments, interesting questions arise. If it was disinformation, why put it in a French magazine instead of in an open source American magazine? The answer to that question might lie in the fact that a foreign origin might tend to lean a Soviet intelligence analyst away from the disinformation theory, and give some credence to the story. If it was disinformation, why choose a psychic angle to the story, one that in and of itself would normally generate doubt and suspicion? Specifically, it would be against Soviet dogma. The possible answer to this question is, Yes, that's right. By creating an article about a supposed line of research that would be against established Soviet doctrine, it could get the analyst sitting in Moscow doubting that it was a piece of disinformation.

Coupled with the fact that the Soviets had an idea about American mind control experiments and funding for early parapsychological studies, the *Nautilus* telepathy story might pass for truth, which, given the Russian upsurge in psychic research after its publication, seems to indicate to the Russian military-intelligence establishment that these experiments were the absolute *pravda.*

It is likely that the *Nautilus* story was a rather well-conceived piece of disinformation designed to divert Soviet manpower and money into a decided waste of time. Whatever it was, the story of the telepathy experiments were not declassified until 1981,[5] more than twenty years after it first appeared in an open source French magazine. Keeping a bit of disinformation classified for so long was a nice touch by American Intelligence, or was it something more than that? Regardless of the accuracy of the submarine telepathy experiments, the Russians went full speed ahead in trying to close the magic gap while they were closing in on the missile gap.

Many of the paranormal studies that occurred in the 1960s in the USSR dealt with "the transmission of behavior impulses—or research to subliminally control an individual's conduct."[6] In the Spring 1958 edition of *Studies In Intelligence*, the CIA also was interested in the potential of subliminal influence. In this classified in-house publication, an article appeared entitled *The Operational Potential of Subliminal Perception.* This report, declassified almost forty years after its publication, revealed, ". . . it has been demonstrated certain individuals can at certain times and under certain circumstances be influenced to act abnormally without awareness of the influence or at least without antagonism."[7] (While the conclusion certainly had numerous qualifiers, it does indicate that various forms of what would now be called remote influence were being considered in the Cold War—by both sides.)

Besides its pursuit of remote influence methods and media, the Russians during the Cold War years were investigating the possibilities of intercepting and even jamming telepathic messages. Regarding this subject, authors Sheila Ostrander and Lynn Schroeder, in their classic *Psychic Discoveries Behind the Iron Curtain*, conclude that "if the Soviets are right . . . it seems that even a modern sophisticated spy armed with ESP might still have his messages bugged."[8]

Could it be done? Were telepathic signals capable of detection and jamming? Radiation of a variety of sources can be detected, but was telepathy sent by a particle, a wave, or by anything that might be detected with existing technology? Or could it be detected by the same medium as its transmission—a human mind? What of jamming telepathic signals? Could they be affected by electronic methods as could radio communications, or would the jamming aspect require human psychic-powered intervention? Great and important questions, and to date, no declassified information that would enable us to answer them. There was one experiment performed by American scientists that tends to indicate that a human under visual observation has changes in his galvanic skin response while being observed, which might give credence to a theory that a biological sensor may serve as a detector of attempted paranormal perceptual penetrations.

However, in frequent phone conversations with former top CIA psychic spy, Joseph McMoneagle, I was once told of his having experienced contact with Soviet psychics during his remote-viewing work in search of intelligence information. (He does not necessarily claim that these meetings with remarkable spooks in Wonderland were what they appeared to be.) Whether or not the interaction of psychic spies in the nondimensional realm was actually true or only apparently true, it gives additional support to the possibilities that telepathic interception and perhaps jamming is possible. If it is possible, then this could reduce the potential threat that psychic spying holds. If, on the other hand, telepathic communication cannot be intercepted or jammed, then psychic espionage has the potential to be the most dangerous form of intelligence collection and transmission.

Electronic ESP

As the years passed, the Soviets would become more involved with what they had called psychotronics—the electronic enhancement of paranormal abilities—which put electromagnetics and extrasensory perception together in a marriage of doctrinal convenience. At the core of the psychotronic research was the search for the power to remotely control the minds of men, which of course is what a life-defying totalitarian state should be doing in order to maintain its tyranny.

In an article in the Moscow *Times* in July 1995, reporter Owen Matthews, declared, "Reports have emerged of a top secret program of psychotronic brainwashing techniques developed by the KGB and the Ministry."[9]

The skeptic now rears his head and says, "Aha! If the Russians were capable of all of this wonderful mind control, why did the Soviet Union fall in one lifetime? Why couldn't they control the population, their economy, their ethnic populations with all of this remote influence?" Explanations range from the Soviets having in their research unleashed an extradimensional power that nearly destroyed it (more on that theory later in this chapter), to the more easily digested theory that remote influence and mind control in the Soviet Union is bunk. Searching in the ruins of Russia to try and find a middle-ground reason why mind control could not put all the Soviets together again, we examine the physical milieu in which Soviet mind control would have had to work.

First, there were devastating economic problems in the Soviet Union, caused by military expenditures that crushed the chances for Soviet economic development in more financially productive and useful areas. Second, there was a large and hostile variety of ethnic groups antithetical to the communist regime. Further, there was widespread corruption in the country. Historical lesson number one in the history of the military-occult complex: Greed, anger, sloth, and the rest of the seven deadly sins will outfight psychic power every time in the realm of geopolitics.

Remote mind control, if it exists, is a subtle force, a subliminal force. (Now, perhaps there are people reading this with access to classified information who are chuckling at this pronouncement, but from the available open data, this appears to be true.) A growling, hungry stomach, a burning hate for what is perceived as one's oppressor, the unending greed of a corrupt official, are forces to reckon with that far outweigh the focusing of a psychotronic device. Or so it appears.

The post-Soviet Russians are supposedly using remote viewing "for solving practical tasks in geology, construction, engineering, and ecology."[10] They have studied psychokinetic effects on increasing seed germination, mental healing of irradiated mice, and mental influence as it impedes or enhances certain brain-wave patterns on sensorily isolated humans.[11]

There *are* a variety of private remote-viewing concerns that claim to be employed, among other things, in geological and mining searches, so the Russian claims with respect to their present uses of the paranormal are credible. To date, it appears they haven't quite mastered the technique because their stock market has taken a beating, and my in-country sources confirm that the cupboard is bare for those Russians without adequate political and criminal connections.

In a declassified Defense Intelligence Agency report on Soviet parapsychological research, it was revealed that "Many scientists US and Soviet feel that parapsychology can be harnessed to create conditions where one can alter or manipulate the minds of others. The major impetus behind the Soviet drive to harness the possible capabilities of telepathic communication, telekinetics and bionics are said to come from the Soviet military and the KGB."[12]

In *Psychic Discoveries Behind the Iron Curtain*, it was claimed that "there is every indication from multiple sources that psi (or psychic) research with military potential is well financed by the Soviet Army, secret police and other paramilitary agencies. Soviet scientists doing psi research in non-military areas often have trouble getting money."[13] The above may serve as further explanation for why the psychotronics of the Soviet Union failed to keep it alive. Like its economy, the Soviet paranormal research program was too heavily dressed in battle fatigues. Not enough research was done for the commercial uses for psi.

Had the Soviets enjoyed an economy with a chance for survival, what could their researchers have achieved? Bulgarian parapsychologist Georgi Lozanov, back in the glory days of Soviet psychic research, was heard to say, "Our support is from the highest levels of government, the highest. We never have to worry about money here. We can go ahead on any project, in any area of the paranormal."[14]

Besides the fact that this quote flies in the face of what *Psychic Discoveries Behind the Iron Curtain* concluded, it still indicates—for military and intelligence purposes—that the Soviets had more funding for paranormal projects than did the Americans. Could they have gained a tactical and strategic superiority over America, had their economy allowed their form of government to survive?

An interesting, yet academic question, for the Soviet Union crumbled under its own centralized bureaucratic weight. A more interesting historical fact of the military-occult complex is the degree of paranoia Soviet paranormal research generated in American intelligence analysts in the late 1960s and early 1970s. The above-referenced declassified Defense Intelligence Agency report warned, "The potential applications of focusing mental influences on an enemy through hypnotic telepathy have surely occurred to the Soviets. . . . Control and manipulation of the human consciousness must be considered a primary goal. Soviet knowledge in this field is superior to that of the United States."[15]

The analyst who wrote that report on Soviet mind control was ignoring more subtle American mind control techniques. We had Madison Avenue, the heavyweight champion of the world when it came to mindbending the public, and Madison Avenue was much more heavily funded than the Soviet psychic researchers. This is more than a facetious comment. The use of drugs and electromagnetic instrumentation to control the human mind seeks a direct connection and a direct influence on physical structures and processes directly connected with human mental functioning. Advertising instead uses images designed to trigger certain associations and emotional responses, which are then reflected in changes and effects on the brain's physical processes and, perhaps, structures. Physical forces, of course, can effect chemical changes and mechanical effects. Emotional forces and images are manifested in the brain and body by chemical and biological changes.

Mechanical Mind Wars

In any event, the Soviet Union is no more, but Russians are still around. The KGB has changed its name but not its function, and while communists might be somewhat less in number, Russian criminals are on the rise in proportions that make the Colombian cartels look like pikers. We may presume the research continues into mind control. A study of electromagnetic warfare claims that "The Soviets have led the way in learning about the risks of electropollution. . . . They've apparently been the first to harness those dangers for malicious intent. In Soviet experiments with rats in 1960, five minutes of exposure to 100,000 microwatts reduced swimming time in an endurance test from sixty minutes to six."[16]

That was then, and this is now. In testimony before a U.S. Senate subcommittee around Thanksgiving 1997, an expert witness testified, "microwave beams can be modulated with voice signals such that when the beam is directed towards a subject's head, he 'hears' the voice."[17] Almost forty years ago the Soviets were weakening rats with microwaves, and now there is testimony that methods exist to implant thoughts in an unsuspecting person via microwave beams. How far advanced in such research are the post-Soviet Russians?

A report on the *Military Development of Remote Mind Control Technology*, by scientist Turan Rifat, claims, "There is reason to believe that their (Russian) research in the biophysical domain became so advanced that they opened doorways to other continuums and themselves fell prey to malevolent forces."[18] This idea is possibly borrowed from the reported claims of a retired former Pentagon analyst, Lieutenant Colonel Thomas E. Bearden. Internet sources report that Bearden claims that Soviet psychic experiments aroused the collective unconsciousness of man, an entity he calls *Zarg*.[19] Zarg is an extradimensional entity and to date has not yet posed for any publicity pictures.

Bearden, who is the CEO of a private research and development corporation, is on the cutting edge, or the fringe, depending upon your orientation, of psychotronics. He is a member of and has served on the board of directors for the United States Psychotronic Association. He has a master's degree in nuclear engineering, and attended the Army General Staff College. The man therefore has some credentials.[20]

The patent office does have registered mind control devices, some dating back over twenty years.[21] The Eastern Bloc did heavily invest in paranormal research, and major universities have parapsychological study departments—Amsterdam and Edinburgh, for example. Thus, the paranormal research should be taken seriously, and in the case of potential enemies, closely monitored. If microwave radiation can serve as a carrier for voice messages, if such things as pulsed microwave audiograms really can implant thoughts in the minds of men, our boys in the basements and alleyways of espionage had better know about it.

If remote-viewing techniques can eventually lead to a significant improvement in the accuracy of the intelligence obtained by those methods, it will be a revolution in the world of espionage.

We should not be lulled into a false sense of psychic security by the destruction of the Soviet Union, for this particular bear, while it may have matted fur and vodka on its breath, still has plenty of nuclear, biological and chemical weapons, and may have who knows what else up its psychic sleeve.

CHAPTER 14

PSYCHIC RUMBLE IN THE JUNGLE

The Supernatural as PsyWar Tool

Besides a long history of military and intelligence organizations trying to really use the occult practices of sorcery and magic as an aid to defense and conquest, there were many times when the trappings and suits of the occult were used in psychological operations, or as they are referred to in military jargon, PSYOPS.

In the Far East

Back in the 1950s, during the rebellion in the Philippines, U.S. Air Force General Edward Lansdale, then head of CIA PSYOPS in the islands, used the legend of Philippine vampires to chase the Huk rebels from their various areas of operation. The *asuang*, or Philippine vampire, struck terror in the hearts of the superstitious population, a fact exploited by the CIA. When a Huk patrol would pass by, the last member of the patrol was silently captured, and then killed. Two holes were punctured in the Huk's neck, and he was hung upside down to drain the blood from his body. The corpse would then be left where it would be found by his comrades—a victim of the vampire. Did it work? According to documentary sources, when the Huks found one of the vampire victims, they also found another place to play.[1]

Lansdale was to work his magic in the very early days of United States involvement in South Vietnam. He hired North Vietnamese astrologers in the mid-fifties to predict the downfall of the Vietminh. Lansdale also concocted a plan to have Castro deemed the antichrist, using pyrotechnics and projected images to make the Cubans think the end of the world was coming. This particular mission in the military-occult complex never flew, however.[2] In Vietnam, another technique used by U.S. PsyOps forces was the use of helicopter-borne loudspeakers to project ghostly sounds to frighten the North Vietnamese and Vietcong. The Vietnamese were very concerned with proper burial, and the use of the cries of wandering spirits was aimed at weakening their will to fight.

In 1967, the Joint U.S. Public Affairs Office, the directorate of propaganda in Saigon, issued a report on "The Use of Superstitions in Psychological Operations in Vietnam." It was designed to suggest ways to exploit the enemy superstitions in a hostile and destructive manner, while using the same tactics in a supportive rôle with friendly forces. Superstitions were targeted, according to the report, ". . . because it permits with some degree of probability the prediction of individual or group behavior under a given set of conditions."[3] One of the examples of the use of superstition in Vietnam was the use of the ace of spades as a death omen. American GIs would often leave these cards at battle scenes and on patrol in enemy territory. Did this brilliant strategy terrorize the enemy with any effect? No. It was discovered in a survey that ". . . the ace of spades does not trigger substantial fear reactions among most Vietnamese because the various local playing cards have their own set of symbols, generally of Chinese derivation."[4]

One of course wonders why our brilliant PsyWar strategists were not aware of this fact in the first place. The JUSPAO report acknowledged, "Here then was an incorrect identification of a superstition coupled with a friendly capability to exploit the presumed condition. It didn't work."[5] In describing the failure of the American forces to acknowledge the superstitions of the "friendly" forces, the report relates an after-action report of a patrol in the jungle. "The advisor who was brand new, stopped them (the Vietnamese troops) and found hanging around their necks, dangling from their belt or in their pockets objects of stone, wood and metal. The noise would have surely revealed our position, so the advisor collected all the amulets and sent them back to the camp area. This proved to be a bad mistake. Before we had penetrated deeply into the forest we had lost half the men. The other half would have been better off lost, because they believed it was their time to die. They had been deprived of the protection of the good spirits. Needless to say we came back without accomplishing our mission . . ." From the above examples, the report concluded, "Failure can lead to ridicule, charges of clumsiness and callousness that can blacken the reputation of psychological operations in general. It is a weapon to be employed selectively and with utmost skill and deftness. There can be no excuse for failure."[6]

Surprising honesty from a government-generated report. The jungles of Vietnam and the Philippines saw the PsyWar efforts of the military-occult complex use magic as a psychological weapon of war. So did the jungles of Africa. In the mid-1960s, the presence and parasitic relationship of the military-academic complex was becoming well known. Protests on campus were to become an all-too-common occurrence as students sought to dislodge recruiters from campus and put a stop to military-funded academic research. (This was one of the factors that prompted Stanford Research Institute, the site of the early remote-viewing studies of the CIA, to disassociate itself from Stanford University.)

In Africa

There were times that the military-academic complex and its government-sponsored research strayed deep into the territory of the military-occult complex. An example is found in the 1964 report from the American University's Counterinsurgency Information Analysis Center (CIAC) entitled "Witchcraft, Sorcery, Magic and other Psychological Phenomena and Their Implications on Military and Paramilitary in the Congo." The report was funded by the U.S. Army.

In this work, the superstitions and magical practices of the Congolese military rebels were analyzed as potential sources for successful psychological warfare. "Magical practices are said to be effective in conditioning dissident elements and their followers to do battle with government troops. Rebel tribesmen are said to have been persuaded that they can be made magically impervious to Congolese Army firepower."[7] The Chinese Boxers had made the same incorrect presumption sixty years earlier. In analyzing the part played by the supernatural in the uprisings of the Congo, the study determined, ". . . it was the disruption in government machinery which forced the younger members of the tribes to seek the urban centers in an effort to improve their situation, and pushed the older members back towards traditionalism and its beliefs in magic and witchcraft."[8]

This situation bears a closer analysis, as it is one of the common themes evident in the history of the use of occult practices by military and intelligence organizations. When the Congo lost its Belgian rulers and became independent it also lost European efficiency and benevolent paternalistic rule. The competency of the Belgians in administration and the provision of basic human services was not paralleled in the new native government. Quite the contrary. The production and distribution of basic necessities collapsed. Health and hygiene declined. The tribes, who benefited from the Belgian administration that led on the local level through and by the tribal rulers, faced extinction. The young *"evolues"* (the evolved ones) who were impressed with themselves and their new European ways split off from the traditional tribal customs, leaving the villages both geographically and politically.

When science is not well developed, or when a former technologically supported society declines in the availability and quality of its technology, magic will once again rise up as a political and military weapon. When the Congo lost the Belgians, the gap widened between European-influenced Congolese and those who held fast to tribal customs. The gap grew to violence between the factions, and rebellion reared its head. The rebels were to use tribal traditions as a political weapon.

The CIAC report concluded, "The current uprisings in the Congo, and for that matter, elsewhere in Black Africa, gain impetus from the insurgent practice of employing magical procedures to convince tribal insurgents that no harm can come to them by forces of the central government. These tactics are effective because in the Congo, and elsewhere in Black Africa, beliefs in witchcraft, sorcery and magic and other supernatural phenomena are deeply rooted among the people."[9]

What were some of these magical beliefs? One of the most devilish was that of Palo Mayombe. "In the ancient customs of the African Congo," we are told by Carlos Galdiano Montenegro in his work, *Palo Mayombe—The Dark Side of Santeria,* "when an individual was initiated, he went into the bush by himself or with an elder and collected all of the elements necessary to create this powerful spiritual world. . . .

The individuals who received this initiation believed that they were empowered with special magical powers from the spiritual world."[10]

Among these necessary elements is a human skull, human bones, scorpions, tarantulas, lizards, bats, and even termites. These elements go into the sorcerer's cauldron, or *nganga,* and become the foul necrotic source of the wizard's power.[11] Or so believe the practitioners of this African black magic.

With superstitious beliefs as the above, it is no wonder that magic would be used as a psychological weapon of war. The CIAC report declared, "If crops are blighted, if a hut caves in and kills its occupants, if the chief becomes unfriendly, or if a sudden illness or death occurs, bewitching is usually given as the primary cause."[12]

The Congo peoples believed that the magic power had a physical situs in the body and, according to the CIAC report, "The Belgian authorities had to bar the practice of the tribal elders performing autopsies upon the bodies of suspected witches."[13]

When one is planning on using magic and superstitious beliefs as a weapon of war via psychological operations, it is necessary to ascertain the exact nature of the beliefs, the strength in which they are believed, the spread of such beliefs, and the subtle (and not so subtle) differences that occur over different territories of the area of operation. We have already seen the mistakes of the ace of spades cards in Vietnam, and how mistaken attitudes toward magical beliefs can spell ineffectiveness, or even have a negative "boomerang" effect on psychological warfare.

The CIAC report discussed the use of superstition as a counterinsurgency tool. The forces employing same "must be able to compile and analyze a large quantity of specific and detailed information embracing the entire spectrum of superstitious beliefs." Magic was to be used for "limited tactical objectives rather than broad strategic concepts or solutions to fundamental problems."[14]

If only those strategists in Vietnam had read this 1964 report of the CIAC. They never would have wasted time on the ace of spades gambit. Magic as a PsyOps tool worked well in the limited tactical objectives against the Huk rebels in the Philippines, as we have seen. The vampire scare cleared the rebels out of the area in which the vampire appeared to be slaughtering rebels and drinking their blood. Magic as a PsyOps tool in Vietnam did not succeed, for it was used more as a strategic tool.

The authors of the CIAC report were not writing from an ivory tower, however, and recognized that firepower can be an effective countermeasure against the witch doctor. "Any study of historical examples of uprisings supported by superstitious practices, however, will reveal that vigorous military countermeasures of a conventional nature have produced optimum results in suppressing the insurgency."[15] In other words, on the battlefield, ballistics triumphs over belief. The report made it absolutely clear: "In the Congo, as elsewhere in Black Africa, there is every reason to believe that disciplined troops proficient in marksmanship, and led by competent officers, can handily dispel most notions of magical invulnerability."[16]

The Middle East

While magical practices and beliefs cannot make a soldier bullet-proof, it can inspire him to acts of selfless bravery (or foolishness, depending on your philosophical approach to war), and improve general esprit de corps. In today's terrorist arena, we see how the belief in some glorious afterlife to be visited upon the Muslim martyr gives impetus to those who blow themselves up in car bombs and other suicide missions. It is a very inexpensive way to get the superstitious to kill themselves and others. The stereotypical image of the Islamic fanatic shouting *Allahu Akhbar* (God is Great) as he takes out a busload of civilians, or blows up unarmed people in an embassy, is instructive. The sting of death has been taken from the terrorist who believes that upon his immolation, he will awaken in a cool green paradise, where he will be served wine from the hands of lovely dark-eyed serving girls, or some other such comforting myth. Despite the Aladdin's-lamp nonsense of it all, it works as propaganda, as motivation for martyrdom.

The Islamic fundamentalists are using the occult, aka religion, as a psychological operations tool against Israel and the West. The official newspaper of Yasir Arafat's PLO has published an article that claimed that the tomb of Rachel and Joseph are not Jewish holy sites. The article calls for a PLO liberation of these sites. On December 1, 1997, *Al-Hayat Al-Jadidah* published an article declaring that these tombs "must be liberated" and stated that it is proper "to treat Joseph and Rachel as just two people who died, like anyone else who dies."[17]

In the November 22, 1997 edition of *Al-Ayyam*, a PLO newspaper, the Western Wall in Jerusalem was claimed to be Muslim religious property. "The Jews have no relation to it."[18] Most interesting is the claim in a PLO television broadcast in June 1997 that claimed, "all the events surrounding King Saul, David and Rehoboam occurred in Yemen, and no Hebrew remnants were found in Israel, for a very simple reason—because they were never here." It goes further. "The stories of the Torah and the Bible did not take place in the Land of Israel, they occurred in the Arabian peninsula, primarily in Yemen." The PLO, in a later interview of one of its ministers of information, said "Jerusalem is not a Jewish city, despite the biblical myth implanted in some minds." Arafat said "Abraham was neither Jewish nor a Hebrew, but was simply an Iraqi."[19]

This is a transparent strategy: attacking the religious beliefs of an enemy to attempt to undermine the psychological foundations of their people, and bolster those of your own. (Of course, the PLO does not quite have possession of the state of Israel, do they?) In their desperation, the PLO has brought out the old czarist forgery of the *Protocols of the Elders of Zion* to claim there is a secret Jewish plan to conquer the world. On September 2, 1997, *Al Hayat Al Jadidah* published an article claiming "The conflict between Muslim and Jews is an eternal conflict, similar to the conflict between mankind—the Muslims, and Satan—the Jews."[20] The demonization of your enemy is an old trick in the military-occult complex.

But the Arabs aren't the only ones who used religious fervor and the concepts of a martyr's death to spur soldiers into suicide. The Japanese in World War II were quite good at it also. In the thirteenth century, a Mongol invasion of Japan was supposedly thwarted by a typhoon, which the Japanese believed was sent by the gods, naming this meteorological savior *Kamikaze*, or Divine Wind. The name was to be used by the suicide pilots of Japan, who flew their aircraft into American naval vessels, destroying whatever they could, including themselves. In 1944, the Kamikaze opened at the battle of Leyte, in the Philippines. An American escort carrier was sunk and other ships were damaged. The tactics were repeated at the battle of Iwo Jima. Over 1,900 kamikaze attacks occurred in World War II. The Japanese still lost. The originator of the Kamikaze Corps, Vice-Admiral Takajiro Ohnishi, committed ritual suicide, ripping open his abdomen with ceremonial *tants* in due and ancient form.[21]

It all goes back to the conclusions realized in the aforementioned CIAC report. The exploitation of superstition in military engagements has limited tactical value. It has never succeeded as an overall strategic tool. Thus, the military-occult complex, in its use of superstition in PsyOps, still has much to learn.

CHAPTER 15

CIA PSYCHIC RESEARCH

The USA Embraces ESP

Operation Often

In 1969, the Office of Research and Development of the Central Intelligence Agency commenced a program known as "Operation Often," which was intended "to explore the world of black magic and the supernatural."[1] Remember, this was the CIA that had already performed studies in mind control and hypnosis, faked vampire attacks in the Philippines, and studied the use of superstition and magic in the Congo rebellion. In their quest for data, the ORD scientists went on a nationwide trek, interviewing psychics, palmists, and other poseurs from the fringe of reality. The CIA men referred to themselves as researchers from the "Scientific Engineering Institute."

The use of strategically placed psychics around the Soviet Bloc was contemplated by the folks at ORD. Unfortunately, it was realized that it is tough to understand telepathically received thoughts in a language you cannot speak. Clairvoyants were also used to detect "evil" people in the United Nations building. (Either the experiment didn't work, or nobody in the building was bad, because the psychic detected no evil personages in the UN.) Castro's palm prints were obtained, and palmists on government salaries analyzed them. One of the brilliant conclusions about Fidel's fingerprints were that the owner of the palms was "perhaps a person high in the church, possibly a future Pope."[2] To be fair, a communist dictator in a banana republic *is* akin to a pope. He is overtly worshiped by his flock and he enjoys infallibility, at least until the next successful coup.

In 1971, three astrologers were on the CIA payroll, and among their tasks was to determine effective means of combating airplane hijacking. The illuminating conclusions of the star gazers included the training of stewardesses to seduce hijackers, passengers being forced to travel in their underwear, and the playing of the Cuban national anthem before takeoff and the arrest of anyone who stood up.[3]

The ORD funded a course in sorcery at the University of South Carolina. Two hundred and fifty students took it. Lest the reader laugh at the foolishness of the CIA, it should also be noted that Patrice Lumumba University in the Soviet Union (named after one of the Congo rebels) taught a course in Voodoo.[4] Why? Why all of this use of supposed mumbo-jumbo for military and intelligence purposes? The answer is simple, really. Large groups of people are superstitious. Of these people, the superstitions and beliefs they hold have demonstrable effects on the way they live, work, and think. To study these superstitions and beliefs and to determine the causal relationship between belief and behavior can have enormous benefits in the field of manipulation of both individuals and masses of people.

Remember that the military is an ultra-powerful manipulative tool. Perhaps the ultimate tool. Intelligence organizations are not just for information gathering, analysis and dissemination. Not in reality. They are organizations also dedicated to the control of humanity. Control of politics, resources, and minds. Is this paranoia? Is this fantasy? There is no doubt that the CIA has an operational arm—a strong arm. People who train people to kill, blow up things, and operate clandestine propaganda radio and other broadcast facilities are not just in the information-gathering business. The CIA and similar entities are tools of policy, both overt and covert, of their respective governments. Since the mind controls the man, the organization that controls the mind controls that man.

Psychological operations based on magic and superstition are inexpensive. They do not require a great deal of manpower or mechanical maintenance. If a piece of paper from the sky can get one soldier to lay down his arms and retreat, or change sides, there is a definite gain. If a superstition can be used to increase the will of one's army to fight, it would be foolish not to exploit it. So when the CIA funds studies in sorcery, and the Soviets teach voodoo, it makes a sort of sense, in light of the above.

Until mankind can free itself from superstition, until he can throw off the fetters of religion, these blemishes on man's reasoning ability will be used to manipulate him. In business, in society, and in the realms of armed conflict and tactical and strategic intelligence, the "jelly spots" of belief will continue to be exploited. But even when man is free of folly and faith, there may remain a residue of the paranormal that has a place in the worlds of the military and the intelligence services which function as their eyes and ears. There may be powers in man that are as miraculous as the tales told in the various holy scriptures of the various true religions.

Operation Often was the ancestor of a major study of psychic power that was to commence in the mid-1970s, starting at Stanford Research Institute in California: a study that was to develop a methodology and series of protocols wherein the age-old ability of clairvoyance was to become a more scientific intelligence collection tool, known as remote viewing. It is this development in the history of the military-occult complex that we shall next explore. It is where faith and folly become irrelevant, and the final frontier of the powers of the mind of man are explored on the outer edges of reality.

CIA RV at SRI

In Menlo Park, California, the Stanford Research Institute (now called SRI International), and the high-caliber scientific minds that labor within conduct cutting-edge research in a wide variety of areas. In the 1970s, with initial government funding provided by the Central Intelligence Agency, an investigation into the care and feeding of psychic spies was undertaken. The study of remote viewing was to establish a form of ethereal espionage that would remain secret (to most of the public at least) until the mid-1990s.

One of the scientists involved with the early days of the SRI psychic research was Dr. Harold Puthoff, a laser physicist. He went from amplified light to amplified mind studies in 1972. The study of psychic spying heated up after a visit from an artist and psychic, Ingo Swann, to the SRI labs. After a few performances of psychokinesis and clairvoyance by Swann, Puthoff recognized the potential espionage uses of psychokinesis and clairvoyance (which was to be rechristened and repackaged at SRI as remote viewing).

It should be remembered that government interest in the paranormal extended back at least until World War II, and that funding of parapsychological research (by the Navy) was a fact of life as far back (at least) as 1952, as we have seen in the chapter on the Soviets. Thus, CIA funding in the 1970s for psychic espionage research was not as avant garde as it might appear.

Dr. Puthoff was an excellent choice for the research program, as he had served in uniform in Naval Intelligence and as a civilian at the National Security Agency. The intelligence services were concerned about a psychic gap between the United States and the Soviet Bloc. DIA reports warned of Russian dominance in the field, and books like *Psychic Discoveries Behind the Iron Curtain* were telling tales of super psychics, psychotronic weapons, and other such science-fiction-sounding wonders in the Warsaw Pact world.

Stanford Research Institute was chosen as the research facility for the development of psychic spying because, as Puthoff explained, "[CIA] had been on the lookout for a research laboratory outside of academia that could handle a quiet low-profile classified investigation and SRI appeared to fit the bill."[5]

The initial tests involving psychic Ingo Swann were an indication of what the mind of man could do without going through the normal sensory channels. Swann was able, through mental effort alone, to control the movement of a magnetometer that was specially shielded, and was able to determine the contents of sealed containers. In one sealed box experiment, Swann said, "I see something small, brown and irregular, sort of like a leaf or something that resembles it, except that it seems very much alive, like it's even moving."[6] What was in the container? A live moth, which fit the Swann description rather well.

Perhaps from an intelligence point of view, the fact that Swann was able to determine that the object was alive was more significant than his accurate description of it. The ability to remotely ascertain whether or not a subject is living has obvious utility in hostage situations (as well as others), which might be resolved upon intelligence provided psychically along with input from more traditional espionage sources. The technology to remotely detect life has existed for some time. (Your author, at one time, attempted to interest certain intelligence agencies in a device to be implanted in a tooth that would enable a receiver to detect life in the tooth's wearer. They weren't interested.) But implanted sensing devices can easily be detected, and would most certainly be searched for by a sophisticated enemy. To be able to determine living status without a mechanical means would be invaluable. Eventually, remote viewing was, on occasion, to demonstrate the ability to determine whether or not a subject was alive.

In the early part of the SRI research, the CIA overseers of the program tried out their own remote-viewing skills and many of their efforts, "generated target descriptions of sufficiently high quality to permit blind matching of descriptions to targets by independent judges."[7] The successful performance of a psychic experiment by a would-be skeptic is perhaps the best method of converting him to a true believer.

Early experiments involved the use of a sender, or someone sent out to the site to be remotely viewed within a certain time range, wherein the remote viewer would be attempting to acquire the target. This method of experimentation had its problems, however. It was difficult to separate what might have been a telepathic phenomenon from a clairvoyant or remote-viewing phenomenon. Later in the research, outbound beacons were found to be superfluous to remote viewing, and geographic coordinates were used to designate the target, in what was called CRV or Coordinate Remote Viewing. Eventually, even these were done away with, and random numbers were assigned the target to be remotely viewed.

When geographic coordinates were used, the project was referred to as "Scanate," which was a short form of "Scanning by Coordinates." The replacement of outbound senders and beacons by geographic coordinates was evolutionary. First, it reduced the possibilities of mixing different forms of psi phenomena, making it more likely than not that telepathy was not operating. Second, it proved that remote viewing could be operationally useful in areas where the presence or undetected insertion of an agent was impracticable or outright impossible.

The research continued, and in 1973, remote-viewer Pat Price was to astound the researchers of psychic spying by accurately describing a sensitive military site chosen as a training target, including remote reception of actual code words. Interest in ESPionage skyrocketed among those with a need to know about what was going on at SRI.

Price was also to remote view several communist military sites. In

July 1974, he remote viewed what was referred to as an unidentified research and development facility at Semipalatinsk, in the Soviet Union. Given the geographic coordinates, and only told it was an R&D site, Price was able to draw surprisingly accurate details of the actual site.

With clear demonstrations of the power and possibilities of remote viewing as an auxiliary intelligence collection device, it is revealing that the raison d'être of the program was not so much to develop remote viewing as a collection tool, but to evaluate its threat when used by hostile intelligence agencies.

The development of remote-viewing protocols and methodologies was undertaken and underwritten with relatively small funds, compared to other military and intelligence spending. Its cheapness to develop, and the likelihood that it could not be detected or defeated, demonstrated that remote viewing could become the most cost effective, and potentially dangerous intelligence collection method in existence—dangerous, that is, if the accuracy and reliability of this psychic spying method could be enhanced enough to become operationally effective.

In the 1970s, President Carter's administration turned to remote viewing when spy satellites failed to locate a downed military plane. It is reported that then–director of Central Intelligence, Stansfield Turner, hired a female psychic "which enabled CIA to locate the plane."[8]

In a conversation I had with Turner in January of 1998, the former DCI made it clear that he was not a big fan of psychic spying, never putting much faith into it. He recalled his rather darkly humorous remark about Pat Price, made more than twenty years ago, stating that since Price died, the intelligence establishment "hadn't heard from him." (Actually, Turner remembered the joke, but forgot that when he originally quipped this line in the 1970s, he was talking about Price.)

Despite a lack of across-the-board enthusiasm in the intelligence community for what was being investigated at SRI, it was clear to the scientists involved that they were on to something. Dr. Harold Puthoff, the laser physicist involved in the remote-viewing research, said, "The integrated results appear to provide unequivocal evidence of a human capacity to access events remote in space and time, however falteringly, by some cognitive process not yet understood."[9]

Another researcher, also a physicist, Dr. Russell Targ, stated, "We learned that the accuracy and reliability of remote viewing was in no way affected by distance, size, or electromagnetic shielding, and we discovered that the more exciting or demanding the task, the more likely we were to be successful."[10] A conclusion, if accurate, of tremendous import to an analyst assessing the intelligence potentials of remote viewing. Satellites, listening posts, and other forms of media for signal intelligence collections are remarkable. They are, however, not unlimited in the scope of possible intelligence collection. There are times that a satellite cannot see, times when the electronics of a listening post, either ground-based or airborne, cannot hear.

Remote viewing, being free of spatial and temporal restrictions, may have unlimited potential for intelligence collection. A remote viewer in a room in Maryland or Moscow might be able to send his mind out into the ether—or anywhere on (or off) the planet. And the government wouldn't have to spend a lot of money on it either. Besides the cost effectiveness, there is the added benefit of almost no risk to the remote viewer engaged in spying. He cannot be captured, shot, interrogated, or used as a trade. Whether or not it is possible to harm him via what is called remote influence is another story, which will require further research and the declassification of more studies.

Scientist and statistician Dr. Jessica Utts reviewed the results from SRI and concluded, "Using the standards applied to any other area of science, it is concluded that psychic functioning has been well established."[11] Utts, in her "Assessment of the Evidence for Psychic Functioning," wrote that the majority of the SRI remote-viewing experiments were of the "free response" type, allowing an open description of the target by the remote viewer. These experiments yielded better results than "forced choice" experiments, where the viewer had to select the proper target from a narrow pool of possibilities.

It may be that the performance pressure created by forced-choice experiments interferes with the free flow of data obtained psychically. It parallels the old magical maxim that "lust for result" is contrary to effective spell-casting and ritual work. When more carefully analyzed, this is understandable. Given a finite amount of energy to devote to a task, any task, the more of said energy that can be focused on task performance, the better. When the performer of a task divides his energy, part toward performance, and part toward anticipation or anxiety about the results of performance, he has diluted his power and diminished the available energy for the completion of the task. Therefore, whatever creates performance pressure will likely detour performance energy, thereby lessening the chances for satisfactory results being obtained.

Further, by presenting several choices to a viewer, he is in essence being "front loaded" with information, which can force an analytic overlay onto the data he obtains by psychic functioning. Analytic overlay is the tendency to prematurely or incorrectly interpret and analyze raw psychically obtained data. As an example, a viewer might receive input of a series of wavelike forms, and conclude that he is viewing an ocean shoreline, when he might have actually derived input from an oscilloscope. The methods and protocols taught viewers during the SRI research were designed, in part, to reduce instances of this analytic overlay.

Another conclusion to which the SRI researchers came was that, in the field of remote viewing, some viewers are better than others. "There was a group of six selected individuals whose performance far exceeded that of unselected subjects."[12] One of these viewers, designated as no. 372, was Joseph McMoneagle, about whom we will learn more in another chapter (and who was interviewed especially for this work). McMoneagle was the most accurate viewer of the program (and is still involved in remote-viewing research at the time of this writing).

Pat Price was also recognized as a psychic superstar. In their 1974 article entitled "Information Transmission under Conditions of Sensory Shielding," Targ and Puthoff spoke of Price's "ability to describe correctly buildings, docks, roads, gardens, and so on, including structural materials, color, ambiance and activity, sometimes in great detail." The scientists admitted, however, "The descriptions contained inaccuracies as well as correct statements."[13] The above conclusion is important. In the private sector of psychic research and development, there are persons claiming that anyone can become a successful remote viewer and obtain results that are 100 percent accurate. It is easy for a student of the history of the military occult-complex to be taken in by these grandiose claims. Remember, though, that the SRI researchers never claimed complete accuracy when they acknowledged that psychic functioning is real, that it does exist. They further specifically concluded that the ability to remote view is not equally distributed among all humans. Just as in any other field of endeavor, some are more skilled than others—regardless of training, regardless of technique. "Neither practice nor a variety of training techniques consistently worked to improve remote-viewing ability," Utts was to conclude in her analysis.[14]

The interviews I conducted with the two most respected remote viewers, Joseph McMoneagle and Mel Riley, affirm the SRI conclusions. Remote viewing is real, but it isn't always right, and not everybody can successfully do it. "Given our current level of understanding," said Utts, "it is rarely 100 percent accurate and there is no reliable way to learn what is accurate and what is not. The same is probably true of most sources of intelligence data."[15]

In my conversations with McMoneagle, it came to light that in the research, a computer was used to try to make the remote-viewing sessions more accurate. Statistical analyses of viewer perceptions versus target features were undertaken, to try and use the computer as a sort of visual translator of the viewer's recorded perceptions. For example, if Joe Viewer constantly or consistently input a broadcasting antenna as a castle, this would be programmed into the computerized working aid. If he saw an elephant psychically when he is actually remote viewing a tank, this too would be noted. Then, when during an operational tasking, this remote viewer, Joe, visualized an elephant standing by a castle, the computer would come up with a numerical possibility that it might be a tank near a broadcasting tower. The foregoing is a generalized description of the computer work performed; the actual methods and the results must, as of now, remain classified. When such computer work was used, the remote viewers ideally would remain ignorant of the existence of such a working aid to avoid the generation of analytic overlay, thereby destroying the accuracy of their psychic perceptions.

In an independent evaluation of the early SRI research, it was admitted that remote viewers "produced manifestations of extrasensory perception sufficiently sharp and clear-cut to justify serious considerations of possible applications."[16] The evaluator was to warn, however, that "existing ignorance of the basis of paranormal phenomena together with the capricious and unreliable nature of the channel dictate that information derived from this source can never stand alone and must be used with caution. Extrasensory information should at best supplement normal information or guide its collection, but should never serve in place of it."[17]

The research at SRI was not the first time that the government spent money on psychic research to determine its utility as a military and espionage tool. It was, however, the most sustained effort by the United States to incorporate psychic spying in its arsenal of intelligence-collection techniques. The research was to continue, and other laboratories were to make their contributions in the field of remote-viewing research, but it all started in Menlo Park, California, at SRI. The bigger questions are: has it ended, and if not, where will remote-viewing research end?

CHAPTER 16

THE KRESS REPORT ON PSYCHIC SPYING

The CIA Tells It Like It Really Is

The CIA-sponsored research at Stanford Research Institute had been going on for several years when a report on the project appeared in a classified in-house CIA periodical, *Studies In Intelligence*. In the Winter 1977 issue, Dr. Kenneth A. Kress offered his article "Parapsychology in Intelligence—A Personal Review and Conclusions." This favorable report was declassified in 1996, well after the American Institute of Research report was issued that diminished and disparaged the usefulness of psychic spies. (More on that report in a later chapter.) This early evaluation of the research is instructive vis-à-vis the real view the Agency took with respect to ESPionage.

Dr. Kress reports, "This record is likely to be of future benefit to those who will be required to evaluate intelligence-related aspects of parapsychology." Now more than twenty years since its publication, this prediction has come true. While those who have monitored the story of psychic spying since its exposure in 1995 are familiar with the conclusions of the negative AIR evaluation, many are not aware of this earlier and more favorable report.

It is admitted in the report that the CIA "took the initiative by sponsoring serious parapsychological research." Yet, it took another eighteen years before the CIA would officially admit it. First and foremost, the general public's reaction to spending millions of taxpayer dollars on ouija board wonders would be somewhat less than favorable. It was therefore politically expedient to wait two decades to admit it. Second, when one studies the available literature; and takes the time and opportunity to talk to the actual psychic spies who performed their wonders at SRI and later at Fort Meade, the conclusion becomes clear that psychic spying can be an effective method of intelligence collection, despite a percentage of inaccurate detail. Kress says of the results obtained from the research that "Tantalizing, but incomplete data have been generated by CIA-sponsored research."

The Kress report dealt with the two most-studied extra-sensory powers deemed potentially useful for spying; psychokinesis and clairvoyance, which would later be called in certain laboratories anomalous perturbation and anomalous cognition. At the Stanford Research Institute, where the main focus was on controlled clairvoyance, the term "remote viewing" was coined as a more palatable, less provocative label for the phenomenon.

It should be remembered that government interest in the powers of the mind goes back at least until World War II, when hypnosis was used to create multiple personalities in couriers, and the research was being done to try and create the perfect assassin—programmed to kill, programmed to have amnesia afterwards. Direct government funding of psychic research was to occur at least as early as 1952, when the Navy put its money into the psychic research being done by Rhine at Duke University.

We have already seen the use of the supernatural as a psychological warfare tool in the Philippines and Vietnam as early as the 1950s, and in the Congo in the 1960s, and in the very early 1970s, Project Often had astrologers on the government payroll. But it was at SRI where the first major efforts in researching the potential for extrasensory perception as an intelligence collection tool was to take place.

In the Kress report, it is revealed that in 1972 scientists "met with CIA personnel from the Office of Strategic Intelligence (OSI) and discussed the subject of paranormal abilities." Two of the early scientists involved with the research were Russell Targ and Harold Puthoff, both men with a hard science background. It was to be a demonstration of psychokinetic ability by a professional psychic, Ingo Swann who, by willing it, moved the shielded magnetometer at SRI that clinched the financing deal. If the mind of a man could affect magnetism, computers, which were becoming indispensable in intelligence, might likewise be affected. The Agency came up with the funding. Swann was also to demonstrate his remote-viewing ability, and the Kress report says the results were "so startlingly accurate that the OTS (Office of Technical Services) and ORD (Office of Research and Development) representatives suggested that the work be continued and expanded."

Kress became a project officer in the early research. (Initially OTS put up $50,000 for research in 1972.) The early findings were encouraging. One of the test subjects could cause temperature changes via psychokinesis another could read the contents of sealed envelopes, (putting a new spin on the "flaps and seals" techniques of the CIA, those methods used to surreptitiously read the contents of mail). But all was not sunshine at the project, for there was difficulty in replicating these results. Replication of results is the scared cow of scientific research, and Kress "began to have serious feelings of being involved in a fraud." But he wasn't. He was expecting normal scientific behavior from a phenomenon that is more akin to an art than a science. You can't sit Michelangelo down in a lab, hook him up to a variety of biometric machines and say, "Okay Mike, paint a masterpiece." You will have a hard time doing that with a psychic—at least in the beginning.

In 1973, Kress was no longer to feel like a fraud. Former police commissioner and incredibly talented psychic Pat Price became involved with the research at SRI and demonstrated what could be done by a talented clairvoyant. Price, in remote viewing a military facility, "provided a list of project titles associated with current and past activities, including one of extreme sensitivity. Also the code name of the site was provided."

As we learn more about the government-sponsored remote-viewing research, we see how difficult it is to obtain specific word information as Price obtained. William Colby, then director of Central Intelligence, was "favorably impressed" by the results. A new research program was funded by the Agency, beginning in 1974. This project did not seek to prove the existence of the remote-viewing ability in certain people; that was already a given. This project was to develop psychic spying and make it operationally useful for intelligence purposes. Psychics were analyzed via psychological and biometric testing in order to see if there was a correlation between the ability and certain physiological and psychological measurements.

A study of the operational reliability of psychically obtained intelligence was made. One of the remote viewers was targeted against a Soviet "URD" facility in Semipalatinsk. (URD stood for unidentified research and development facility). The viewer was Pat Price, and he successfully "saw" a large crane that was actually at the site. After this, he was quickly asked to sign a secrecy agreement. He did. Then he went on to accurately remote-view features at the facility that were confirmed in intelligence photos. What was interesting about this is that Price described features that did not exist at the time he viewed them, but had been there before. It was the confirmation by recent photos that demonstrated that not only could remote viewing be useful in present time, but in the past as well. Certain assumptions about the nature of time itself were being challenged by the remote-viewing research at SRI.

Of course, no signal reception is perfect, and in Price's remote-viewing descriptions there was "noise"—in other words, there were inaccuracies. Kress says in his report however, regarding Price, that "he did nevertheless produce some amazing descriptions, like buildings, then under construction, spherical tank sections and the crane." A physicist who reviewed the data at the time at the behest of the project's director concluded, "A large body of reliable experimental evidence points to the inescapable conclusion that extrasensory perception does exist as a real phenomenon, albeit characterized by rarity and lack of reliability."

The 1977 Kress report should be held in the left hand when the interested student of the military-occult complex holds the derisive 1995 newspaper articles about CIA psychic spies in the right hand. The reporters of the mid-1990s were joyfully lampooning a program that a variety of top hard science researchers in the seventies were affirming as positive proof of psychic powers. The reporters did not have access to the data.

During one mission, Price was given an operational intelligence assignment at SRI. Foreign embassies were targeted, and Price was to locate and report on their code rooms. He "came up with information that would allow a member of the audio team to determine whether Price was likely to be for operational use in subsequent operations." (An audio team is a group of agents who break into embassies and plant surveillance devices.) Price was shown exterior photographs of the buildings and given their geographic coordinates. "In both cases Price correctly located the code rooms. He produced copious data,

uch as the location of the interior doors and colors of marble stairs
and fireplaces that were accurate and specific," according to the Kress
report.

In what was to be his final remote-viewing assignment, Price was
targeted against a Libyan terrorist training facility. He accurately described an underwater sabotage training area that was located near the
camp, and he made a "map-like drawing of the complex." The CIA
Libyan desk officer then requested a more detailed remote-viewing run
and Price obtained a requirements list from the Agency. This mission
was never completed; Price died of a heart attack prior to his scheduled
remote-viewing session.

At this juncture, we can engage in all sorts of speculation about the
timing of Price's death. Was he somehow killed by enemy spies who
were aware of what he was doing for the government? Was there an
unknown side effect of remote viewing that was physically dangerous
and sometimes fatal to the remote viewer? (Many of those who were
engaged in the remote-viewing program were, in fact, to have fatal and
near-fatal illnesses.) Nobody knows. He did have a history of heart
problems, and it is quite possible that his final heart problem did what
final heart problems usually do—it killed him. Later on, when then-
DCI Stansfield Turner was talking about Price's ability, the Admiral
quipped, "he died, and since then we haven't heard from him." (Turner
was Carter's CIA hatchet man, and helped kill a lot of careers when
the Agency fell out of favor with the President. He was never a fan of
RV).

The Kress report was to make reference to other observed paranormal phenomena. "Apparently, certain individuals called point men who
led patrols into hostile territory had far fewer casualties from booby
traps and ambushes than average . . . the Army gave extensive physical
and psychological tests to a group of unusually successful point men
and came to no conclusion other than that perhaps paranormal capabilities may be the explanation."

The Kress report detailed other funding sources in the government
than the CIA for paranormal research. The Navy and the Air Force
Foreign Technology Division contributed money to the research that
was being done at SRI. "How is it," asked Kress in the conclusion of
his report, "That the phenomenon remains controversial and receives
so little official government support?" He recommended that "agencies
must commit long-term basic research funds and learn to confine at-

tention to testing only abilities which at least appear reproducibl
enough to be used to augment other hard collection techniques." On
agency or another did just that until the mid-1990s, and focused o
remote viewing both for experimental and operational purposes. Mos
of the results of that work are still locked away, classified from pryin,
public eyes, in boxes gathering dust in some CIA storage room—boxe
that may contain enough evidence to completely revolutionize the pres
ent concept of the cognitive capabilities of humanity.

Over twenty years ago, hard scientists and practical intelligence me
well experienced in dealing with truth and lies were witnessing wha
became an inescapable conclusion: the mind of man was not bound i
its perceptions by space or by time. An inexpensive, low-tech, probabl
undetectable and undefeatable method of intelligence collection ha
been discovered. It was not totally accurate, but there were times whe
it compared favorably with other "earthbound" collection methods
Kress's article, in its entirety, appears in the appendix of this book, s
that the reader may learn directly from the source. Psychic spying *di*
take place; on occasion, it worked admirably well.

CHAPTER 17

MISSIONS IN THE MIRACULOUS

Planes, Missing and Astral

Project Bluebird

It is the 1970s. A plane lands in Riyadh, Saudi Arabia. On the plane is then U.S. Secretary of State, Henry Kissinger. He had made many such trips to the Middle East, although he does not know, as he takes this flight, that this trip will be a memorable one. The plane lands; Kissinger and his wife, Nancy, are whisked away in a waiting limousine. The limousine is overrun by a Libyan hit team, and shots are fired. Kissinger is not hit, but his wife is killed in the gun battle.

Do you remember reading this? Well, if you don't, do not despair for your loss of memory, for the above event never actually happened. Intelligence authorities were told it would happen, however, and the source of the information was paranormal. Project Bluebird was perhaps responsible for saving Kissinger's life. When the plane did arrive, Kissinger was whisked away in a limousine at high speed, and the hit team never caught up with him. That is one interpretation. Another, more likely than not, is the advice as to the possible hit was relayed to the appropriate authorities (without, of course, revealing the source of the information), and the advice was just plain wrong.

What was Project Bluebird? It was an operational attempt via psychic means to penetrate the mind of Moammar Khadaffi (assuming that his mind could be penetrated by anything other than a well-placed bullet). The viewer, during the session wherein the assassination was "witnessed," screamed—he was in a cold sweat. Intelligence sources revealed that indeed, Kissinger was in-flight on his way to Riyadh. Saudi and American security officials were notified of the possibility, and the source was merely referred to as "being of unknown reliability." However, the viewer who psychically saw the Kissinger hit had a reputation for accuracy in the remote-viewing field. This unnamed psychic had previously remote-viewed secret U.S. underground compounds, and was therefore, in the field of psychic spying, a name with which to conjure. According to press reports, Kissinger was never told of the prediction, and when asked, never remembered any high-speed limousine ride after the flight in question.[1]

Besides the above being a fascinating tale in the history of the military-occult complex, the newspaper article that reported it gives us an insight into the world of intelligence disinformation. In a December 3, 1995 article in *Newsday*, a major Long Island, N.Y., newspaper that reported the psychic incident, the reporter wrote, "The CIA, which dumped its psychic program in 1977 because it saw no value in it, insists it was only research and was never used in operations."[2] A beautifully plausible-sounding statement made with the authority of a reporter for a major news publication. One need not be a remote viewer to envision Mr. John Q. Public reading this account with his morning toast and coffee, and snickering about how crazy those in government can be, how they can waste money on nonsense like psychic spying. But at least he is comforted by the knowledge he receives from the article, that the CIA never really thought much of this psychic stuff, and would never use it operationally. Besides, it all ended eighteen years before Mr. Public was reading about it.

Too bad for Mr. Public. What he had read was nothing but pure, unadulterated government disinformation. The program was only about five years old in 1977 (on the research side). The military psychic spying program, under the name of Gondola Wish, would go into operation in 1978. and in 1977, the year that the CIA supposedly dumped its psychics, the Kress report was circulating in classified circles in the CIA, detailing how there was something to the program, and that it had been useful operationally. The remote-viewing program was to officially close down in 1995, just before the *Newsday* article appeared, and even that "fact" is highly debatable.

The Kress report, which appeared in the 1977 *Studies in Intelligence* periodical, clearly stated, "A large body of reliable experimental evidence points to an inescapable conclusion that extrasensory perception does exist as a real phenomenon." An operations officer in the remote-viewing program stated for the Kress report, "It is my considered opinion that this technique (remote viewing)—whatever it is—offers definite operational possibilities."[3] This Kress report was not declassified until 1996, months after Mr. John Q. Public was chuckling about the Libyan hit team incident from Project Bluebird. The declassification of the report did not make it to *Newsday*, and it certainly wouldn't be widely publicized. Only those in the know or interested in the field would find out about the Kress report. (Or those who read this work.)

What did hit the newspapers in 1995 was an announcement of the end of the Stargate Program, the $20 million that the CIA supposedly invested in psychic spying, and that an evaluation commissioned by the Agency declared it had no value. The supposed failure of psychic spying was widely reported. The actual successes of psychic spying, those that have been declassified, are ignored in the major media. Rest assured, this is no coincidence, but a carefully orchestrated disinformation campaign to keep the public ignorant of the fact that, Yes Virginia (and oftentimes in Virginia) remote viewing can work—operationally.

The Bluebird scenario, although wrong, was a realistic scenario. Since the normal brain sometimes cannot distinguish between actual fact (mirages, hallucinations, etc.) and what is vividly imagined, to expect the portion of the brain (wherever and whatever it might be) that engages in remote viewing to have this ability is being rather demanding, to say the least.

If nothing else is learned from the reader's perusal of this history of the use of the paranormal in military and intelligence operations, learn this—the reality of psychic spying is like an iceberg. What we see gives us an indication of its reality. What is still submerged, when explored, will give us an appreciation for the depth and scope of the phenomenon. Normal intelligence collection methods are most certainly not foolproof. They are most certainly not one hundred percent accurate. We cannot expect a higher standard of reliability from an under-researched, under-funded new collection method, which involves a power of the human mind, that is only beginning to be intelligently explored. Another psychic-spying mission came somewhat closer to tangible results than Project Bluebird.

Recon in Wonderland

Perhaps appropriately, on the day before Halloween, 1991, a National Guard Pavehawk helicopter went down in stormy waters off Long Island, N.Y. Ironically, the aircraft was attached to the 106th Air Rescue Group based at Westhampton Beach and was attempting to rescue a stranded sailor sixty miles offshore. Failing in its attempts to refuel from a tanker plane while airborne, the helicopter was intentionally ditched in the water. Four of the five crew members were shortly rescued. The fifth was missing. Technical Sergeant Arden Smith, then 32, was never found again.

A joint service rescue operation was undertaken in the storm-tossed waters, with military personnel searching around the clock. No sign of the airman was found. Rescue efforts, like luck, are not ever-lasting, and the search was called off. On November 12, 1991, Arden Smith was officially declared dead. Yet a week after this fatal declaration, the search was mysteriously renewed. Even though the Marines, Navy, Air Force, and Coast Guard had not found Smith, a psychic claimed to know where he might be found—alive. The government listened. The psychic, who had been consulted during the more traditional search efforts, now assured the officials that the airman was alive, and indicated an area of the Atlantic that should be searched for the survivor.

On November 18, 1991, and continuing for several days thereafter, search planes went out on their mission to verify the psychic's advice. Nothing. An additional search was undertaken around Thanksgiving of that year. A spokesman for the Air National Guard Rescue Unit stated at the time, "The psychic met with Marianne Smith (the airman's wife), and based on information they were able to come up with, the psychic was able to pinpoint another area to search." Again, no airman was found. However, survival materials were found in the area indicated by the psychic.[4] This story comes from open source material, specifically, *Newsday*. It gives rise to some interesting questions. Was the psychic truly a freelance agent, or was he or she part of the (then) Stargate government remote-viewing program? If the psychic was a freelancer, were the official government psychics tasked in the search? (The official answer is no, but don't you believe it.) This type of operation was tailor-made for the Stargate viewers. The fact that survival materials were found in the psychically indicated area also speaks for a degree of expertise in remote viewing that would unlikely be found in the civilian sector in 1991. Alas, we must wait for some report on the matter to be declassified before we can say we know for sure.

The Pavehawk helicopter incident may be labeled a partial success. No, the missing airman was never found, neither dead nor alive, but survival materials *were* found. It is no great leap of logic to state that where there are survival materials, there probably was an airman nearby, either trying to survive, or already dead. Of course, the media has a tendency to fudge facts, or get them wrong unintentionally. We don't know how accurate the psychic was, as there was no working tolerance specified, to determine what "found nearby" might mean. Was it within meters of the indicated site, or miles?

Another factor to consider is that an expanse of open ocean is relatively featureless and therefore difficult to remote-view with pinpoint accuracy. Therefore, if the psychic was even close in guessing the whereabouts of the survival materials, this might be deemed an operational success. More useful information is missing from the media story. We do not know how much the psychic in question was "frontloaded"—how much information and feedback he or she was given about the helicopter crash. As we have already seen, one of the "noise" factors that affect the accuracy of remote viewing is analytic overlay. This tendency to prematurely draw conclusions about what it is that is being viewed (as opposed to what is being seen) is a negative factor in remote viewing that often can be accelerated and amplified by frontloading—giving a psychic too much information before and/or during a viewing session.

Perhaps, in the helicopter incident, if the methods and protocols of remote viewing had been more carefully observed, the airman might have been located. On the other hand, from a more skeptical point of view, we might opine that the said airman was aging shark excrement by the time the psychic exclaimed he was still alive. What we know for sure is that, based on psychic guidance, military men and materials were engaged to find a missing airman. That involved time, effort, and expense. Triggered by remote viewing, this case of reconnaissance in the ether is another true mission "flown" in the history of the military-occult complex.

CHAPTER 18

CAST OF CHARACTERS

Rogues and Heroes in the Psychic Trenches

ESP VIPs

The field of psychic spying is a small one; the players—the known players—few and far between. To personalize this history, and to make the reader familiar with the public personages whose books, courses, and claims he might run across now and in the future, we shall survey the cast of characters who flew their missions in an astral plane. We shall learn about the lives and personae of the psychic soldiers at the eve of the third millennium.

Ed Dames

One of the most controversial stars of psychic spying was, and still is, Edward Dames, or, as he still frequently calls himself in civilian life, "Major Dames." The "Major" was a major player in psychic spying in the 1980s and now cruises the ether in civilian clothes, looking like a psychic surfer or beach boy from beyond. His blond bangs and San Diego accent seem appropriate for someone who worked in the military-occult complex as a psychic soldier. However, some of the tales he tells and claims he makes may be viewed as paranormal in more ways than one, as we shall soon see. But first some biography.

Dames enlisted in the U.S. Army while Vietnam was heating up in 1967. He started out as a ground-pounder with parachute wings, but never saw the war in southeast Asia. After about a year with the infantry as his military occupational specialty, Dames became a member of the Army Security Agency. He was sent to school to learn Mandarin Chinese, and became one of those gentlemen who should not listen to the conversations of other gentlemen—but do. He served in Taiwan, listening to broadcasts from the mainland, a GI translator for the National Security Agency. (China, during the Vietnam War, was naturally a hot intelligence target. While your author was attending Czech language training at the Defense Language Institute in Monterey, California, Chinese linguists were in abundance.)

Dames left the Army in 1974, went to the University of California at Berkeley and by some strange coincidence, studied Chinese. The transition to civilian life was not to his liking, and after his education, he joined up again with Uncle Sam and his merry military men. The return of Dames to the military is easy to understand. When a very young man enters the military (Dames was seventeen), and is performing top-secret intelligence work at a time when most of his buddies are working at a 7-eleven or the equivalent, this can be pretty heady stuff. To then learn upon discharge that all of your highly skilled ability is worthless in the real world is somewhat demoralizing. (Your author also joined up at the age of seventeen, was also discharged in 1974, and went from top secret translator/linguist to civilian shipping clerk; an occupational shock, to say the least.) The second coming of GI Dames saw him as a second lieutenant in military intelligence. He drew a three-year tour in Germany, assigned to monitoring Soviet and Czech communications, which for the most part, had to be rather dull. (It was for me.)

In 1983, however, Dames's career got a whole lot more interesting. He started training to be a psychic spy. He attended the Monroe Institute in Virginia to learn the experience and use of altered states of consciousness, by using the "Hemi-Synch" process developed by the institute's head, Robert Monroe. Essentially, this process alters brain wave frequencies by the input of slightly different sound frequencies in each ear, and supposedly assists the owner of the brain in achieving different mental states that are conducive to, among other things, psychic perception. Dames also attended training at the Stanford Research

Institute, and was instructed in the methods of remote viewing preached there—predominantly Coordinate Remote Viewing, or CRV, which was developed by a civilian psychic, Ingo Swann. (Even more on him later on.)

So far, this history of "Major" Dames is not disputed. I have confirmed his stay at the Monroe Institute with Nancy McMoneagle (the former Nancy Honeycutt, stepdaughter of Robert Monroe, who trained Dames). Among other members of the remote-viewing unit, it was not in dispute that Dames was trained at California's SRI. Past this point, however (according to a pre-existing controversy on the Internet), there seems to be a disparity concerning Dames's involvement and responsibility in the remote-viewing chapters of the history of the military-occult complex. Dames writes on his website, "The US Army began a funded study at the Stanford Research Institute to systematize psychic phenomena and develop a working tool by which non-psychics would also be able to utilize psychic functioning. . . . Mr. Dames became the operations and training officer of this team."[1] Close, but not quite, according to other members of this "team." CIA was one of the original funding sources of SRI, not the Army, and the program of research began around the mid-1970s. The remote-viewing unit, under one name or another, was formed in 1978. According to Joseph Mc-Moneagle, remote-viewer Dames entered the unit in 1984.[2] Ergo, the program research began about a decade prior to Dames's involvement, and the operational unit started six years prior to Dames becoming *an* operations and training officer, not *the* operations and training officer. When Dames was assigned to the remote-viewing unit, he was not tasked as a remote viewer, but as a monitor and lecturer. According to Lyn Buchanan (in another website), one of the team at the time Dames was there, "The decision was made before Ed ever came to the unit that he would not be allowed to be a viewer. Ed's reputation, before he ever came to the unit, was that he would get one perception, decide what the target was, and the rest of the session was an attempt to prove himself right."[3] If true, then this was a serious drawback, not only for a remote viewer, but for an intelligence professional dealing with normally obtained data.

In my interviews with Mel Riley and Joseph McMoneagle of the remote-viewing unit, along with my three decades of personal psychic experiments, it becomes clear that much psychically obtained input is often symbolic, not literal. Being symbolic, it is open to interpretation;

being open to interpretation, it is often subject to misinterpretation. For example, the symbol of a circle can be to one man the symbol for the sun, for another, a representation of a pizza with anchovies. Prejudging symbolic data (target preconceptions) can make paranormal perceptions worthless. An open mind, devoid as much as possible of ego involvement, is the sine qua non for the effective use of psychic input.

Even when fragmentary data obtained from psychic means is literal, it is sometimes not logical. For example, one may perceive a sharp-pointed object in a horizontal position, which—in the three-dimensional world—is a sharp-pointed object in a vertical position. It is the sum total of impressions that may have value when using remote viewing. It is the unbiased analysis of that sum that can enhance the value. It takes a special and unusual type of mind.

When dealing in the sphere of normal intelligence activities, rarely is one source of data relied upon for analysis, and especially for operational taskings. A gestalt of information is desired; collateral confirmation is the key. Signals intelligence confirming human intelligence, confirming open source material, etc. When it comes to spying, the more confirming data from different sources, the better.

It should be remembered that remote viewing is not the only method of obtaining real-world intelligence via psychic means. It is merely the most regimented form of data collection in the ether. It is the method perhaps best designed to minimize premature conclusions and analysis.

In my twenty-four years of Tarot card divination, I have made many startlingly accurate conclusions about those who have queried me. Specific names, specific locations, job functions, diseases, etc. have all been obtained from the analysis of symbolic data. I have about a ninety percent accuracy rate (and no, James Randi, I don't want to accept your challenge, but thanks).

On the other side of the psychic coin, there have been times when during my readings I have been blind, stupid, and about as perceptive as cheddar cheese. Most of these failures I attribute to preconceptions and jumped to conclusions about the querent. Ergo, the ego caused interference with the messages from the ether. The desire to accurately perform, paradoxically, can interfere with the ability to accurately perform.

According to other individuals in the position to know, Dames did not function as a remote viewer during his government service. He instead became one of the operations and training officers, monitoring remote-viewing sessions, scheduling room assignments, and giving some lectures. Not according to him, however. In his public response to the 1995 negative report on remote viewing from the American Institute of Research, Dames posted the following: "Dames is the man who actually helped create the psychic espionage unit, heading its operation for almost a decade, leading all of the major operations, and serving as its only training officer during the project's entire twenty year history."[4] This is an amazing accomplishment but, according to his former colleagues, it just isn't true, that's all. In response to this, Paul Smith, who was one of the remote viewers in the unit at the time of Dames's service, says (on the Internet), "The fact is, during his time assigned, he probably was for a year or so the deputy commander of the unit. What being deputy commander means is that if anything happens while the boss is away, you get blamed for it."[5]

McMoneagle, who was the premier remote viewer of the military, and the only man who was with the program from its inception in 1978 until its demise in 1995, says Dames left the unit in 1987. Now 1984– 1987 is three years on this planet, and even in the fifth dimension, or the ninth circle of Hell, it is a damned sight short of a decade for leading an operation. Dames was a relative latecomer, and he was out about eight years before the program ended.[6]

Regardless of the ongoing dispute about Dames, he did serve in the remote-viewing unit, he did obtain training in the methodology and protocols of remote viewing, and he did make a contribution to the world of the psychic soldier. Then he became a civilian, and the long, strange trip really got strange. In 1989, while still in uniform, Dames formed the PSI-TECH Corporation, an enterprise dealing with remote viewing and the training of remote viewers. Dames called his particular spin on clairvoyance (with more rules) Technical Remote Viewing®.

Dames used to say in his website promotional materials, "Since 1983, when Mr. Dames began teaching and employing these incredible skills, he has perfected remote viewing methods and techniques, employing his Technical Remote Viewing® training and operations protocols, which guarantee his commercial clients an unprecedented 100 percent data accuracy rate."[7] One wonders if this claim is as documented as it is unprecedented. Unfortunately, Mr. Major Dames never responded to my two e-mail requests to give input into this work, so we might never know how accurate this accuracy claim is. On his more recently reviewed website, he refines this claim: "100% surety is placed upon ensembles of jointly corroborating data."

Now to claim 100 percent accuracy in remote-viewing data acquisition is paranormal, to say the least. In my frequent conversations with Joseph McMoneagle, the best remote viewer the government ever had (and sometimes the only one), I learned that he had an approximate 50 percent accuracy rate as far as correct target acquisition, and of targets acquired, a 50–85 percent accuracy rate as to data obtained. In speaking with another exceptional remote viewer from the government psychic spying program, Mel Riley again, no such accuracy claim as 100 percent is made. But Dames, according to himself, is the best. "Rather than being forced to stand by and witness the disintegration of his unit's effectiveness and the loss of remote-viewing technology, Major Dames retired from the U.S. Army, taking the original team's best and brightest with him to form his Beverly Hills, California–based company, PSI-TECH."⁸ Oh? Dames retired after he had his twenty years in, and he did so several years before the remote-viewing program ended. He did have the temporary assistance of some of the viewers of the psychic spy program, but not for very long. And his company was not originally based in Beverly Hills, it was in New Mexico.

PSI-TECH started teaching Technical Remote Viewing® in ten-day sessions for $4,500 a clip. Later, Dames increased his market and more widely disseminated his methods by offering video-taped training (about eight hours worth) for $300. Dames tells us, "PSI-TECH's instructional video tapes will provide you with rigorous, step by step instruction . . . taught by the world's foremost instructor, Major Ed Dames."⁹ Maybe he is the world's foremost instructor. Maybe you can learn Technical Remote Viewing® in eight hours of taped instruction. Mel Riley and Joseph McMoneagle lean toward perhaps eighteen months of personalized full-time instruction, but they aren't selling tapes, and differences of opinion make a horse race.¹⁰

Besides being the "world's foremost instructor" of remote viewing, Dames has become the Nostradamus of the '90s, making all sorts of predictions that the end is nigh. Many readers might be familiar with Art Bell's syndicated radio program, wherein various facets of the edge of reality are popularly examined. Dames has made several appearances on Bell's show, and on the January 30, 1997 program, talked about a Telstar 401 satellite that was destroyed by an alien UFO. He further spoke of how PSI-TECH was employed as a remote-viewing agency during the Iraqi war. "We not only located the biological warfare or chemical canisters, we entered the bunker . . . the command bunker of Saddam Hussein and downloaded all his battle plans."[11]

Now as I researched the available documentation on remote viewing, and spoke with two of remote-viewing's superstars, it became apparent that items such as letters, numbers, and specific words are extremely difficult to remote-view. (Perhaps because the psychic function may be right-brain dominant, and words and numbers are left-brain dominant—although this theory is as of yet unsubstantiated.) Downloading battle plans would probably deal with both numbers and words, and if what Dames claims is true, he has taken remote viewing into a higher plane (no pun intended). So, how can we tell? We can't, but we can look at some other claims of PSI-TECH, and perhaps these might have an effect on our opinion of Dames's Technical Remote Viewing®.

In the Art Bell radio show, Dames spoke about the Hale-Bopp comet, which many readers will remember was implicated in the mass suicide of a group believing their real home was contained in said comet. "A cylindrical area of the comet," said Dames, "a cylindrical area that is hollow . . . in that cylindrical region there is a space, and in that space there are particles . . . and those particles form a kind of organic soup. The meteor showers that will be associated with Hale-Bopp are going to be of a very interesting type because they are bringing in a plant pathogen . . . an engineered plant pathogen."[12] And what will said pathogen do? "It will quickly infect everything that's green . . . beginning with the trees. There will be no food for cattle, there will be no food for milk cows . . . all the food that we eat will go away." "Global economic collapse beginning mid-98" said Dames.[13] True or false? This chapter of the book was written past the mid-1998 point, and as I am writing this, I am enjoying the afterglow of having consumed a rather nice shell steak. Reasonably priced, tasty, and the restaurant had plenty to sell. The place was packed, as a matter of fact. We all had plenty of food, presumably the steaks consumed were once cattle that had been fed, and everybody paid for their meals.

This book, at the time I write this, is to be on the market in the early months of 2000. So if you are reading these words, and are still well fed, and can afford groceries, and see trees, and drink milk, and eat steak, guess what? Dames, who claims 100 percent accuracy—is wrong! If, on the other hand, you are an archaeologist in the year 3000, deciphering this work, and are having difficulty with words like steak, cows, and trees, well, heck—maybe Dames was right.

This engineered pathogen kills 80–85 percent of the world and is of alien origin. How sure is Dames about this? On the show, he says, "In the economic collapse and in the pathogen, 100 percent, or I wouldn't be talking about it on your [Art Bell's] show."[14] It is respectfully suggested that the reader is in the best position to determine the accuracy of this statement. As you peruse this work, is the vast majority of the world dead? If so, Dames was right. If not, then this 100 percent accuracy claim is pure, unadulterated bunk.

Dames does admit to certain phenomena that block his ability to remote view. Angels. "The only experience that I and my team have had in something blocking us," says Dames, "is with angels."[15] When not involved with angels in the astral world, Dames is seeing aliens on planet Earth. "There is another race here . . . a colony of humanoids that do not look very dissimilar from us."[16]

In a 1998 appearance on the Art Bell radio show, Dames predicted nuclear war in Korea, and killer solar flares that will wipe out most of us before 2000.[17] So, if the alien pathogen doesn't kill us, if the radiation from the Korean nuclear war doesn't fry us, we can all look forward to an unpleasant death from solar flares.

Dames warns would-be remote viewers, "If someone is emotionally unstable, they should not be learning this (remote viewing) because it will throw them over, probably it may very well throw them over the edge."[18]

One of the exciting things about writing on Dames at this time is not knowing whether he will be correct. The readers will have the advantage over the author, because they will be, at the earliest, reading these words in early 2000. You will know if Major Ed is right or if he is wrong. It will be easy to tell. If you are reading this, he is wrong. If you are dead, and not reading this, Dames might be right (although results may vary for the individual).

As we progress in detailing the lives and thoughts of the major players in remote viewing, certain common traits of the cast shall appear. Belief in UFOs is one. Belief in present or past civilizations on Mars is another. Belief in aliens is a third. These are not the type of pronouncements that tend to add to a witness's credibility on the stand, in the press, or on the podium. They do, however, make great copy, they do attract large crowds, especially of the New Age variety, and they have the potential to make their pundits wealthy, and/or famous. What makes the study more interesting is that, in this arena, we are dealing with highly intelligent people, people who functioned well in more normal military environments, and people who, one way or the other, have shown leadership abilities. This is not a granola-gathering of fruits, nuts, and flakes. Ed Dames, whatever he might be, retired as a major in the U.S. Army, studied at Berkeley, learned a rather difficult language, and served his country honorably. His energy, intelligence, and ambition are indisputable. His notoriety, while on the one hand may diminish the public perception of remote perception, on the other hand promotes the possibilities of remote viewing as a military and civilian intelligence gathering tool. While it would be easy to dismiss him as just another California kook, it would not be accurate to do so.

When we examine the less flamboyant, and probably more able and experienced military remote viewers, their lives, and their beliefs, we will find some facets incredible. We will also see evidence that has been documented, proven, indisputable; and remember, what is being read about, the tales that are being told, are only the declassified ones. There is much that still remains hidden in cartons behind locked doors. Doors open only to a select few, in some of the most secret spaces in the world.

While psychic perception has been around since the days of the troglodyte, it was not until the late twentieth century that methodologies and protocols were designed to maximize accuracy and minimize error. It is a scientific, a laboratory approach to psychic phenomena, especially that of clairvoyance with controls. It is a study that has shown imperfect yet indisputable results. Remote viewing is a pathway that leads to a revolution in man's concept of himself and of his sensory limitations (or lack thereof). The men who participated in military remote viewing and who are now continuing with the research on the civilian side, are truly pioneers, and no matter what else may be said of Ed Dames, he is out there searching on the final frontier of mind.

Having examined the most flamboyant of the military psychic spy team, Mr. Major Maverick Ed Dames, we shall now explore the world of a man who runs a psychic detective agency, using former U.S. remote viewers as astral gumshoes, in search of missing persons.

Lyn Buchanan's Psychic Detective Agency

Texas native Lyn Buchanan was involved with the government remote-viewing program from 1984–1992. Trained as a Russian linguist, Buchanan was attached to INSCOM, serving under the command of General Albert Stubblebine III. In fact, it was an interview with Stubblebine in 1984 on an Augsburg army post that led to Buchanan's involvement with remote viewing. Stubblebine believed that the sergeant had used psychokinesis to "crash" a computer. Buchanan confessed that he had. Joining the program, not as a viewer, but as a training officer and manager of the unit's database, Buchanan, who had a history of paranormal experiences, participated in the RAPT training at the Monroe Institute, and served at Fort Meade. Buchanan reported to have had an out-of-body experience at Monroe, which was a normal paranormal occurrence at the institute.[20]

After his military service, Buchanan worked with his former commanding officer, General Stubblebine, lecturing and giving remote-viewing seminars at various New Age conventions. A falling-out with Stubblebine led to Buchanan's forming PSI, which stands for Problems, Solutions, Innovations, and is a private for-profit remote-viewing enterprise. (Fallings-out among psychics are commonplace. Take large egos, increased sensitivities, and you have the recipe for confrontation.) Buchanan also maintains what he calls the Assigned Witness Program, which offers no-cost remote-viewing assistance to law enforcement agencies engaged in missing persons work. Mel Riley and David Morehouse, two former psychic soldiers, are some of those who have participated in the Assigned Witness Program. The success of their efforts is unpublicized, ergo, unknown.

In an interesting synchronicity it was another (albeit unrelated) Buchanan who first discovered the paranormal art of psychometry, or clairvoyance via objects. Supposedly, events leave psychic traces on objects located in the situs of the events, and these can be read by sensitives. Psychometry is a major tool employed in psychic detective work, and Joseph Rhodes Buchanan wrote the book on it in 1885. It was called, appropriately enough, the *Manual of Psychometry*.[21]

The modern Buchanan describes for us what a viewer sees during a session. "At the beginning of every session you get mainly words or very vague concepts."[22] Later in the session, "the signal gets stronger and the impressions more real."[23] It gets even more interesting at times, as Buchanan reveals. "You can sometimes enter a sort of virtual reality where the things coming from your subconscious appear to be totally real."[24]

In speaking on the government remote-viewing program, and the monies expended therefore, Buchanan says, "We worked in buildings which had been condemned right after World War II, we used furniture and equipment a lot of which we had gotten from Property Disposal. What you must remember is that there were two sections to the project. The research at SRI in California, and the operations side at Fort Meade in Maryland. The quote of $20,000,000.00 accounts for both sides of the project. You have a handful of soldiers sitting in a condemned building on an Army base. Who do you think got all the money?"[25] Having served at Fort Meade, I witnessed many such buildings and can assure the world that the money was not heavily spent on luxuries for the remote viewers. The millions of dollars spent on paranormal research were from various government coffers, and the spending spanned some twenty years. This is a drop in the military budget-bucket.

With significantly less funding than that supplied by the government, Buchanan operates PSI. His company claims to be able to "access and describe places and events so inaccessible or so hostile that no other form of data collection is possible." According to Buchanan, "In the most extreme example, a controlled remote viewer (CRV being Buchanan's particular spin on the phenomenon) can enter a guarded building, pass beyond bolted doors and search locked file cabinets to read papers no one is supposed to see . . . all without tripping alarms, being spotted by guards or dogs, or being featured on closed-circuit TV."[26]

Can a psychic detective really get his man? Colin Wilson, in his work, *The Psychic Detectives*, says, ". . . our normal picture of the world is falsified by the dullness of our senses and the narrowness of consciousness."[27] Hopefully, Lyn Buchanan, remote-viewing entrepreneur, former psychic soldier and figure in the history of the military-occult complex, is one of those people, one of those pioneers of consciousness who will add new truth to our world picture without invading individual or commercial privacy.

Another citizen of the psychic espionage elite is David Morehouse. His story follows.

David Morehouse

Former Army Ranger (sans combat experience), and mail order (Lasalle University) Doctor of Philosophy, Dr. David Morehouse is a self-proclaimed martyr of the government remote-viewing program, and the author of the highly readable *Psychic Warrior—The True Story of a Soldier's Espionage and Awakening.* His is an important story in the history of the military-occult complex, because a portion of his story is simply "factoid" and not fact. Students of this subject need to know the difference between history and what may be historical fiction, especially when it comes to the reality of something as bizarre as the use of the paranormal by armies and spies.

Morehouse was a career Army infantry officer. In his book, he reported that a stray M-60 round, which struck his helmet during a Middle East military training exercise, opened his eyes to a world of new perceptions. He tells his readers, "As the months passed, I actually came to believe that I could see forward in time, or predict the outcome of certain events. It was an odd feeling having my mind's eye open all the time."[28] Well, if it really was so odd, what is even more odd is that when telling his colleagues about the bullet incident, he "mentioned that it had only given him a headache afterwards."[29] The phenomenon that Morehouse refers to actually *did* happen to Joseph McMoneagle, the best remote viewer the government had. McMoneagle had a near-death experience in 1970, which did change his level of perception, and eventually led him to become a psychic spy for Uncle Sam.

In talking with a neuroscientist and professor at New York University's Center for Neural Science, the author of this work was informed that trauma to the head is not a pathway to the realm of the spirit. It might cause brain damage, which might cause hallucinations, but the reader is herein advised not to take a club to his cranium in order to see into the great beyond. It just plain won't work.

In the author's note in Morehouse's book, he says, "I tell this story as I saw it and lived it."[30] The reader is again reminded that familiarity with the personae of the public pundits of the paranormal in the military-occult complex is important. As more and more documents concerning the various government psychic-spying programs become declassified, as more information on the subject becomes available, more people are going to be exposed to the claims and commercial interests of those who seek to promote remote-viewing courses, make millennium predictions, and generally stroll about the ether as experts of ESPionage.

The public needs to know the real story that can be told, and be aware that much of the story cannot yet be told. Fact must be separated from fiction, especially regarding a topic that sounds fictional ab initio. Morehouse presumably has made a decent piece of change from his book, the paperback rights, the movie options, the television options (if any), etc. That is fine; he is entitled to the money for the work that he penned. And it is a great read, but its accuracy has been called into dispute.

Contrast the David Morehouse and Ed Dames types in remote-viewing wonderland with the Joseph McMoneagle and Mel Riley varieties. We have already read about the Dames claim of 100 percent remote-viewing accuracy, and in this chapter we bear witness to the historical creativity of Morehouse. Money is a legitimate motivation, but in the case of McMoneagle it is the research into the revolutionary field of remote viewing that stirs him. Riley just speaks of having done his soldier's duty, and now immerses himself in Native American culture.

I spoke frequently with McMoneagle, and on several occasions with Riley, and the differences between these two veterans of the military-occult complex and David Morehouse are significant. In my conversations with Mel Riley, I was told that his participation with Morehouse in the book *Psychic Warrior* was conditioned upon the work being released as an opus of historical fiction. Obviously in its publication this did not turn out to be the case, as no mention of this appears in Morehouse's book.

Riley and McMoneagle kept their government secrecy agreements. To be fair, Morehouse was involved in remote viewing for a short time, and was apparently capable. Further, he was not convicted of revealing any military secrets, and therefore should be presumed innocent of such allegations. Moreover, Morehouse, served honorably for most of his military career and achieved Ranger status, which is by no means a minor physical accomplishment. From 1988 until 1990, Morehouse left the realm of the ground-pounder and was involved with the Sun Streak program of psychic spying. He had previously been an ROTC officer at Brigham Young University, entered the regular army as a second lieutenant in 1979, and served with distinction prior to joining up with the remote-viewing program. When arriving at the Fort Meade remote-viewing unit, Morehouse was informed by his colleague, Lyn Buchanan, "What we do here is train individuals to transcend time and space, to view persons, places and things remote in time and space, and to gather intelligence information on them."[31] And that is just what they did.

The program was, of course, highly classified. Morehouse must have thought his wife had a clearance and a need to know, because in his book he admits, "Every night I told Debbie all the particulars of the day's training and let her read my secretly copied notes."[32]

I held a top secret security clearance for a number of years. It was made absolutely clear to me (and everybody else in my situation) that unless somebody had a specific clearance for our information, and had a need to know, they were not to be informed of any classified matters. That included friends, mothers, tax collectors and wives. It is understandable why a man in a remote-viewing unit might want to tell his wife all about it, but Morehouse was a soldier with a clearance. No matter how amazing the work was, no matter how life-changing, it was top secret.

At the times he was remote viewing, Morehouse states "I felt myself rising into darkness . . . I felt blind, lost, helpless and cold."[33] Now that is nice, dramatic, and entertaining to one's readership, but it isn't usual remote viewing. It is similar to what is referred to as extended remote viewing but the majority of the RV work does not involve out of body experiences or any such thing.

In speaking with Mel Riley and Joseph McMoneagle, in performing the extensive research that is required to write a history of the military-occult complex, I saw clearly that remote viewing was a rather mundane-appearing procedure. Its results were sometimes amazing, but if one was to film somebody sitting in a chair and drawing scribbles on a piece of paper and talking into a tape recorder, you wouldn't get boffo blockbuster box office footage.

The remote-viewing program, Sun Streak, in which Morehouse participated was used against drug dealers, among others, and supposedly cargo ships and drug-processing facilities were successfully targeted. "From the ether," writes Morehouse, "we hunted Pablo Escobar and other drug kingpins, accessing their minds to reveal elements of their plans that could not have been obtained by any other means."[34] From other sources, which I cannot disclose, I learned that remote viewing was used in the search for missing DEA agents as well. There is no hard data available to uncleared historians regarding the effectiveness of remote viewing as used against the criminal narcotics cartels of the world. However, there is no reason to believe that remote viewing would be any less (or more) effective a tool in the realm of contraband interdiction than it would in any other sphere of operations.

Morehouse also states that he left the remote-viewing unit about a year after being an operational viewer (as compared to his training period), and departed on the day of the Iraqi invasion.[35] After his stint in the psychic realm, Morehouse the Ranger became Morehouse the rebel. "By this point in my career," he says, "I'd grown sick of intelligence prima donnas . . . and some of their private lives! A few staff members hardly bothered to conceal extramarital affairs."[36] This moralizing of Morehouse did not preclude him from allegedly engaging in relations with the wife of an enlisted man, and being brought up on charges of adultery and sodomy, among others.[37] He was discharged under other than honorable conditions in January 1995, and the charges against him were dropped.

Rangers learn to be resilient, and Morehouse was certainly that. Retiring from the Army under somewhat less than a shower of accolades, he already had a book on the remote-viewing program in progress. He was co-authoring a work with Ed Dames, who at the time was his good friend and partner in a private corporation engaged in remote-viewing for hire, PSI-TECH, formed in 1989. When Dames read the typescript of Morehouse's proposed book, he reportedly referred to the book as a screenplay and called the book "heavily fictionalized." The book (which reportedly received an advance of $100,000, shared between the authors) was to be published by Harmony. The deal did not see fruition. However, the work, like the Phoenix, rose from the ashes, and a different version of it was published by St. Martin's Press, as *Psychic Warrior.*

Hollywood showed a great deal of interest about the story of a soldier who remote viewed the Iraqi war—and learned that the American troops were exposed to chemical or biological agents, which the government wanted to cover up. They were intrigued by the persecution of this martyr of the metaphysical—Morehouse. There was only one minor problem: Morehouse was out of the program before he could have remote viewed the Iraqi War for the government. He was, however, still in the Army, and may have remote viewed these events elsewhere. There are also serious doubts among his fellow remote viewers as to the degree of persecution Morehouse claimed to have suffered. "Suddenly it all seemed clear to me. The DIA wanted to make sure that a chemical or biological agent had been released on U.S. troops, but they didn't want anyone else to know."[38] Jim Schnabel, author of the excellent *Remote Viewers—The Secret History of America's Psychic Spies,* noted in his book, "Former colleagues will also be surprised that Morehouse was asked to detrimentally remote influence Saddam Hussein. Morehouse had heard the story from another remote viewer and apparently thought it was a good enough story to insert into his new version of events in *Psychic Warrior,* despite the fact that he had left DT-S (the unit's designation) by the time Iraq invaded Kuwait."[39]

Schnabel visited Morehouse in 1994, when the latter was in an army psychiatric hospital.

"Morehouse," says Schnabel, "is the only member of the remote-viewing program ever to have been hospitalized for psychiatric reasons."[40]

As to the accuracy of the Morehouse book, scientist and author Schnabel levels harsh criticism "To tag every piece of fiction in the Morehouse book would mean commenting on virtually every page."[41] He may be a "creative" writer, but colleague Lyn Buchanan says Morehouse was "a good remote viewer, and [Buchanan] never found anything which would make me question his remote-viewing ability."[42]

Be that as it may, this "good remote-viewer" had to hire a private investigator when one version of his manuscript for *Psychic Warrior* was allegedly stolen. Apparently Morehouse could successfully and remotely spy on drug dealers, Iraqi leaders, and others, but he could not find his own manuscript with his psychic powers. "The FBI has been notified, and several investigators have been retained by the author," warned Morehouse. He also offered a $10,000 reward.[43] With regards to the missing manuscript, Morehouse referred to it as "a hodge-podge compilation of the author's writings, editor's notes, rewrites and a great deal of completely fabricated material—probably written by whomever perpetrated the theft."[44]

Remember that psychic perception is more of an art than a science, and even a good remote viewer can have days that yield no results. Morehouse is certainly one of the more flamboyant characters in the military-occult complex, and it is both necessary and easy to be critical of much of what he claims. However, neither in the written research, nor in my interviews with the real stars of the military remote-viewing unit, was there ever a claim that Morehouse was an inept viewer or that he was not at times accurate in the intelligence he brought home from the heavens. The above being true, Morehouse will go down in the history of the world of psychic spying as one of the participants in a program that was on the cutting edge of what might become a standard intelligence collection technique in the twenty-first century.

Joseph McMoneagle

History will reveal that the best of the remote viewers for American intelligence was Joseph McMoneagle. He may be referred to as the Babe Ruth of psychic spying for all of the operational home runs he hit while serving in paranormal espionage. Every worthy endeavor of man has its heros, its champions. Men who, outstanding in their fields, combine an exceptional level of ability with a substantial humanity. They are examples of demonstrated accomplishment unaccompanied by arrogance. Exceedingly rare breeds, these. In the field of psychic spying, such a man is Joseph McMoneagle. Joseph McMoneagle is not exactly a household name. Few outside of certain segments of the intelligence community, and aficionados of the paranormal in espionage have heard of him. This will change.

Born in Miami, Florida, in 1946, McMoneagle enlisted in the U.S. Army in 1964 to begin one of those long, strange trips that occur with regularity in the highly irregular world of the military-occult complex. An uncommon soldier, he was placed into the haven for the uncommon—military-intelligence.

Perhaps as an omen, perhaps a herald for his future endeavors, while stationed with an Air-Sea Rescue Unit in the Bahamas in the fall of 1965, McMoneagle witnessed his first UFO. It was not to be his last sighting, nor was it to be his last experience with something that could be deemed out of this world. The Air-Sea Rescue Unit was actually an intelligence listening post targeted against certain Cuban and other interests operating in the region. What the UFO actually was is unknown.

What McMoneagle was to become was the top psychic spy for Uncle Sam.

McMoneagle did his time in Vietnam, coming close to being KIA in a helicopter accident. After completing his duties there, he wound up in Germany, working for what was then called the Army Security Agency. (ASA was the outfit that dealt with such things as SIGINT, or signals intelligence, and COMINT, or communications intelligence. They were soldiers, but under the control of civilian spy agencies, mainly the National Security Agency. In this arena, joint service operations are normal, and there often is interaction with friendly foreign intelligence organizations, especially the Brits. Your author served with all four services during his intelligence stint, sharing a border listening-post mountain site with the French and the Germans. I frequently sent top-secret kinds of "stuff" to our friends in Grosvenor Square, England, wherein is found the Government Communications Headquarters (the British version of NSA).

In 1970, McMoneagle was in Austria, having dinner with friends. On this particular occasion, it almost became his last supper. McMoneagle was given something to drink during dinner. Whether it was shaken or stirred is unknown, but McMoneagle shortly afterwards went into convulsions, swallowed his tongue, and ceased the rather necessary function known as breathing.

He was brought to the hospital, dead. While the emergency room crew feverishly worked on him, a somewhat less-tangible McMoneagle was floating nearby, watching the action. He had his first (but not his last) NDE or near-death experience. He saw the Great White Light that seems to be a fixture in NDEs, and in describing the experience, McMoneagle later says, "While this is happening you have a sense that you're not alone, the unconditional love is so overwhelming."[45]

Whether or not the visions and feelings were experiences of another dimension of human existence or the hallucinations of anoxia is a determination the reader must make for himself. McMoneagle was there, we weren't, and given his accuracy in the realm of psychic spying, we may want to give him the benefit of any doubt. (On the other hand, another champion of psychic spying we will read about, Mel Riley, who suffered a heart attack, "died" (albeit not permanently) and saw nothing. In my phone conversation with Riley in the summer of 1998, he related no sensory experiences at all while he was lying "dead" at his wife's feet.)

In any event, the NDE McMoneagle experienced was the trigger for the frequent manifestation of spontaneous OOBEs (out of body experiences) and flashes of psychic insight, which McMoneagle referred to as "spontaneous knowings." (Your author, among his other more worldly endeavors, has been a practitioner of ceremonial magic for nearly thirty years. Anyone with any degree of intelligence [no pun intended] who engages in the frequent creation of altered states of consciousness will [or should] experience the type of phenomena McMoneagle calls "spontaneous knowings.") While engaged in ritual work—or more technological versions of psychic endeavors—and often while not so engaged, insights will pop into the brain—solutions to problems, new approaches, new ideas. It is a sign of progress, of evolution of the thought processes, of the growing open relationship between the dark subconscious where symbols and images are the lingua franca—and the conscious mind. It can be exhilarating, or it can be decidedly otherwise.

McMoneagle was to suffer depression and frequent thoughts of suicide after his NDE and the accompanying psychic manifestations. "My reality, as I understood it, was completely shattered," he was later to say.[46] McMoneagle, while serving overseas until 1978, kept a lid on his supernatural sojourns, not wishing to terminate his career in the military with "extreme prejudice." However, upon his return to the United States, as fate would have it, he contacted the pocket protector types who were researching the paranormal at California's government-funded "think tank," SRI. (Stanford Research Institute, which formerly was attached to Stanford University.)

SRI was engaging in the study of "anomalous cognition in the presence of sensory shielding," which was a rather technical way of saying remote-viewing. Remote viewing is itself a rather modern way of saying clairvoyance, although McMoneagle might not exactly agree with this statement. Clairvoyance is "clear-seeing" in French, and Joseph McMoneagle was to certainly demonstrate that ability on numerous experimental and operational occasions.

With CIA funding, SRI's scientists—and these were people with advanced degrees in the "hard" sciences—were out on the last frontier of mind, experimenting with an apparent human ability to obtain information via extrasensory methods; seeing there without being there.

McMoneagle became involved at SRI, and also spent more than a year at the Monroe Institute in the southeast United States, perfecting his out-of-body abilities. The purpose behind all this was not to write articles about it for *FATE* magazine. The purpose was to evaluate remote viewing as an intelligence collection tool. Given the giggle factor, or potential for political egg on the political face, the work and the funding source were highly classified. If remote viewing worked, it could be a revolution in intelligence collection methods. Information could be obtained without risk to agents' lives; and without paying for airplane tickets and hotels, which appealed to the cloak-and-dagger clerks and top-secret bean-counters at CIA.

With the SRI studies, experiments led to experience, experience to expertise, and methodologies and protocols were developed. McMoneagle proved to be a stellar test subject. But as usual when dealing with the realm beyond reality, the experiments were not without their emotional effects. In describing his early work at the Monroe Institute in controlling his out-of-body experiences, McMoneagle said, "When I first began working with Bob Monroe to develop my out-of-body abilities, my first few separations were accompanied by a sense of something in the room that was so primitive it was almost demonic." What was this "something in the room?" McMoneagle confronted it in the ether, and discovered it was his physical body. It was McMoneagle the shade face to face with McMoneagle the shape. He got used to the experience.[47]

Frequently in the literature that deals with astral travel and OOBEs, we read about the confrontation with the "dweller in the threshold" or "crossing the abyss" or some such other melodramatic purple-prose description. Perhaps this dweller, this abyss, is the inborn attachment of man to the hard walls of three-dimensional reality, which creates discomfort and disorientation when a journey beyond dimension occurs. Perhaps the primitive demonic force that is sometimes experienced in an OOBE is the unfettered conscious mind confronting the primitive sections of the subconscious mind, which could well be the generator of psychic experiences. (There is more than a passing relationship between lucid dreams and OOBEs.)

The experiments in remote viewing and the work on OOBEs were causing profound changes in the mental matrix of McMoneagle. In his book, *Mind Trek*, he observes, "By the time I was into my third year of the remote-viewing experience, I realized that somewhere or some place in the beginning I had taken a high dive from the edge of a cliff and as a result was not stumbling around in a rather featureless canyon wondering where the path out might be. I was stuck somewhere between the "I believe" and "I know"." McMoneagle became unstuck.

"What had actually happened was quite simple. Through no deliberate effort, I modified a sufficient number of personal realities or concepts to unhinge my understanding of time and space, or at least the way I had been originally taught and understood it to work."[48] This modification of personal realities or concepts was to lead to a substantial body of experimental data and operational evidence that the mind of man (or at least the mind of the man McMoneagle) was not subject to the boundaries of time and space in its capacity to see, to learn, and to know.

We may be more, much more than the slide rule and stethoscope set tells us we are. We may be far beyond the evolutionary result of lightning on a mixture of inert gases. Our perceptual limitations may transcend the constraints of the concept of linear past, present, and future, and the horizon may not be the terminus of our vision.

The work of men like McMoneagle has taken what at first was fantastic—perception without material sensory observation—and made it fact. The theoretical has become operationally practical. (The CIA commissioned an evaluation of the remote-viewing program by another government-funded think tank, the American Institute of Research, or AIR. The conclusions of the evaluators, made public in 1995, bore little reality to the facts of the effectiveness of remote viewing, for the evaluators were informationally malnourished. They were reporting on studies without anywhere near full access to the data. More on this later.)

McMoneagle was the only remote viewer to be with the program from the early SRI days of the 1970s until the supposed termination of the program in 1995. His talents were tasked by the CIA, the DIA, the DEA, and other alphabet-soup governmental entities. Most of what he did is still classified; however, some examples of successful psychic spying may be revealed.

The orbit of Skylab in the late 1970s was decaying, and the remains of the spacecraft were to hit the Earth. The people of the world were naturally concerned about the location of the impact point, not wishing to be standing there at the time of contact. McMoneagle remote-viewed Skylab and accurately predicted its crash site eleven months before the event took place in 1979.

Once again, it is 1979. The boys in intelligence are curious about the goings-on in a certain large building in the Russian port of Severodvinsk. A photo of the building is given to McMoneagle to remote-view, and he described construction of an unusually large submarine.

His efforts were doubted until soon after his viewing—when the Typhoon-Class, supersized submarine rolled out of the building on McMoneagle's psychically perceived launch date.

It was 1981. The terrorists of the Red Brigade kidnaped United States General James Dozier—and the CIA was rather keen on knowing his whereabouts. McMoneagle, in a remote-viewing session, not only named the city where he was being held—Padua—but described the building in which Dozier was located.[49]

Just a few of the more spectacular sightings of McMoneagle. Indisputable demonstrations of what a trained natural psychic can produce in operational taskings for intelligence purposes. What exactly was this remote viewing about, that it could achieve such results? McMoneagle explains.

"Remote viewing is the ability to perceive information about a place, person or thing remote from yourself without any other means of knowing. What differentiates remote viewing from psychic functioning is that it is always done under controls."[50]

As to those controls, McMoneagle says, "The remote viewer as well as anyone else in the room is blind to the target; and the way the target is targeted is blind, you know, so there's no ability to know something about the target ahead of time."[51] This double blind procedure often has interesting consequences. "What we found," says McMoneagle, "especially on the research side, is that the facilitator in the room with the remote viewer inevitably will ask the right question at precisely the right time during the remote viewing. So, in effect, the person asking the questions is being as psychic as the remote viewer."[52]

Assuming the existence of such a phenomenon as psychic functioning, the mutual target ignorance of viewer, facilitator, and monitor is an important protocol. If there are different forms of psi, it would be handy to know which one is taking place in experimental research and operational tasking. A facilitator with target knowledge prior to the session might intentionally or unintentionally transmit this information to the remote viewer via telepathy. Further, the conclusions or prejudices of the facilitator, what has been called analytic overlay, might also be transmitted, destroying the purity of the remote viewer's input. Therefore, there might be the functioning of telepathy, where the researcher is trying to obtain data on the functioning of clairvoyance under protocols, or remote-viewing. However, even these protocols might not prevent different forms of psi from functioning during a remote-viewing session.

Let us assume an operational target is selected, and there is no facilitator foreknowledge, and obviously no viewer foreknowledge. The target is, for this example, a listening post on the border between a NATO country and a Warsaw Pact country, and we will choose the year for our example as 1980. The only input in the session is the furnishing of nongeographic coordinates, a series of randomly generated numbers. How could telepathy still be the functioning form of psi, and not clairvoyance? Simple. There are a bunch of East Bloc soldiers running around with earphones, drab uniforms, and functioning minds. They see, hear, feel, and think. Assuming that these impressions can be picked up telepathically, we could easily have a situation where the remote viewer working for the good guys is not perceiving data directly via remote viewing, but is getting second-hand information telepathically—from the people who are actually there. Ergo, how do we know that what we have labeled remote viewing (clairvoyance with rules) is, in reality, telepathic reception from other minds?

The astute reader now raises the objection, "Ah! What of remote-viewing targets where there are no people present? Is the reception of data from this type of target not clearly an example of direct, albeit psychic perception?" As the song from *Porgy and Bess* says, "It ain't necessarily so." We eliminate the time factor; and our prejudice that time is linear. We might now have the functioning of telepathy in retrospect, in other words, the viewer may be picking up telepathic transmission from living minds that were at the target site in the past.

What if remote viewing is done on a target where a human mind has never been? McMoneagle has remote viewed the planet Mars in 1983, and came up with some interesting data. He also came up with the impression that there was a former civilization at the site (indigenous or just visiting), which left a "psychic time capsule." Ergo, we still might have retrospective telepathic transmission, instead of direct psychic perception. Next question. What about the remote viewing of a site in the future? Same problem, different pew. We might have prospective telepathic reception, and not direct psychic perception. In other words, it is possible that what we call remote viewing is not clairvoyance under contractual rules at all. It might be telepathic reception unbounded by, and in, time. Does it make a difference? Is it important whether data can be received via telepathy or direct remote perception? Yes, it does. Our three-dimensional tools of measurement and perception do not rely upon data filtering through other perceivers than the person using the tool of measurement or perception. Galileo, looking through the telescope at the universe, is not seeing through the mind of the pope, he is perceiving directly via his own mind. As we know that Galileo and the pope had some different ideas about the relationship between the sun and the earth, we can see how remote viewing might have greater chances for accurate perception and reporting than has telepathic reception, whether in real time retrospectively, or prospectively.

Having just endured the above, not sure whether remote viewing is clairvoyance in action or telepathy, let us find out how accurate McMoneagle was in his research and operational viewings. "Out of any hundred targets," McMoneagle says, he "can be expected to hit the target 55–60 percent of the time." Of those targets he "will acquire an average from 45–85 correct percentage of information." In 20 percent of the cases, his drawings will be a near-exact overlay of photographs taken of the target.[53] Not too bad for somebody not on the scene. Rather useful as a collateral source of confirmation for intelligence received from other assets or collection methods and sources. You might not want to base an operation solely on information received via remote viewing, and McMoneagle certainly agrees with that.

How does he actually do a remote session? "I have a tape recorder running, so there's certainly a verbal record of what I'm perceiving. . . . I'm just trying to describe elements or parts or pieces of the target. At the same time, I will be doing preliminary sketches, perhaps to try to organize those parts or pieces in some legitimate way. When I'm through, usually what I do is go back through and then try to generate a final drawing."[54]

Between operational taskings and experiments McMoneagle has performed over 4,000 remote viewings. In characteristic humility, he has stated, "In terms of the remote-viewing project there were quite a few individuals within the project that were as good and in some cases probably better than myself. It is something everyone can do to a certain extent."[55] At the time of this writing, McMoneagle has been involved, both as soldier and civilian, with remote viewing for twenty years. He is the proprietor of Intuitive Intelligence Applications, formed in 1984 (after his retirement from military service). This private enterprise engages in using remote viewing as a tool for such purposes as the location of likely sites for mining and drilling operations.[56]

Psychic, soldier, and spy, McMoneagle is truly one of the superstars of the military-occult complex. He remains on patrol out there in the world beyond, pushing back the borders of the last frontier of mind.

Every unit of "stars" has its leader, and in the field of remote viewing, the man in charge was General Stubblebine, a man who both wore, and saw, stars.

Sorcerer General

He has a master's degree in chemical engineering from Columbia University. From 1981 to 1984 he was the head of the U.S. Army Intelligence and Security Command. He attained general rank in his military career. Impressive, yes? Here is a quote: "I will also tell you that there are machines on the surface of Mars, and there are machines under the surface of Mars that you can look at, you can find out in detail, you can see what they are, where they are, who they are . . ."[57]

General Stubblebine, with his advanced scientific degree, with his command achievements, is perhaps the highest-ranking member of the military-occult complex. He is proof positive that the military mind can also be the magical mind, for our General (retired) not only believes in Martians and UFOs, but he once had the nickname of General "Spoonbender," because he was a big fan of Uri Geller and psychokinesis.

"As far as UFOs are concerned," says our General, "they can be accessed, they can be tracked, we have looked at the propulsion system for them . . . you can track them back to where they came from."[58] (Now, no doubt most of the readers of this historical work are capable of tracking UFOs back to where they came from; however, your author is not so skilled.) Stubblebine once interfaced with General Noriega; he graduated from West Point, and had been in command of the Army's intelligence school at Fort Huachuca, Arizona.[59] He is not exactly the average guy. He is not exactly even the above-average guy. He is a former Army general, yet he expounds on flying saucers, machines on Mars, and the like.

The General was, during his career, dedicated to the study of human

performance enhancement, and had worked with the hyperkinetic in-
fomercial motivation guru, Anthony Robbins, engaged in neurolinguis-
tic programming, and was also behind the U.S. Army Project Jedi
where soldiers used modeling techniques and mental imagery to improve their ability to shoot the .45 caliber pistol.

If Timothy Leary would have sought a military career, he might have
been General Stubblebine. Spoonbender Stubblebine would hold parties where high-ranking officers would attempt to mentally mold various items of silverware.[60] The General believed that psychokinetic
power could be used as a military weapon, not only to mess with the
mess kit utensils of the enemy, but to discombobulate their computer
systems, which are, by and large, the brains behind modern weapons
and military communications. He was also a fan of remote viewing, and
for a time was in charge of the program.

After retirement, Stubblebine was involved with a variety of private
fringe science organizations ("fringe" here should not be taken as a
pejorative term, but be viewed more in the light of "cutting edge" for
paranormal fans, or "borderline" for others). In 1992, our sorcerer
general gave a speech at the International Symposium on UFO Research sponsored by the International Association for New Science.
(The General was married to a UFOlogist.)

On speaking of remote viewing at the symposium, Stubblebine said
to the audience, "I can go anywhere on this earth, I can go into any
closet, I can go into any mind . . ."[61] "There is a huge bank out there,
all you got to do is go access it. Who can access it? Anybody, anybody
can access that data bank alright [sic] . . ."[62]

One of the people that Stubblebine had brought in to try and access
that data bank was a civilian psychic named Alex Tannous. Even
though the psychic reportedly wore makeup and eyeliner, his image
was tarnished when he managed to come up with less than zilch as a
remote viewer.[63]

Those who can remote view worked hours that would make a
banker jealous. "Each session incidentally is about a forty-five minute
session. We find that you go much beyond forty-five minutes and you
are beginning to run into lapses or a lapse in the energy field . . ."[64]

One wonders whether Stubblebine might have been remote viewing
overtime when he issued the following statement to the 1992 audience
at the symposium regarding the aforesaid Martian machinery: "It's

moving, the machinery is moving, so I don't know if it's from a leftover civilization, its got a long-life battery, its better than any of the dolls we put out in Christmas, I tell you, Okay?"[65] The above gives the flavor of the General's speaking prowess. Disjointed, colloquial English. One would expect better from an officer of general rank. (Whatever his remote-viewing skills might have been [he was not a viewer] his platform skills aren't exactly out of this world.) Why mention his speaking ability? Speaking ability sometimes betrays thinking ability, and when we have an officer in command of an intelligence unit who believes in UFOs, spoonbending, and Martian machines that are moving, one does have the right to stop and say, "hmmm."

It is symptomatic in the lesser lights of the military-occult complex to have demonstrated accomplishment and pulp-magazine silliness co-existing in the same soldier. However, the great ones, like McMoneagle (whom we have already visited) do not suffer from this undesirable combination. They may have opinions of life on Mars, they may have seen flying saucers, but their thinking is articulate, their speech convincing, and in talking with them one gets the feeling, if not of credibility, at least of actual possibility for the theories they propound.

One of the more interesting tidbits of Stubblebine's remote-viewing speech to the symposium was his claim, "There are indications that some countermeasures are possible. We have bumped on indications of countermeasures ..."[66] Unfortunately he is not specific, perhaps either because he is wrong, or because he cannot be specific for security reasons. In any event, the fascinating possibility that countermeasures could exist against remote viewing must give us pause. In order for countermeasures to work, the measures must be capable of detection. Ergo, we posit the question, is remote viewing detectable? If so, is it detectable by mechanical means, psychic means, or both? If it is detectable by mechanical means, does remote viewing then cause some form of electromagnetic radiation to be transmitted?

If it is detectable by psychic means alone, are we saying that what is essentially clairvoyance with controls may be telepathically intercepted, without intentional mind-to-mind transmission? What could be the countermeasures? Electromagnetic radiation of an inhibitory frequency? Psychic jamming? All interesting questions, without presently unclassified answers being available. (There might not even be classified answers available. Whatever our opinion of General Albert Stubblebine

III might be, he is one psychic soldier that makes us think about the possibilities beyond the realm of matter. For that at least, we must be grateful to him.

We had mentioned before that psychic spying might be more of an art than a science. In fact, the protocols of remote viewing were based on the work of an artist-psychic, Ingo Swann.

In Comes Ingo

Artist, writer, psychic Ingo Swann could well be called the grandfather of the remote-viewing program. He literally wrote the book (or at least the manual) on remote viewing, which trained the psychic spies of the 1980s. (Not everyone was trained by Swann, nor does everyone agree that his methods are gospel remote-viewing methodology and protocol. Nevertheless, Ingo Swann is largely responsible for the research that took place.)

Swann was an Army veteran of the late 1950s, and saw service, appropriately enough, in the Far East. After discharge, he sought to establish himself as an artist in New York, and participated in some psychic experiments at the American Society for Psychical Research. A visit by Swann to the Stanford Research Institute in the summer of 1972 was the springboard from which he—and America—jumped into the dark waters of psychic spying.

Dr. Harold Puthoff, a physicist with leanings towards parapsychological research, was at SRI, searching for funding for a project on the edge of reality: the use of the paranormal as a possible intelligence-collection device. Cloak and clairvoyant dagger. Swann, during his visit, was able to mentally affect the output of an electromagnetically shielded magnetometer at SRI. It was a clear demonstration of psychokinetic power, and word got around.[67]

Puthoff, looking at the government as a possible funding source, let out the word about Ingo's ability. The CIA took the bait hook, line, and sinker. Two agents came to SRI, referred to as "East Coast scientists,"[68] And, during Swann's various tasks at SRI, "The two East Coast scientists were in constant attendance."[69] Swann says, "No one will believe it now, but neither Puthoff nor I remember their names."[70] But those two East Coast scientists remembered what they saw at SRI, and the CIA opened its purse strings to finance the beginning of experiments in psychic spying. Swann was asked to sign a security agreement, and did. He was cleared for level Secret. He claims to have held a Top Secret clearance during his Army days.[71]

We have already read about some of Swann's doings at SRI, and Jim Schnabel's book, *Remote Viewers*, does a good job in describing what went on in those days. What has not been made known in the books on remote viewing so far, is the rather unorthodox (and quite possibly correct) view of remote viewing that Swann promotes.

He does not see remote viewing as a paranormal or psychic phenomenon. "When remote viewing was understood," says Swann, "even in its natural state in individuals, it was no longer ambiguous, but seen as a precise set of existing faculties against which the ambiguous term "psychic" was no longer useful."[72]

The Soviet efforts in paranormal research took a similar position. Talents such as remote viewing were not viewed as paranormal, or psychic. They were "psychotronic," or "bioenergetic." The Soviets obviously had to conform their researches with their dogma, and the supernatural was definitely a no-no. Ergo, the phenomenon, which in the West was viewed as an anomalous cognitive talent possessed by certain individuals, was in the Eastern Bloc viewed as a naturally occurring, inherent talent that needed further exploration for its military exploitation.

Swann, while at SRI, came up with the techniques for what was then called Coordinate Remote Viewing, which was the basis for Project Scanate—Scanning by Coordinate. Originally geographic coordinates were used, but then random-number coordinates only were assigned remote-viewing targets. Swann was to develop different stages in the remote-viewing process, where descriptions of psychically input data were drawn or spoken of, in stages of increasing complexity and analysis. The techniques were an attempt to minimize analytic overlay, which was the tendency to analyze what it was that was being viewed, instead of simply what was being perceived. The perception of a round object is reported as a round object, or should be, not analyzed as a dome, or a beach ball, or a container for controlled nuclear explosions.

It was coordinate remote viewing (now called controlled remote viewing) that served as the foundation stone for the training of America's psychic soldiers. Swann says, "It was to be the scope and increase of accuracy which identified the original formats of remote viewing, and especially controlled remote viewing, and which accounted for the long duration of the intelligence community's effort."[73] That effort was to officially last some twenty-three years. (We submit it still goes on.) While many of the readers of this history are experiencing their first exposure to government-sponsored psychic spying, even those who are familiar with the subject are few in number.

Mainstream media either mock the story of Sorcery at the Pentagon, or ignore it as not being generative of sufficient reader interest, and, therefore, publishing profits. It is the investment of courageous publishers (e.g., St. Martin's Press) that is bringing out this fascinating segment of military and intelligence history. Swann correctly observes, "The mixing of the mainstream intelligence community with the fringe area of remote viewing and so-called psychic spying is one of the bigger tales of the 20th century."[74] Yet he is highly critical of the media's reporting of the story. In speaking of the media frenzy of 1995, when the CIA evaluation of psychic spying was revealed to the public, Swann said, "This particular media wave confused all of the important issues beyond recognition and in general held the intelligence community up to ridicule for allegedly wasting taxpayer money on the bewilderment of psychic hoopla."[75]

Swann accurately explains the force behind the doubt and derision that the public and the media cast upon the field of remote viewing and psychic spying. "Even though most support the concept of increasing our knowledge, very few really want to do anything of the kind if it wrecks their existing realities."[76] How true. The religious right would view such things as government psychic spying as United States cooperation with the forces of Satan. As this anachronistic voting bloc carries voter numbers as well as potential significant dollar contributions to local and nationwide campaigns, they are a name to conjure with. Politicians, who wish to seem as mainstream as they wish to appear Main Street (with the exception of a select few of intelligent and courageous individuals), would obviously wish to distance themselves from any government investment in the realm of the paranormal.

Revelations about remote viewing, and the possibility that it may be an inherent species talent, not just an anomalous ability in a select few, would be as disturbing to the average man as his sudden ability to lift himself aloft by flapping his arms. The fact that a remote viewer can perceive beyond our concepts of linear time and space, and "see" what should be imperceptible by such a viewing method, not only rocks the political and social boat but it is a revelation of extremely dangerous military and espionage sensitivity.

Swann views talents like remote viewing as species-inherent. "The superpowers of the human bio-mind, of which remote viewing is but one, can be defined as those species-inherent faculties which permit human awareness to transcend the conventionally perceived limits of space and time . . ."[77] The development of such species-inherent ability could make obsolete much of our military and espionage equipment and tactics. Swann is not alone in his opinions. In my interviews and frequent conversations with Joseph McMoneagle (who is not by any means a fanatical fan of Swann's RV methods), he has repeatedly stated that everyone who comes into the lab evidences some level of psychic functioning. In speaking with remote-viewer Mel Riley, I heard a similar opinion.

Perhaps we are not yet ready to accept this new talent in ourselves. We may be, all of us, something more, something much more than we thought. We just might not yet be ready to hear it, or consider it.

In his proposition that what we call psychic powers are not anomalous cognitive talents for an elite, but are inherent within the species, Swann hints at a darker motive in those who sneer at the possibilities. "It is interesting indeed, why in our scientific times," he says, "there should be such a pogrom that victimizes our species' superpowers of bio-mind with its marvelous spectrum of sentiency. It may be that someone somewhere, doesn't want that marvelous spectrum to be identified and developed."[78]

Yet the government, in various departments, did fund the research. The CIA provided the initial funding. The Navy contributed. The DIA took over the program, and various other elements of the federal establishment, like the DEA, the Coast Guard, and the FBI, used the talents of the government remote viewers as an adjunct to their operations. That same government who provided the money was, in 1995, extremely efficient in its dissemination of an evaluation that disclosed that remote viewing was not useful as an intelligence collection tool. That report, and that evaluation performed by the American Institute of Research, shall itself be fully examined and evaluated.

How accurate were the remote viewers? Swann says, "The 15 percent accuracy cited in recent public statements on behalf of the CIA is the baseline which ordinary non-gifted and untrained persons often do achieve. This figure was identified very early in the SRI research phase. The minimum accuracy needed by the clients was 65 percent. In the later stages of the development [training] part of the effort, this accuracy level was achieved, and often consistently exceeded."[79] It was Swann who trained America's psychic spies and achieved a level of accuracy sufficient to satisfy the CIA, regardless of what disinformation is being distributed via the official 1995 evaluation of the program.

This should not come as a surprise to anybody, as Swann acknowledges, "The key players in the development, training and use of remote viewing remain under the strictest security constraints. They can't talk, but I at least honor them for their commitment to the welfare of the nation even if within a controversial area. Similarly, the documentation supporting the real story is archived under top security wraps."[80]

When Swann wrote that, it was the end of 1995, prior to the publication of Morehouse's *Psychic Warrior*, Schnabel's *Remote Viewers*, and this book, of course. It was also prior to the declassification of the 1977 *Studies in Intelligence* report of Dr. Kress, which acknowledged the possibilities of remote viewing early into the research and described some of its operational successes.

The wraps are slowly coming off and the story, the true story, is slowly emerging. Swann, the professor emeritus of remote viewing, lives in Greenwich Village, producing intriguing paintings, and writing his history of remote viewing—a history that has been rejected by the primary publishers of America's books. It does appear in the new frontier of available knowledge, the World Wide Web. In that history, we learn that remote viewing worked. "Remote viewers did help find SCUD missiles, did help find secret biological and chemical warfare projects, did locate tunnels and extensive underground facilities and identify their purposes. Not all of the time, of course, and sometimes imperfectly so."

But we must remember that no method of intelligence collection is foolproof. No tool remains sharp without attention and proper grinding. "Regardless of official and media misdirecting," says Swann, "The general world knows now that remote viewing exists. Soon other nations will utilize it for their own interests."[81] When that happens, we shall all live in interesting times.

One other dweller in the dark of the world of magic and the military needs to be mentioned. He is a man who would rather reign in Hell than serve in the Army. He is Michael Aquino.

The Devil's Own

One of the darker denizens in the history of the military-occult complex is former U.S. Army Lt. Col. Michael Aquino. A former intelligence officer, a participant in psychological warfare experiments and exercises, Aquino is also a Satanist. He is a classic example of the meeting of the military mind with the magician's soul.

Aquino started his formal pursuit of Satanism when he joined the Church of Satan in San Francisco, under the rulership of former burlesque-house organist and lion tamer, the late Anton Szandor LaVey. He was to rise to great heights in LaVey's organization, being ordained a priest in 1970, becoming author of some of its ritual workings, and then, when the inevitable conflict occurred between the egos of these particular devils, Aquino split from LaVey's organization and in 1975 formed the Temple of Set.

Aquino first came under LaVey's Church of Satan influence in 1968, while Aquino was serving as an intelligence officer. He bought into the philosophy and eagerly accepted administrative duties with the church. (It was somewhat a deviation from another organization he had participated in, the Eagle Scouts!) Disenchanted with LaVey's brand of Satanism, our Army officer received a revelation on June 21, 1975, from the Prince of Hell himself, appearing in the guise of the Egyptian god Set. It was set and match for Aquino, and this meeting with the arch-fiend resulted in Aquino penning the demonically inspired, *The Book of Coming Forth By Night*. (It is apparently the right of all founders of religious movements to credit divine or demonic inspiration in the books that they write, which inevitably serve as scriptural authority for the author's leadership of the movement.)

Aquino put on the satanic uniform of the day. LaVey had shaved his head, and because doing so would be somewhat derivative, Aquino trimmed his hair into a widow's peak and plucked his eyebrows. In case this wasn't bizarre enough, he also had **666** tattooed on his scalp.

Aquino has been accused of being rather partial to Nazi occultism and fascist ideals. But such accusations were lightweight, compared to what happened to him in 1987.[82] Aquino, Vietnam veteran, army officer, and Satanist, was accused of being a child molester. The San Francisco police were investigating his participation in allegations of child abuse coming from the Presidio of San Francisco's Army day-care center. Aquino's home was raided. He sued. The final outcome of the

186 ● THE PSYCHIC BATTLEFIELD

investigation was nil. No charges were brought. The San Francisco police investigation turned up nothing. A subsequent U.S. Army investigation likewise found no evidence against him. One wonders if these investigations ever would have taken place but for his public profession of his Satanic beliefs.[83]

Aquino is interesting because he had top-level security clearances, and twelve of his Setian disciples were also members of Army Intelligence. (Again, the elitism, the desire for hierarchical structure runs deep in the veins of both soldiers and sorcerers. Magic, like the military, provides both.)

In 1983, Aquino was to visit the SS castle at Wewelsburg, Germany, where fifty years earlier, Himmler, who believed himself to be the reincarnation of tenth-century Germanic King Henry the Fowler, held Nazi rituals. Aquino was to perform his own magic workings in the castle, and continually study Nazi occult methods.[84]

Aquino has recently been involved with legal action (as a plaintiff) in the California courts. In a suit in San Francisco, he brought an action against an Internet content provider, Electriciti. The cause of action was for negligence and intentional infliction of emotional distress. Aquino had been accused of ritual Satanic abuse (a phenomenon that occurs in talk shows, but rarely in the real world), child molestation, and governmental fraud. Aquino, who was awarded the Meritorious Service medal by the Secretary of the Army, was understandably upset about these accusations, especially when formal investigations had failed to result in any charges against him. According to Aquino, Internet postings caused him and his wife emotional distress, and subjected them to threats and insults. Aquino was seeking, inter alia, $100,000 in punitive damages.[85] He had also sued for the removal of his name from the Army CID (Criminal Investigation Division) file concerning the allegations of child abuse. He lost.

We have a man of obvious intelligence and military accomplishment, who openly avows his allegiance to Satan (albeit in Egyptian dress). It is not until after this avowal that he is accused of terrible crimes—crimes of which he was not only never convicted, but never even indicted. Since, in the author's many years of criminal law experience, I feel it safe to say that a grand jury could indict a bagel and cream cheese for high treason, it is apparent that Aquino is, and must be considered innocent.

Aquino is one of the more glaring examples of how open and notorious occult interest can be fatal to not only a military career, but to a private individual. His Satanic involvements, coupled with his blatant admiration for the Nazis and their supposed occult traditions have purchased for this former lieutenant colonel with an intelligence background, a world of hurt. Is it unjust? Of course it is. Is it typical? Unfortunately, yes. But until the paranormal, in any and every form, ceases to carry such emotional baggage in the real world, those who participate in its study and practice may not only achieve mastery, but martyrdom.

CHAPTER 19

1984

The ESP Begins to Leak

In the world of psychic spying, 1984 was an eventful year. Top remote-viewer Joseph McMoneagle retired from the Army to work on the civilian side of the research (although still heavily involved with the government programs). New remote-viewing recruits like Lyn Buchanan and Ed Dames entered the field. Of greater significance, the classified program developed several major leaks, and the public began to learn about the military-occult complex. Stories in the newspapers about Sorcery in the Pentagon, appeared. Books like *Mind Wars* were published by major New York houses. As usual, disinformation and misinformation flowed in abundance.

The *New York Times* article, "Sorcery at the Pentagon,"[1] had sources denying government involvement in psychic spying. However, in the same article, a former DIA head of general officer rank, Daniel Graham, was quoted as conceding "that the military had spent considerable sums on psychic research." The article concluded with, ". . . the government has indeed been suckered into some hocus-pocus scheme for waging war by necromancy."[2] Was this article written in honest ignorance, or was it an intentional placement of government-planted disinformation? The reality in 1984, when the article appeared, was that there had been more than a decade of government-sponsored research into the experimental and operational uses of remote viewing, the military program was in its seventh year, and there had been successful operational uses of the technique. The government had not been suckered in, but instead had gradually increased funding for its paranormal research programs as it became more and more evident that there really was something to ESPionage.

As to the poetic claim that the government was waging war by necromancy, this was mostly (not totally) nonsense. There had been occasions when military paranormal research tried to contact dead agents, but that was a tiny part of the program. The majority of the remoteviewing program dealt with ways of "accurizing" the technique, and using it as a quasi-clairvoyant method of intelligence collection—always as an adjunct, and not as a sole source for data.

It was at least an interesting coincidence that this leak of disinformation occurred in 1984 (no doubt sponsored by the real-world Ministry of Truth, the CIA). The Orwellian overtones of a psychic big brother made good press, but the press did not make good on the real story. About six weeks after the "Sorcery at the Pentagon" article appeared, a slightly less derisive and derogatory report was published from the "Science Desk" section of *The New York Times,* with the less-pejorative title of "Pentagon is Said to Focus on ESP for Wartime Use."[3] The opening paragraph of this article was a blockbuster. It spoke of millions of dollars of Pentagon money being spent "to perform various acts of espionage and war—penetrating secret files, for example, locating submarines, or blowing up guided missiles in midflight."[4] Again in the article, the government "denies that it is spending money on psychic research."[5] Again, the government was lying.

There was a quote from a university professor of philosophy in the article, who opined "You can't get it [ESP] in the open laboratory."[6] Said professor was then the chairman of CSICOP, a high profile antipsi organization, whose letters stand for the Committee for the Scientific Investigation of Claims Of the Paranormal. However, in 1984, there had been abundant proof in the laboratory (at SRI) that ESP did exist. There had been abundant proof of ESP recognized by the CIA seven years before this pundit pontificated. (The Kress report in 1977.) The people who denied ESP were either government employees who were under orders to offer disinformation, or those who simply did not have the need to know, and therefore didn't. It would be another dozen years before the Kress report would be declassified, and when it was, the newspapers were strangely silent about what was revealed therein. (Perhaps they just didn't know.)

The year 1984 was also to see the publication, by St. Martin's Press, of Ronald McRae's *Mind Wars.* (St. Martin's is a publishing house on the forefront of the paranormal, having published not only McRae's work, but Morehouse's 1996 *Psychic Warrior,* and, come to think of it, this book also.) Another book, *Mind Race,* was published in 1984 by some of the scientists at the SRI remote-viewing research project. A well-known parapsychologist, Martin Ebon, offered his book *Psychic Warfare* in the same year.

Was it a coincidence that all three books were published in the same year, and that year was 1984? Was it a clever marketing technique of the publishing houses to release this type of book in a year as heavily laden with big brother overtones as 1984? Or, more interesting perhaps, was it approved by the government? The leaks came from government. They had to. They started to flow in 1984, and poured out of the publishing houses and the press. Was it an intentional disinformation campaign aimed at our Cold War adversaries to make them fear a psychic gap—as had occurred with the planting of the Nautilus Telepathy Experiments in 1960? We may never know.

Perhaps George Orwell was a psychic.

CHAPTER 20

AN AFFAIR WITH MONROE

Military Minds in Alternate States of Consciousness

It is a place of blue sky, rolling verdant mountains, and sparkling fresh waters. A place to relax, a place of rediscovery, of rebirth, if you will. The Monroe Institute, located in Faber, Virginia at the foothills of the Blue Ridge Mountains is a place where minds are introduced to alternative states, out-of-body experiences occur, and lives are forever changed in outlook. It was here that, in the 1980s, the United States Army Intelligence and Security Command, INSCOM, sent its future psychic soldiers.

As we have already learned, this time was the era when INSCOM was headed by General Stubblebine, aficionado of the Paranormal. It was at the Monroe Institute that certain government remote viewers came to be opened to a new way of perception, a new way to access and organize data. The founder of the institute, Robert Allan Monroe, was the son of a physician mother and professor father. At first, Monroe's career gave little indication of its ultimate destination. He was a radio broadcaster, a producer, director, a writer of music. His first venturing on his way to being a paranormal pioneer was in sleep learning. In 1958, Monroe's research led to an out-of-body experience. This served as a springboard from which he jumped into consciousness research, especially that which involved the use of sound frequencies to induce altered mental states. Monroe was to obtain patents on several devices and in 1974 founded his institute.[1]

One of the consciousness-changing methods of the Monroe Institute, the Hemi-Synch® process, was to be used on the INSCOM trainees. The Hemi-Synch® process involved inputting two slightly different sound frequencies into each ear of the subject, which in turn would create a third brain frequency resulting in an altered state of consciousness. This patented and trademarked process saw the subject with earphones on his head, lying in a specially constructed chamber, wherein light intensity and color could be controlled, music piped in, and other sensory controls could be initiated. The chamber was referred to as a CHEC, a Controlled Holistic Environment Center, and looked something like a walk-in closet with bedding and wires.[2]

The sensory-controlled environment, in concert with the Hemi-Synch frequencies, resulted in out-of-body experiences for some of the INSCOM participants, enhanced perception for others, and for one possibly induced a nervous breakdown.

In my September 1998 interview with Nancy McMoneagle (who back in the INSCOM trainee days was Nancy Honeycutt, Director of the Monroe Institute and trainer of the psychic soldiers), I learned the true details of how one would be psychic turned psycho during his Monroe training.

Apparently, the soldier had lied on the questionnaire given to all Monroe students. Having examined the application, it is my testimony that the questionnaire specifically requests information on drug usage, and prior involvement with mental health professionals. Apparently, this soldier never disclosed a past psychiatric history (which of course made sense career-wise).

While undergoing the Hemi-Synch process, the soldier, wide-eyed and perspiring profusely, demanded to go to the separate administration building where Nancy McMoneagle was working. He informed her that he knew "who she really was," although who that was he never revealed. He then took off his shirt, holding a pen threateningly in his hand, and claimed that he had been trained to kill with said pen. (Can there be a secret military unit trained to kill with ballpoints?) Jim Schnabel, in his *Remote Viewers* book, has this trooper running around naked, but Nancy says no, he was just shirtless. (She maintained her cool, suggested that she get some coffee, and returned with some de-caffeinated psychiatric assistance.)

Remote viewing was not taught at Monroe; that course was given at SRI. But Monroe served as a booster to loosening up the linear thinking that was contrary to good remote-viewing technique. Stubblebine had been there. General Spoonbender, as he was often called, wanted his troops to have the same training. Back in 1983, the approximate cost per soldier for the week or so they spent at Monroe was $750. Now it is double this, but we are, at the time of this writing, talking fifteen years later.

INSCOM called the training RAPT—for Rapid Acquisition Personnel Training. The Army training program was quite similar to the civilian courses, but the semantics were sometimes changed to protect the bureaucratic innocents. Two Monroe training sessions took place, the third was canceled after the aforementioned freak-out by the psycho soldier. But military involvement with Monroe did not end. Listed as a board advisor to the institute is one Franklin Holmes Atwater, aka Skip Atwater, who was also a member of the Army remote-viewing unit. He has written widely on the Monroe technologies, and in a recent article explained the Hemi-Synch process. "When brain waves move to lower frequencies and awareness is maintained, a unique state of consciousness emerges. . . . The Hemi-Synch process offers access to a wide variety of altered-state experiences for those wanting to explore the realms of consciousness."[3] It was this exploration of the realms of consciousness that was behind the government remote-viewing re-search. The term Hemi-Synch derived from hemispheric synchroniza-tion where the right and left brains were placed in synch, creating optimal thinking—or so it is claimed.

The work at Monroe continues today. Its Gateway program offers participants a new view of themselves, the functioning of the mind, the purpose of their lives. The Institute is also an important milestone in the modern history of the military-occult complex, and a significant component in the training of the psychic spies of the 1980s. Alumni of the INSCOM training would later go on to perform their own private research into the final frontier of the mind's potential, and all have benefited from the research and development of Robert Allan Monroe and his dedicated staff of researchers.

During my Christmas 1998 visit with the McMoneagles, I had occasion to walk the grounds of the Monroe Institute and enjoy the panoramic view of the foothills of the Blue Ridge Mountains. If ever there was a place for mental quiet, a base from which to launch mental transcendence, it is the Monroe Institute. Expect human perceptual revelations to come from this quiet, rural Virginia haven in the century to come—a probability and a prediction.

CHAPTER 21

BY ANY OTHER NAME

Aliases of the
Remote-Viewing Project

During the field day the press had when the government's investment in psychic spying was made public in 1995, the name associated with the entire effort by the uninformed journalists was Stargate. It had a nice ring to it, like Star Trek, Star Tac, etc. But it was an error to refer to the twenty-plus years of paranormal research by the military and intelligence services as the Stargate Program.

Late in 1977, the first operational remote-viewing program, complete with tiny office and tiny budget, was christened Gondola Wish. Its mission was to use specially trained personnel to clairvoyantly spy on intelligence targets. (Since clairvoyance has an aura of tea leaves and spinster seances about it, remote viewing was the government neutral name given to the art of seeing there without being there.)

Two of the original recruits in Gondola Wish were to be of immense help in the creation of this history of the military-occult complex—Joseph McMoneagle and Mel Riley. The program did not last long and was terminated after a relatively few missions. The unit consisted of part-timers, military personnel from other intelligence units who did temporary duty in the astral plane for Uncle Sam. They proved that the concept worked—sometimes. The results were sufficiently impressive to bring in larger funds, more office space, and a new name—Grill Flame.

Housed in two small buildings on the grounds of Fort George Meade, in Maryland, (which was also the military post housing the headquarters of the National Security Agency), the unit was to receive its operational taskings from the Defense Intelligence Agency.[1] McMoneagle and Riley, still with the renamed unit, were both to remote view a Chinese nuclear device, describing in similar terms developments in bomb technology that the everyday normal intelligence analysts did not think were yet available to the Chinese.[2]

In 1983 the program's name again changed, this time with the traffic-like moniker of Center Lane. This unit came under the direct control of General Albert Stubblebine III, about whom we have already learned. He was a firm believer in the paranormal, and an aficionado of spoon bending a la Uri Geller. It was during the Center Lane program that (then) Captain Edward Dames was to join the unit, not as a remote viewer, but as a training officer and monitor. We learned in a former chapter about Dames—his grandiose claims of having been the creator of the remote-viewing program, and having the ability to perform 100 percent accurate remote-viewing missions.

It seems to be a tendency (with some refreshing exceptions like McMoneagle and Riley) for those involved in the arena of psi research and practice to have rather large egos, and a rather small regard for truth. Those who started out as participants in a paranormal experimental intelligence unit were later to speak with authority about moving Martian machines, and pregnant extraterrestrials living under the earth's surface. Angelic encounters, demonic rendezvous, and enough astral phenomena to keep Industrial Light and Magic busy with special effects for years have been described by some of the remote-viewing veterans.

The four new recruits of the Center Lane program, Dames, counterintelligence specialist Paul Smith, another Army captain, and a civilian intelligence analyst had undergone mind-expansion training at the Monroe Institute in Virginia. One of the trainers there was Nancy Honeycutt, who was later to become Mrs. Joseph McMoneagle.

Honeycutt assisted the trainees in using the Hemi-Synch process of attaining altered states of consciousness, developed at the Monroe Institute. As described earlier, this process involved the input of tones of slightly different frequencies into each ear, which supposedly created a third brain-wave frequency in the trainee. Out-of-body experiences were common during the training at the Monroe Institute. (Nancy McMoneagle, by the way, is an excellent astrologer, increasingly in demand. The author had his horoscope cast by Nancy, and even as a veteran of many psychic faire fakers and divination dummies, I was impressed by her accuracy.)

The aforementioned head of the Center Lane unit, General Stubblebine, was to have his head lopped off as unit boss when the powers that be felt that he was too far out, even for remote viewing. He later became involved as a retired military man with various civilian organizations exploring paranormal phenomena.

Control of the unit was taken over by the Defense Intelligence Agency's Scientific and Technical Intelligence Directorate, and in 1985 the well of Army financing dried up. However, this psychic-spying phoenix again rose from the ashes under the name of Sun Streak. It was during this phase of the unit's history that Army Ranger David Morehouse came to spy. He would later publish an account of his exploits, entitled *Psychic Warrior.*

Along with the military types, Sun Streak housed some tarot card readers to "read" the astral plane for intelligence information. The soldiers looked down at the civilians, who did not fit in with the RV mold and their technical training. This was an unfounded prejudice. Your author has used tarot cards as a prognostication and consultative medium since 1975. I have been able to obtain information that was factually accurate by these means—often. Is there any inherent psychic power in the cards? Doubtful. The tarot is merely a tool, a crutch to engage one's power of psychic functioning. In my conversations with both Mel Riley and Joseph McMoneagle about remote viewing, the three of us agreed that various tools and techniques are fine to use, so long as the results manifest.

Sun Streak fell into disfavor with the traditional military and intelligence types, and in 1991 or so, the program received its final designation—Stargate. It was the Stargate program that came into the public eye when a CIA-funded evaluation claimed the program was of no intelligence value, and in 1995, the final plug was pulled on the paranormal spying for which the government had paid for some twenty-plus years. That report, which shall be discussed in detail, was prepared by the American Institute of Research and referred to as the AIR report. Based on fragmentary data, its authors denied access to the classified files hidden in some secure room, the AIR report was, by and large, full of hot AIR.

From Gondola Wish to Stargate, the government remote-viewing program was to prove itself of operational value, and to shed light in a dark corner of the potential of the human mind. It was a light the government didn't want America to see.

CHAPTER 22

THE OTHER
"WORLD WIDE WEB"

The Information Theory of
Remote Viewing

Something Borrowed

On July 4, 1998, Independence Day took on an additional meaning. It was on this day that the *Defense Intelligence Agency Training Manual for Remote Viewing* (originally authored in 1986) appeared on the World Wide Web: free at last. I contacted several of my intelligence sources (who must remain nameless) and learned that they believed the manual was authentic. Thus, the method to the madness of remote viewing became free to anyone with an Internet service provider.

The manual will be dealt with in detail in the next chapter, where it shall be analyzed and commented upon in depth. For our purposes here, however, we will look at the theoretical part of the manual that deals with the well of information from which remote-viewing information might be obtained. We will see that this theory, embedded in what was once a 1986 classified document, existed in a popular paperback published sixteen years before, for all to read.

Whether or not the government theory for the source of remote-viewing data was borrowed from said paperback's author is a matter of conjecture, which I will leave to the analysis of the reader. (My rather controversial opinion is that it was borrowed.) Submitted as Exhibit

One is the following quote: "Remote-viewing theory postulates a non-material matrix in which any and all information about any place or thing may be obtained through the agency of a hypothesized signal line. The viewer psychically perceives and decodes this signal line and objectifies the information so obtained."[1] The above was from the DIA remote-viewing manual. Now we offer a quote taken from a book authored by the first student to graduate with a degree in magic and thaumaturgy (wonder-working) from—where else? the University of California at Berkeley.

In his book, *Real Magic*, author Isaac Bonewitz states, "Plugging into the switchboard would seem to be a type of psi phenomena, in that the same variables are involved. You could conceive of this plugging in as a kind of telepathy with the switchboard or as a kind of super introspection."[2] The similarity of concepts is obvious. The government's original remote-viewing research took place in Menlo Park, California, starting around 1972–1973 at the Stanford Research Institute. The book by Bonewitz, which was published in 1970, was issued by a San Francisco publisher. The times are close, the book and research emerged from the same state, and the theories speak for themselves vis-à-vis similarity. "This matrix can be envisioned as a vast three-dimensional geometric arrangement of dots, each dot representing a discrete information bit."[3] That quote comes from the DIA manual. "The vast net of billions of interlocking metapatterns with their innumerable subpatterns is what I call the switchboard."[4] That quote comes from the Bonewitz book. Again, the similarity of concept is noteworthy, yet in the resource listings of the DIA manual, there is no mention of the book *Real Magic*. This, of course, makes sense, when you figure a government field manual isn't going to be very eager to quote a popular work on Sorcery 101. In his book, Bonewitz says, "I find it perfectly possible that all clair senses and possibly even the various forms of hyper cognition (super fast thinking) may all be functions of the switchboard. Perhaps we merely plug into the switchboard to pick up the data we then interpret as clairvoyance or clairaudience."[5] "When the viewer is prompted by the coordinate or other targeting methodology, he accesses the signal line for data derived from the matrix."[6] That is from the DIA manual. In examining the above quotations, is it not likely that the author(s) of the DIA manual had at least come across the Bonewitz Switchboard Theory? We may imagine that researchers into psychic phenomena would be reading everything they could get their hands on that would be relevant to the research, whether it came from respected sources of parapsychological research, or popular literature on the subject. If true, it would have been difficult for the DIA people not to read and review the Bonewitz material. The above argument is conjectural, true, but the similarities of theory, and the means by which the theory is expressed might point to what is called in law the doctrine of *res ipsa loquitur* (the thing speaks for itself).

The Bonewitz Switchboard or the DIA Matrix demonstrate the modern tendency toward mechanistic viewpoints and explanations when it comes to paranormal research. In analyzing, or attempting to analyze phenomena that appear to directly run contrary to physical laws, our paranormal researchers, dressed in their lab coats, wearing their pocket protectors and fingering their slide rules, like to maintain the trappings and suits of science. It makes sense to do so. When you are being funded by such a fuddy-duddy source as Uncle Sam, especially by his military-intelligence establishment, you need to have a hard science approach. (Otherwise, your funding might get pulled, and you have to go back to less exciting research, like how to destroy the world with lasers, electromagnetic pulses, and plasma weapons.)

The Russians were famous for their electromagnetic and radio metaphors for psi phenomena, even though the research didn't quite back up the metaphors. (As an example, ESP has been shown many times to be able to operate in conditions where electromagnetic waves are shielded, thereby making it unlikely that EM waves are serving as a carrier of psychic information.)

Our scientists like to label psi phenomena with twentieth-century terms and concepts, seemingly forgetful of the fact that psi phenomena existed thousands of years before anybody ever thought that something like radio or other electromagnetic-spectrum waves existed. Again, given the politics of government research, they cannot be too harshly castigated for this fault.

As interesting as the question, "Did the DIA authors of the remote-viewing manual steal Bonewitz's Switchboard Theory," is, what is more interesting to consider, whether or not the theory is correct. Is there some sort of material, or nonmaterial depository of universal information capable of being accessed, or at least detected? If so, if there is what the DIA manual calls a signal line, can this signal be amplified or altered?" Fascinating questions, with no declassified answers as of yet. The matrix/switchboard theory seems to have some obvious parallels with Jung's concept of the Collective Unconscious, but as we will see with remote viewing, there have been missions to places where no man has gone before and, therefore, no race memory should exist. (Mars has been remote viewed by several respected and talented viewers, for example.)

Only a few of the remote viewers in the research program could consistently hit the viewing target. Does this reflect on individual talent, or does this mean that the switchboard/matrix is not accessible to everyone? Is belief in the switchboard/matrix a sine qua non for obtaining data from it? Again, interesting questions with no publicly available answers yet.

Many might scoff at believing in this other world wide web of information, yet, according to a 1991 Gallup poll, "The majority of the American population believes in the authenticity of one or more paranormal processes."[7] Therefore, the concept of another world wide web which can be accessed by the mind alone might find acceptance by the majority of believing Americans.

The theme of this book is that there has existed throughout time, in the shadows, a relationship between the military, the spies, and the paranormal world—a military-occult complex. Whether or not the switchboard/matrix exists or not, one thing is beyond doubt. Our government invested our tax money to try to find out.

CHAPTER 23

BY THE BOOK
The DIA RV Manual

If it has anything to do with the government, especially the military, it necessitates a manual of instruction, complete with redundancies, theoretical presumptions and a jargon. The field of remote viewing was no exception, and in May 1986, under the auspices of the Defense Intelligence Agency, a remote-viewing training manual was issued. It was to become the government gospel of psychic spying. This manual went public on Independence Day, 1998 on the Internet, for those who knew where to look, and it revealed the methods and protocols used by many, but not all, of the remote viewers employed by the intelligence services. Authorship of the manual was attributed to Ingo Swann, who subsequently denied the honor, but regardless of the purported author, the methods are certainly those developed by Swann, are as the techniques of the coordinate remote viewing (CRV) variety.

In the Introduction to the manual, a brief description of the remote-viewing session logistics details "a remote viewer and a monitor [who] begin by seating themselves at the opposite ends of a table in a special remote viewing room, equipped with paper and pens, a tape recorder and a camera . . ." It is interesting to note, even in this brief introduction to the procedure, the government mind-set of authority, subtly bordering on an adversarial relationship between monitor and viewer. Why must the monitor be seated opposite the viewer? Why not next to him, in the role of partner, behind him, as mentor, or above him, as judge?

From the inception, the process of coordinate remote viewing has taken on a Missouri flavor of "show me," and perhaps this is proper. The practical intelligence use of psychic functioning could (and often would) result in the collection of information of potential intelligence value upon which strategies and perhaps actual operations might be based. It is possible that the positioning of viewer and monitor served as a mnemonic device to remind the viewer that there would be a critical analysis of the data he produced. It would be interesting to know if there were experiments with respect to monitor-viewer positioning vis-à-vis results obtained, but there is nothing on the subject in the manual, or in the available declassified information.

The manual describes the ambience desirable for remote viewing. "The room is homogeneously colored, acoustically tiled and featureless, with light controlled by a dimmer so that environmental distractions can be minimized." This, of course, makes good sense. As physical sensory stimuli are much more strongly received than psychic ones, it is logical to limit those stimuli so the more subtle perceptions are not overwhelmed. This remote-viewing atmosphere parallels the CHEC chambers used during the RAPT training sessions at the Monroe Institute, with their controlled lighting and sound facilities—the same chambers in which military personnel learned to achieve alternate states of consciousness.

The minimization of site-physical stimuli in a remote viewing session may contain within its concept a possible solution (or perhaps a partial one) to the search for remote-viewing countermeasures. Perhaps a visually and aurally stimulating (and thereby distracting) ambience might serve to cloak a possible remote-viewing target. My conversations with government remote viewers indicate that initially this would be so, but trained remote viewers would be able to circumvent such distracting stimuli. Whether or not this is actual truth or intentional disinformation cannot be determined at this time.

In remote viewing, it is the higher mental functioning of the viewer that can serve as an impediment to the accurate reception of data. In a field that is analysis heavy, like intelligence, this perhaps is one of the greatest challenges to the viewer—to turn off and tune out the analytic functions of the brain. The DIA Manual says, "While it is extremely useful in a society relying heavily on quantitative data and technological development, such analytic thinking hampers remote viewing by the manufacture of what is known as analytic overlay or AOL." Perhaps this might be one of the reasons that traditional science is so hostile to the reality of psi powers. It is the very part of the mind that hard scientists use to achieve their technological wonders that is denigrated to the role of noisemaker, when it comes to remote viewing.

The above being true, it is ironic that the scientists who were initially investigating remote-viewing phenomena were physicists. This analytical mind, while being a hindrance to remote viewing, does not seem so at first, for in the initial remote-viewing exercises undertaken by subjects, there is what the DIA Manual refers to as a First Time Effect, or beginner's luck. It appears that initial remote-viewing efforts, perhaps due to their novelty, and the unfamiliarity of the brain in processing such efforts, are more accurate than subsequent attempts. It is the training and the methods and protocol contained in the DIA Manual that help restore the viewer to a level equal to or better than these initial successes.

During my initial remote-viewing attempts while participating in online experiments originating from the University of Amsterdam's Parapsychology Department, I also experienced the "first time effect." My enthusiasm for my remarkable first-time success was soon dampened by subsequent tries when the results were less than spectacular. The Manual states, "This effect is hypothesized to result from the initial excitation of hereditary but dormant psi-conducting neuronal channels, which, when first stimulated by psychoenergetic functioning, catch the analytic system off guard . . ." In understandable English, a first attempt to employ psychic function turns on the lamp before your rational mind has the chance to put a shade over it.

Even though the official explanation of the first-time effect is laden with governmental gobbledygook, it is perhaps the most monumentally radical language—revolutionary language—ever to have appeared in a government instruction book. There, in black and white, is the serious official pronouncement that there actually are hereditary but dormant psi-conducting channels in existence, and in human beings. Uncle Sam, in one of his many voices, has admitted that we are born potential psychics. The government in its admission has thrown down the gauntlet to the twin pillars that support it in mainstream America—religion and science. This challenge to the myths and measurements of both is an attack on the definitions of the nature of man, and of the parameters of his mind.

Unfortunately, almost nobody knew that this manual, which contained governmental admission to psychic power in humanity, even existed. Most are learning of it for the first time in this work. (As an aside, it would be interesting to study more mundane governmental manuals to see what metaphysical wonders might be hidden among the awkward, stilted language of officialdom.)

The psychic functioning of man is highly sensitive to interference. The DIA Manual warned of inclemencies, which were "Personal considerations that might degrade or even preclude psychic functioning. Muscle pains, colds, allergies, menstrual cramps, hangovers, mental and emotional stress." The manual said these negative influences "could be worked through and ultimately are only minor nuisances." Hunger and a pressing need to eliminate body wastes were the only inclemencies that caused psychic functioning to come to a dead halt. Indirectly, the government was giving meditation (a mind-quieting process) its seal of approval when it spoke of these inclemencies and their effect. As we read between the lines in this DIA-sponsored textbook, we see a government guide that not only admits to psychic functioning as existing, but endorses (by implication) meditation as a method of optimizing psychic functioning.

While the manual's specifics on remote viewing are amazing enough to find in a government publication, the philosophical and metaphysical conclusions that may be reached via analyzing the manual are borderline incredible—not in their concept, but in consideration of the publisher. (We will see in chapter 25 how the government officially sponsored an evaluation of remote-viewing that is decidedly [and designedly] negative nine years after it published the DIA manual.)

In dealing with the various descriptive stages through which the reporting of psychically perceived input must travel, the remote-viewing manual gives us insight (no pun intended) into the differences between sensory perception and that which would be classified as extrasensory. In the beginning reporting stage of remote viewing, an ideogram (one or more lines) is drawn by the viewer as a gross representation of the target site. The manual gives examples: ". . . the Gobi desert being predominantly flat, wave sand, would produce . . . a horizontal ideogram.

The Empire State Building, however, would produce some sort of vertical response . . ."

There is an important caveat in the manual: "A crucial point to remember is [that] the objectification of the ideogram is completely independent either of what it looks like, or its orientation on paper." In other words, the Gobi desert might appear in a vertical orientation, the Empire State Building in the horizontal. "In stage one there is no viewer site orientation in the dimensional plane," according to the manual. Thus, while through physical sensory channels initial perceptions will normally be oriented properly in space through extra-physical viewing, spatial orientation of a target feature is not likely. Could this be an indication that extrasensory perception takes place in an extra-dimensional milieu?

While I was participating in an on-line experiment, a series of concentric circles were perceived as if looked upon directly from above the centerpoint. I also perceived an image of a waterfall, turbulent water in a vertical orientation. In reality, the actual target was a rope bridge over water, with the concentric circles being the supports of the bridge, but from a viewpoint as if directly perceived in front of the viewer, and the water was in a horizontal orientation. Had this been an actual operation, even though the spatial orientation was incorrect, the predominant structural features were perceived, and the site-specific turbulent water was likewise seen via psychic functioning. This could very well have had significant operational utility.

The DIA manual, in speaking of initial ideogram production, states, "Most viewers tend to establish well-worn patterns in executing ideograms on paper. If such habits become established enough, they can actually inhibit proper handling of the signal line by restricting ease and flexibility in proper ideogram production." If true, this ideogram phenomenon might also allow for creation, over time, of an individually based psychic translator, which could serve to externally "accurize" the remote viewer's perceptions. Here's how such a psychic translator might be created and utilized: over time the ideograms of Captain John Doe, remote viewer, are compared with the target sites. Percentage relationships between ideogram and actual target features are recorded. These results may be entered into a computer to produce probable conclusions of site features based on Doe's ideograms. Some of my information sources within the remote-viewing program, who requested anonymity, have confirmed that such computer analysis was actually performed.

With improvements, a rudimentary psychic perception conversion device might be constructed, able to more accurately interpret the psychic input from the viewer. With developments in measurement of brain electrical output and pattern analysis, coupled with electronic and neuroscientific progress, we might be able to turn a remote viewer into a rudimentary psychic television. This is a bit in the future, however. Right now, there is not a definite correlation between electrodermal readouts on an EEG machine and the presence of psychic functioning. Further, our ability to measure the electrical output of specific brain structures is presently limited.

Remote viewing itself is a process of perceptual evolution, becoming more specific in the later stages of a session. Dimensional orientation occurs in what is referred to as Stages II and III. "Generally received only in the latter portion of Stage II, dimensionals are usually very basic," the manual explains. "Tall, wide, long, big."

In Stage III remote viewing, emotional reactions to the target site are input and recorded in what the manual refers to as aesthetic impact. "It must still be borne in mind that an AI [aesthetic impact] response is keyed directly to the individual's own personality and emotional physical makeup, and therefore AI response can differ—sometimes dramatically so—from viewer to viewer." Here again, we have a clue to the creation of a possible accuracy-increasing device for remote perception. It is well known that emotional reactions are biochemical and therefore bioelectrical. As such, they are measurable. Over time, the biometric analysis of a viewer's Stage-III reactions during a session, correlated with actual site data and viewer psychometric (as in psychology, not psychic) performance, might serve to create a computer program that could translate emotions into site descriptions. Such a program would, of course, be viewer-specific, but inasmuch as very few individuals were regularly used in the remote-viewing program, the effort might well be worth the creation of such a program. What we are predicting is the next stage of remote-viewing operations: a man-machine linkup wherein perceptions and emotions may be turned into raw and, later, refined target-site data.

Another implication in aesthetic impact phenomena in remote viewing is the possible creation of an ideal psychological type for remote viewing. In the myriad of testing that has already been done, this has not been discovered. The only correlation found appears to be that those who are not opposed, but are open to the possibilities of the reality of psychic phenomena are more likely to be better at remote viewing. (Not very surprising.)

As remote-viewing continues in a session, another phenomenon, occurring in Stage III, is "mobility." Here, the viewer can "shift his viewpoint to some extent from point to point about the site, and from one perspective to another." We now have psychic perception with dimensional recognition under somewhat conscious control. The viewer has become a psychic camera of sorts, one with remote control. Psychic mobility can also allow a viewer to move from one target to another using what the training manual calls the polar coordinate concept. The monitor tells the viewer to prepare for movement, and new coordinates are given. A distance and direction are given. What is significant is that new targets may be acquired without the viewer having to revert to the initial stages of remote viewing. There does not appear to be a limit to the number of times site movement may occur in a session.

It is apprent that, whatever portion of the mind of man is engaging in psychic functioning during a remote-viewing session, it parallels the development of the brain in its perception. First, gross site descriptions are given via an ideogram, a very primitive perception. Then dimensionality is perceived, then emotions, eventually leading to specific site descriptions in successful operations. Coordinate remote viewing, as described in the DIA Manual, is a process of psychic perception in specific stages, designed to minimize noise factors. One may liken it to using a tuner to more clearly hear a radio station when there is static.

Retired major Paul H. Smith, a former government remote viewer, and the person credited with the actual production of the DIA Manual, says, "The finished version was printed at the DIA press in May 1986. It was a specialty run and never given an official DIA document number." The manual has been posted in its entirety on the Internet, making it now a public testament to the secret world of the military-occult complex. The existence of this manual, treating an intelligence collection method that for most of its existence has been denied and denigrated, is proof positive that remote viewing, while being a fragment of man's mind, is most certainly not a figment of his imagination.

Lest there be any mistake, remote viewing cannot be mastered by reading the manual. Much can be learned, but like any other skill, proper instruction and proper practice over a considerable amount of time is necessary to perfect this most unusual human talent. Further, the coordinate remote-viewing method of the DIA Manual is not the only means of obtaining psychic perception accurate enough for intelligence work. It is perhaps the most "establishment" method, but by no means universally accepted as the sole method.

In speaking with Joseph McMoneagle, I learned he did not often use the CRV method. In speaking with another top remote viewer, Mel Riley, I learned that there are many methods of psychic perception. Regardless of methods, protocols, and manuals, what has emerged from the government RV program is the de facto acknowledgment that psychic functioning is a reality. It is a reality of operational utility in the arena of intelligence collection. It is a demonstrated proof that man's mind can transcend its physical sensorial limits.

We have surveyed the persons and protocols of remote viewing, reviewing formerly classified documents that detailed the operational successes of remote viewing, and the instruction manual for using the phenomenon. Remote viewing is an inexpensive intelligence collection device, difficult or impossible to detect, difficult or impossible to countermand. Ergo, the government had no choice but to make a public pronouncement that remote viewing had no operational utility, and that psychic functioning might not even exist.

This monumental disinformation document will soon be discussed.

CHAPTER 24

WHITE HOUSE WEIRDNESS

The Star-Crossed Reagans

Given his political leanings, it was appropriate that future president Ronald Reagan and his wife, Nancy, had been close friends in the 1950s with an astrologer named Carrol Righter. Besides benefiting from his predictions, the Reagans attended his monthly zodiac parties. Jeanne Dixon, the late psychic-astrologer, was also a Reagan advisor until Nancy lost faith in her stargazing abilities.

When the rôles of president and first lady attracted the Hollywood couple's interest, Nancy Reagan found herself a new astrologer, Joan Quigley. The stars were not in favor of a 1976 presidential win for Reagan, and he lost the election. However, Quigley predicted that 1980 would be the year for a win for the Gipper. After several months in his new office, Reagan won a starring rôle for an assassin's bullet as John Hinckley, Jr., shot the president, but not, of course, fatally. Reagan would continue, after his close encounter of the ballistic kind, to grace America with his smiling ineptitude, a Great Communicator without a clue.

Quigley, ex post facto, confirmed that she had predicted the assassination attempt, giving a brilliant demonstration of the psychic power of retrocognition, the ability to accurately predict what has already occurred. Nancy Reagan, in response to criticism of her occult leanings, said "I have been criticized and ridiculed for turning to astrology, but after a while, I didn't care."[1] Nancy would consult with Quigley on a regular basis, selecting auspicious astrological times for Reagan's schedule, and doing so over specially-installed phone lines in the White House.

For his part, Ronald Reagan was at first unaware (his usual mental condition) concerning Nancy's stargazing, and supposedly he thought it rather silly. Nancy didn't. "While I was never certain that Joan's astrological advice was helping to protect Ronnie," she said, "the fact is that nothing like March 30 (the assassination attempt) ever happened again."[2] How many students of logic reading this are now mouthing the words, *Post hoc, ergo propter hoc*? This is a typical occult argument. Garlic keeps vampires away. I wear garlic, and there aren't any vampires here, are there? Therefore, garlic really does keep vampires away. (Actually, it doesn't work with Italian vampires, who are rather attracted to the stuff, but that is for another book.)

One political analyst in appraising the Reagan-Quigley connection stated, "It is perhaps the only instance of paranormal forces having an undeniably real impact on the course of U.S. history."[3] (Well, not really. There was Salem in 1692, for example.) The same analyst said, "What a sad and barbaric state of affairs to have our nation guided for the better part of a decade by the empty divinations of the zodiac."[4] Quigley was not only gazing at the heavens for the Reagans; she was looking at some heavenly fees for her astrological prognostications, reportedly about $3,000 a month. For this sum she literally created the President's schedule in accordance with planetary influences.[5] "I base my astrological analysis on the data provided to me by my astronomers and charts calculated by computers," claimed Quigley. This was true. Astronomers admitted there was a sun, a moon, and planets. And her computer program provided a quicker and easier method of calculations than the old ephemeris. But the predictions were not from astronomers, and not from computer scientists. They came from Quigley, who said, "My conclusions are based on accurate scientific material in the same way your doctor supports his diagnosis by the laboratory reports or an economist bases his predictions on statistics."[6] (It is hoped that she is wrong about the doctor part, but I fear that she is quite correct about the economist.)

According to Quigley, Nancy Reagan turned to astrological counseling to beef up her poor public image as First Lady. (Some found her stupid and shallow. Others worked for her spin campaign.) The star advice made Nancy publicly pursue charitable works, anti-drug campaigns, and other promotional vehicles which made her appear more First Lady–like. (The author always admired Nancy's stirring performance in the 1950s sci-fi movie *Donovan's Brain,* which was about a brain without a body—sort of a reverse image of Ronald Reagan.)

While the paranormal influence on a recent president is amusing reading, one must also realize that the same individual who had his schedule controlled by the influence of the stars, the same person whose wife installed special telephone lines to communicate with her astrologer, was the commander-in-chief of the greatest military force in the world. (Quigley and Reagan add new dimension to the Reagan-era term Star Wars.) On the other hand, the star-guided Reagan years were rather profitable for business, so who knows?

The paranormal and the office of the president were, in reality, old-time acquaintances. Lincoln was a believer in spiritualism, as was Grant. The Clinton White House also had some astrological influences on it. Primarily, that of Venus rising.

CHAPTER 25

CIA HOT AIR

ESP, Lies, and Red Tape

On November 28, 1995, the work had been completed, the report written, and "An Evaluation of the Remote-Viewing Program— Research and Operational Applications" was made public. This report, produced by a private think tank, the American Institutes for Research, was sponsored by the Central Intelligence Agency. In this chapter, we shall review and assess said report. In other words, we shall critically evaluate the evaluation.

It is interesting to note how easily obtained this report is, in summary form from the CIA's Public Information Officer and in its complete form via e-mail from AIR. Your author received a fax of the summary within five minutes of requesting it, and an e-mail copy in about the same amount of time. In two decades of dealing with government bureaucracies, it was the first time I saw such a demonstration of efficiency and public service. After reviewing the report for this history, I appreciated the reasons for such efficiency. The CIA was most anxious that any inquiring party would have the conclusions of the evaluation immediately upon request. These conclusions, as we shall see, were mandated prior to the evaluation having commenced.

In the opening paragraphs of the Executive Summary of the AIR report, we see remote viewing defined as "the ability to describe locations one has not visited."[1] Already, we have a diluted and only partially correct definition that betrays the bias inherent in the evaluation.

First, there are many phenomena that may fit the above definition. A good writer, for example, has—or should have—the ability to describe locations he has not visited. Does this make him a remote viewer? A good remote viewer can also describe mental and emotional qualities of a target site, which have nothing to do with location. Ergo, the definition is inadequate as we find it in the AIR evaluation. The definition presages the entire report in its inadequacy, as we shall see. The AIR panel supposedly was assigned the review of the research and operational applications of remote viewing. The foreign assessment of remote viewing was "not within the scope of the present effort."[2] With good reason. For the public to know the truth of foreign research and development in the field of the paranormal and its military and intelligence applications would be disadvantageous for the purposes of the CIA. It might make the American efforts pale by comparison—that is, with the data made available to the AIR reviewing panel.

The two primary evaluators of the remote-viewing program for the AIR report were Dr. Jessica Utts, a professor of statistics with a positive viewpoint on psi phenomena, and Dr. Raymond Hyman, a professor of psychology and decided skeptic. The AIR report noted that the two professors were "viewed as fair and open-minded scientists."[3] The reader must ask himself, How could the report say otherwise? Would they instead have said that the two reviewers are narrow-minded and biased? Or might they have commented that one scientist is fair, the other a narrow-minded pedant? Not likely. In law, this kind of statement given during testimony is referred to as bolstering—the conclusory building up of a witness's credibility. It is objectionable both procedurally and academically.

In reality, the two were chosen, at least in part, because their attitudes towards the paranormal were known, as will soon become clear. It was a good strategy to select evaluators from opposite camps; it gave an appearance of balance to the evaluation—an appearance that is deceiving. "In the course of this review," says the AIR report, "special attention was given to those studies that provided the strongest evidence for the remote-viewing phenomenon . . ."[4] This may be viewed as true when one realizes that the special attention given was to attend to especially avoiding the inclusion of those studies in the data evaluation. Dr. Edwin May, former director of remote-viewing research, commenting on the AIR report, said, "It is estimated that more than 80,000 pages of program documents remain highly classified,"[5] and the

AIR panel did not have access to those documents. "It is unclear whether the observed effects can unambiguously be attributed to the paranormal ability of the remote viewers as opposed to characteristics of the judges or the target or some other characteristic of the methods used," the AIR report concluded.[6] Perhaps the review of those estimated 80,000 documents the panel never saw might have helped to clarify the situation. Dr. May says the evaluators for AIR "failed to contact significant program participants," and "failed to apply consistent criteria for acceptance or rejection of anomalous cognition (another term for remote-viewing).[7] Thus, from its inception, the AIR report is misstating the facts. It claims to have examined the strongest evidence for remote viewing, yet in reality has not even come close to doing so. Why, why would an independent think tank hired to perform an impartial evaluation be so sloppy in its reporting of the facts, so misleading?

The answer does not require a panel of experts to determine. The CIA wanted a negative psi report, and controlled the data access so that such a result would be a foregone conclusion. The AIR report was U.S. intelligence purchased disinformation intentionally formulated to misrepresent the true state of remote-viewing research, and the true operational utility of the phenomenon.

In keeping with this intentional disinformation dissemination, the AIR report stated, "The remote-viewing reports failed to produce the concrete specific information valued in intelligence gathering."[8] The arrogance of the statement is equalled by the ignorance upon which it was based. First, the vast majority of the operational data was classified, and the AIR panel did not have access to it. That was their ignorance. To declare that concrete specific information was not produced is false, and flies in the face of the data that are unclassified. That is arrogance.

In the early days of the research, Pat Price correctly obtained code words from a target site, and accurately rendered structural features of numerous targets. That is concrete and specific. In 1981, Joseph McMoneagle accurately determined via remote viewing that General James Dozier was being held in Padua, and described the correct building. That is concrete and specific. In 1979 McMoneagle and Riley accurately described a Chinese nuclear device at Lop Nor, and a test of a bomb that exploded but failed to go nuclear. That is concrete and specific. The aforesaid AIR conclusion about the failure of operational remote viewing is a concrete and specific misstatement of fact. Put more simply, it is a lie.

The AIR report said "The information produced was inconsistent, inaccurate with regard to specifics, and required substantial subjective interpretation."[9] In some cases this is true, as it is when intelligence is collected by more mundane methods. The backbone of intelligence is cross-collateralization of data—the confirmation of intelligence information from multiple sources And remote viewing was never designed to be a stand-alone collection source upon which to base analysis and operations.

In some cases, the AIR pronouncement is false. Both McMoneagle and Riley were consistent in the Chinese nuclear test site RV operation. We have already detailed the types of specific information that had been obtained in RV operations. Once again, the AIR panel has misstated the facts. Dr. May, criticizing the AIR report, said, "As a way of officially ignoring anomalous cognition's positive contributions to intelligence, only a small fraction of the operational remote-viewing database was examined."[10] The AIR report failed to make that point crystal (ball) clear. May declares that the AIR reviewers "have come to the wrong conclusions with regard to the use of anomalous cognition in intelligence operations and greatly underestimated the robustness of the phenomenon."[11] Then again, that is exactly what the CIA wanted them to do.

If one reads between the lines of the AIR report, we can see why. "At the request of congress, the Central Intelligence Agency is considering assuming responsibility for this, the remote-viewing program. As part of its decision-making process, the CIA was asked to evaluate the research conducted since the NRC [National Research Council] report. To achieve these goals, the CIA contracted with the American Institutes for Research to supervise and conduct the evaluation."[12]

The CIA was the initial funding source for the research. The reader might remember in the chapter covering the SRI program, the "two East Coast scientists" who oversaw the original research. They were CIA. In 1977, Dr. Kress of the CIA wrote his evaluation of the research program in his article in *Studies in Intelligence,* which is found in the appendix of this history. Ergo, the CIA was being asked to take over and evaluate the remote-viewing program which, two decades before this mandate, had supervised and evaluated the extant research and

218 The Psychic Battlefield

 THE PSYCHIC BATTLEFIELD

operational data. Remember that there was a substantial giggle factor involved with RV, and the CIA would not likely be chomping at the bit to regain responsibility for the program. What better tactical move than to commission a blue ribbon panel to conclude that the program had no utility?

The fact that the CIA wanted a review of the research after the NRC negative evaluation of the mid-1980s is also evidence of the fact that the CIA wanted a foregone negative conclusion from the AIR panel, vis-à-vis operational remote viewing. Many of the operational successes preceded the NRC evaluation, yet they were intentionally ignored by the AIR panel. According to Dr. May, the NRC "investigators were not cleared for access to the vast majority of SRI's research."[13] Therefore an AIR informationally impotent evaluation commenced its data pool from the time of the last informationally impotent evaluation, the NRC report.

A CIA Fable

One of the more creative AIR fables about the remote-viewing program is, "In 1995 the CIA declassified its past parapsychology program efforts in order to facilitate a new external review." In addition, CIA worked with DIA to continue declassification of Stargate program documents, a process that had already begun at DIA. All relevant CIA and DIA documents were collected and inventoried.[14] Since the vast majority of the data was not given to the AIR panel, it is impossible for them to accurately conclude what was relevant and what was not. Dr. May confirmed, "Most of the operation remains classified."[15] Ergo, the AIR panel had no idea what was relevant to their investigations because they apparently had no idea of the quantum of data that was extant. May says, "There is compelling evidence that the CIA set the outcome with regard to intelligence usage before the evaluation had begun. This was accomplished by limiting the research and operations data sets to exclude positive findings."[16]

Even the AIR report admitted, ". . . it was neither possible nor intended that we review the entire field of parapsychological research and its applications."[17] Clearly the CIA wanted to cast remote viewing in a dim light, and from an operational security point of view, they were acting responsibly. It must be clear by now, after reading this history of the military-occult complex, that the paranormal had, and has, a place in military and intelligence operations. The real experience obtained from the remote-viewing program bears this out. Since RV is a low cost intelligence collection device, independent of high technology equipment, independent of supporting agents in place, it is a collection method open to any tenth-rate intelligence service, as well as any knowledgeable individual.

Second, as has been stated before, RV is difficult or impossible to detect, and therefore to counter. Given the above, it would be irresponsible for the CIA to promote the truth about the operational utility of remote viewing. The production of a respected piece of disinformation concerning the uselessness of RV in intelligence collection was the proper strategic action to take. Whether it was morally correct, I leave to the determination of other authorities.

In the coming millennium, intelligence services worldwide will not rely solely on the latest technological toy to collect information. More low technology sources will be employed. RV will certainly be one of them, despite government denials to the contrary. RV will be employed by terrorist organizations (at least those who can accommodate the concept within their religious dogma), criminal organizations of sufficient intelligence, and private organizations. There is no need to stimulate such exploitation of RV by issuing an accurate report concerning its operational use and history. Ergo, from an OPSEC point of view, the CIA disinformation contained in the AIR report was a necessity.

From the point of view of responsible reporting to the American public, however, the AIR report was a travesty of scientific evaluation. "The broad goal of the present effort," said the AIR panel in its report, "was to provide a thorough and objective evaluation of the remote viewing program."[18] One of the interesting phenomena about government legislation and government-sponsored evaluations is the tendency to accurately describe the exact opposite of the real intentions behind the creation of the legislation or the evaluation. The AIR report has already been shown to be neither thorough nor objective with respect to the remote-viewing program.

Dr. May comments, "Because of the complexity of the twenty-four-year program, it is impossible to conduct an in-depth and accurate evaluation without significant contact with the program's many major participants."[19] The AIR panel neglected to contact the proper parties—again, by design, not by accident. May says the panel conducted its evaluation "purposefully not interviewing historically significant participants."[20] Had they taken the time to talk to Mel Riley and Joseph McMoneagle, their conclusions about RV might have been entirely different. But they didn't. "Prior to convening the first meeting of the review panel," says the AIR report, "the CIA transferred to AIR all reports and documents relevant to the review."[21] Once again, the qualifier, "relevant," is present. Who determined relevancy to the review? The CIA. Who wanted a negative conclusion respecting operational RV? The CIA.

The AIR report argues, "No one piece of evidence provides unequivocal support for the usefulness of a program."[22] Really? There is an absence of logic in this position. If accurate useful information in an operation, is obtained by RV methods, then within that operation, it has proven unequivocally useful. When McMoneagle and Riley, via RV methods, confirmed a failed Chinese nuclear test at Lop Nor (as they did in 1979), within the context of this operation, this one piece of evidence does demonstrate the utility of RV. It worked, it was accurate, ergo, it was useful.

RV Successes

Successful examples of operational RV abound. They were just ignored by the AIR report writers who were granted permission to interview only those persons who were involved in the program at the time of its suspension in the spring of 1995."[23] Brilliant. When evaluating a program for remote viewing, or for television viewing, you need sufficient data included in your "set." Without it, the evaluation is not worth the paper it is printed on. In a program commenced in the early 1970s, and supposedly terminated in 1995, it would make sense to speak to as many participants as possible over the history of the program, not just those employed at its terminus. If one were to do an evaluative history of World War II, for example, would only the data from the summer of 1945 make for an accurate appraisal?

Yet, remote viewing was treated as the bastard child of the intelligence establishment. Input that could have been had from Riley, McMoneagle, and even Dames and Morehouse was not collected. The 1977 Kress evaluation of "Parapsychology in Intelligence" was not looked at because at the time it was still classified.

Why didn't the AIR panel interview the early participants of RV? "This decision," they said, "was based on the need for accurate current information that had not been distorted by time and could be corroborated by existing documentation and follow-up interviews."[24] Nonsense. Detailed records and documentation were kept as a part of each remote-viewing experiment and operation. Follow-up interviews would have been possible with any surviving member of the RV unit, which could have been contrasted and compared with existing records.

As an experienced litigator in one of the most court-congested states in the most litigious country in the world, I can attest that evidence is frequently presented and evaluated that is often years old. Memories of witnesses, corroborated or contradicted by contemporaneous documentation, are submitted for review by a trier of fact. The system of proof works. Therefore, there was no valid excuse why the AIR panel limited its own resources and quantum of proof with respect to evaluating RV. There was the excellent reason to do so, in that their sponsor mandated a negative finding, but that which is convenient is not always that which is true.

"Although it would have been desirable to interview people involved in earlier operations," admitted the AIR panel, "the problems associated with the passage of time, including forgetting, and the difficulties involved in verifying information, effectively precluded this approach."[25]

McMoneagle was associated with RV from 1978 until the end of Stargate in 1995. I was easily able to contact him and interview him regarding the declassified aspects of RV, and I am just a plain old country lawyer. One would think that the AIR panel, financed by the CIA, might have had an even easier time in obtaining his cooperation. Same with Mel Riley; he was readily available, and cooperative.

As far as difficulties in verifying information, this excuse, too, is tissue thin. Oral testimony is quite frequently examined in light of existing documentation. As RV research and operations were thoroughly documented, there would be no difficulty in verifying orally obtained information. The difficulty for the AIR panel would be in the presentation of the information, not its collection. It would be embarrassing to present the proper quantum of RV data and, at the same time come up with the made-to-order negative conclusion vis-à-vis remote-viewing.

In the interviews that were conducted in the AIR evaluation, "a representative of the CIA attended interviews as necessary to describe the reasons the interviews were being conducted and to address any security concerns."[26] Of course. The necessity of having a CIA man present at the interviews to explain the reason for the interview is clear. A subject is called in to speak to a panel reviewing the operational and research applications of remote viewing—a subject who participated in the program. Was it such a mystery regarding his requested presence before the panel, that it required a CIA man to explain? One of the benefits of having served in intelligence is that one gets to experience first-hand the art of disinformation. Your author sat on the border of a Warsaw Pact country reporting on communist military activity. This was referred to as communication research. A CIA man is present during an interview of an RV program participant to "explain the reasons for the interview." Right.

The second half of the raison d'être for the CIA man's presence during the interview process is the real one: security concerns. The Agency wanted to make sure that all of the beans spilled were U.S. Government–approved. It is real handy to be able to control data input when you want to control conclusory output. That is just what the Agency did with respect to the AIR evaluation.

Dr. Jessica Utts was the first reviewer presented in the AIR evaluation. She concluded, "Using the standards applied to any other area of science, it is concluded that psychic functioning has been well established."[27] This statement seems to be against CIA party line, but including Utts as a reviewer was a disinformation master stroke. The positive position is presented first, the negative last. Any speaker, any litigator desires to be last, as what is last in time is usually most clearly remembered. By including a pro psi evaluator, the CIA maintains its appearance of propriety. Utts admitted, "the evaluation of operational work remains difficult . . ."[28] Sure it is, when you are forbidden access to the vast majority of the data. Therefore, even the positive proponent of psychic functioning was downgrading the evidence for operational utility, and that, of course, is just what the CIA ordered. "Another problem with evaluating this operational work," said Utts, "is that there is no way to know with certainty that the subject did not speak with someone who had knowledge of the site, however unlikely that possibility may appear."[29] Of course, we could just as easily conclude that there is no way to know with certainty that Dr. Utts did not speak to someone who told her what to conclude in the report, "however unlikely that possibility may appear."

The above speculations are without value. It appears that even the pro psi evaluator is loath to "hit the nail on the paranormal head," and conclude that psychic functioning occurred operationally. The point is, it is often impossible to prove a negative, especially when dealing with a subject as slippery as remote viewing.

Dr. May concluded about the reviewers for AIR, "the investigators failed to apply consistent criteria for acceptance or rejection of anomalous cognition. The investigators were troubled by possible non AC alternative explanations for the statistically significant laboratory results, yet ignored similar alternatives for the failed operations."[30]

Utts, in her analysis of the SRI experiments, concluded, "Distance between the target and the subject does not seem to impact the quality of remote-viewing," and "electromagnetic shielding does not appear to inhibit performance."[31] Those two conclusions placed side by side are enough to give a counterintelligence professional a month full of sleepless nights. An agent you can't see, an agent you can't locate, can spy on a target regardless of distance—a target that might be impossible to protect from such a collection method as RV. Not exactly something a smart spy agency would want to shout to the world.

The CIA is not stupid (most of the time). They knew that there would be an outcry against the AIR report by those in the know, and by those who thought they were in the know. They knew that the foreign equivalents of the RV researchers would be chuckling over the erroneous conclusions of the AIR evaluation. But they also knew that John Q. Public is basically intellectually lazy, and likes to be spoon fed its information. Thus, the Agency's creation of a blue-ribbon panel to evaluate psychic spying (negatively) was the smartest political move it could make, concerning a program they did not want to touch with a ten-foot public pole. "How is it," asked former program director Dr. May, "that the CIA and AIR could not find compelling evidence for the operational utility of anomalous cognition? They clearly chose not to look."[32]

The second AIR reviewer was Dr. Raymond Hyman, a psychologist. Hyman denied not only the operational functioning of RV, but disagreed with the conclusions of Utts regarding the proof of its existence in the laboratory. "Although the research program that started in 1973 continued for over twenty years, the secrecy and other constraints have produced only ten adequate experiments for consideration."[33] How could Hyman conclude this when he did not have access to the vast majority of the data obtained over the twenty-some-odd years of the program? He could conclude it because I believe he was selected by the CIA to make this conclusion. "Both critics and parapsychologists have agreed that the lack of consistently replicable results has been a major reason for parapsychology's failure to achieve acceptance by the scientific establishment."[34] Whether true or not, it is irrelevant to the specific data and results of remote viewing. There was sufficient replicability of results for the program to continue in excess of twenty years, and it was the research side of the program that received most of the $20 million that the government admitted spending on RV research. Utts correctly observed, "Few human capabilities are perfectly replicable on demand." She recognized, "Even if there truly is an effect, it may never be replicable on demand in the short run if we understood how it works. However, over the long run in well-controlled laboratory experiments, we should see a consistent level of functioning above that expected by chance." Utts concluded, "replicability in that sense has been achieved."[35]

One says yes, one says no. What did the former director of the program say? Dr. May, every bit as much a scientist as Dr. Hyman, said the AIR panel "ignored the conclusions of one of their own investigators who showed that the government-sponsored research had already been conceptually regulated."[36] "I cannot provide suitable candidates for what flaws, if any, might be present," said Hyman. "Just the same, it is impossible in principle to say that any particular experiment or experimental series is completely free from possible flaws."[37] It was impossible to say that because Hyman knew there were no flaws in much of the research. He couldn't find any flaws, and couldn't admit that fact without a qualification that in itself was flawed. "Despite the claims Ray Hyman is making in the media," says Dr. Utts, "we were shown very little of the operational remote-viewing work."[38] "I don't know how he can substantiate the claims he's making about remote viewing being useless for intelligence . . . he has very little data on which to base that conclusion."[39] As a concession of sorts, Hyman admits, "The case for psychic functioning seems better than it ever has been. Further, I do not have a ready explanation for these observed effects. Inexplicable statistical departures from chance, however, are a far cry from compelling evidence for anomalous cognition."[39]

Perhaps a ready explanation for the operational successes of remote viewing, of which Hyman and his colleagues had little information might be that RV works. Perhaps Dr. Hyman does not have a ready explanation for RV because the real explanation—its existence and utility—is one that the government cannot afford to offer. Dr. May scores a direct hit on the AIR evaluation when he says, "As a result of AIR negligence, their report contains numerous errors of fact and errors of assumption."[40] Hyman defends. "It seems obvious that the utility of remote viewing for intelligence gathering should depend on its scientific validity."[41] Why? The utility of HUMINT collection methods are not scientifically replicable, yet they produce some of the most useful and hard-to-obtain data. The bribing, seduction or intimidation of a potential intelligence asset is not the type of phenomenon that can be replicated in a laboratory, but historically these methods have clearly demonstrated their effectiveness.

"If the scientific research cannot confirm the existence of remote-viewing ability, then it would seem pointless to try to use this non-existent ability for any practical application."[42] Put in this way, his point is unassailable. Unfortunately, RV, according to Utts, has been confirmed in the laboratory, RV was used as an intelligence-collection method for at least twenty years, and there is sufficient declassified proof of the successes of operational RV to allow us to toss Hyman's objections in the round file without filling out any forms in triplicate. "From both a scientific and operational viewpoint," said Hyman, "the claim that anomalous cognition exists is not very credible until we have ways to specify when it is and when it is not present."[43] Had Hyman reviewed the existing data and documentation from the twenty-plus-year history of the program instead of the crumbs provided by CIA, even he might not have reached such a conclusion. Protocols and methods were in place to assure that RV was the functioning agent during the operations. Extensive written and recorded documentation was collected during the RV sessions, which would enable any competent researcher with full access to the data to determine when RV was operating.

Hyman states, "Whatever information we get from this survey is extremely limited for the purposes of judging the utility of remote viewing in the operational domain."[44] Funny, but this quote wasn't included in the executive summary faxed out by the CIA's public information office. The AIR panel concluded, "Direct evidence has not been provided indicating that this paranormal ability of the remote viewers is the source of these effects." They then say, "There is no evidence that the phenomenon would prove useful in intelligence gathering."[45] Classic examples of disinformation. The successes of Price, Riley, and McMoneagle, and the unsung others of remote viewing, are belied and betrayed by these CIA-sponsored conclusions. If the techniques were useless, why were they funded and continued in excess of twenty years?

"The evidence accrued from research, interviews and user assessments all indicate that the remote-viewing phenomenon has no real value for intelligence operations at present."[46] Unfortunately those who proffered this conclusion had little access to the research, declined to interview the most likely participants, and were not party to classified user assessments of RV. This would tend to erode any confidence one might wish to mistakenly place in the AIR panel, even in the presence of their mythical blue ribbon.

Dr. May observes, "CIA had strong and valid reasons not to want the program. The Agency was soundly criticized in the press for mishandling the Ames case and other excesses, so they did not need another controversy."[47] The Company operates often in the shadows, where the public eye does not see, but first and foremost it is a political tool, a political weapon controlled by politicians and the political process. Therefore, it must always appear rational, proper, defensible, right. Remote viewing is a political time-bomb that the CIA did not wish to handle anymore, and ergo, as May correctly stated, "What is obvious is that the evaluation domain of the research and particularly the operations were restricted to preclude positive findings. The CIA did not contact or ignored people who possessed critical knowledge of the program, including some end users of the intelligence data."[48] The AIR report, said May, "knew exactly what they were doing, they wanted to demonstrate a lack of intelligence utility for anomalous cognition."[49]

There is a time for secrecy and a time for revelation, a time for disinformation and for the exposition of truth—even in the world of intelligence. It has been the purpose of this history of the military-occult complex to reveal (as much as possible) what has been concealed concerning the five-millennia-old relationship between the weapon bearers and the wand wavers of the world. The cooperative efforts of our soldiers, our spies and our psychics did, over time, develop a method to the madness, which helped to enhance the accuracy of paranormal perception and created an operational psi collection tool for our intelligence services.

It is hoped that in the century to come, which inaugurates a new millennium, the minds and eyes of our public and our politicians will be sufficiently opened to acknowledge the reality of remote viewing, and the reality that man is much more than we have previously thought.

The AIR report is an important document in military-occult history, not for its veracity, but for its existence as a government sponsored piece of disinformation concerning the reality of psychic functioning in the arena of intelligence work. In having dissected its faults, it is hoped that some light has been spread in the shadow world of psychic spies. Our history ends herewith, and what follows is a promised prognostication of things to come in the future of the military-occult complex.

CHAPTER 26

THINGS TO COME

The Future of the Far Out

We have journeyed far together in the dark and narrow world of the military-occult complex.

From the martial magic of Yahweh's followers in Bible times to the techno-shamanic methodologies of the Stargate program, we have surveyed the mystical tripartite marriage of psychics, soldiers, and spies. While the official government statement on psychic spying was, "it ended in 1995," we must view that proclamation with a skeptical eye. At times, the techniques of remote viewing worked operationally and amazingly well. While the Pentagon and the "Company" might fund dozens of total failures, they don't toss out that which works—even if it is only sometimes.

As controversial as the following opinion might be, as much as it will be denied and derided by official government spokesmen, it is the contention of your author that psychic spying still continues, covertly, of course, but constantly. There is a future to government and private psychic spying, and even though this book is referred to as a history, it is a history of the paranormal realm, a place where time and space concepts do not apply. Therefore, in good psychic-soldier tradition, we shall consider the things to come in the world of remote viewing and beyond. We shall attempt to draw the possible pictures one might find in the military-occult complex of the twenty-first century.

In our precognitive attempts, we shall blend logic and intuition, proceeding from the known and normal to the unknown and paranormal. It will be the passage of linear time that will render a verdict as to the accuracy of our predictions, which are herein respectfully submitted.

Future Funding

First of all, there is a future to psychic spying, and where there is a future, there will be funding. The vast majority of funding for remote viewing and other paranormal talents of intelligence value will come from the private sector—corporations, foundations, and individuals. Already, those who served in the government remote-viewing program have started and are operating private remote-viewing enterprises, which are being utilized by private industry—especially the natural resource industry. Like the dowsers of old, the remote viewers are finding oil, gas, and other strategic resources for those in corporate America sufficiently enlightened to appreciate the possibilities and profits from paranormal research and development. The successes that are experienced in this area will draw additional R&D funding. As it is not a coincidence that those who grow fat on oil and gas profits often establish private philanthropic (and tax-advantaged) foundations, we should also see funds coming from these organizations.

People talk, and people will talk about the paranormal. With greater, and more open, industrial and foundation funding and interest in remote viewing and its potential, we should see certain wealthy individuals getting on the bandwagon. (Call for you, Ms. MacLaine.) The funds necessary are a pittance compared to normal R&D expenses a corporation might spend to bring out a new product. The major inhibiting factor in private funding, at least overt funding, of course will be the giggle factor. However, those corporations that have paid exorbitant sums to have some motivational guru lecture their people and fire them up (at least until the seminar is over for five minutes), may be willing to invest in a cutting edge technology like remote viewing.

With private funding and private management, remote-viewing techniques should develop more quickly than when under the ten thumbs of government control. As the techniques and accuracy improve, we will probably see some covert funding from the government again. Remember, most of the money went to the research side of remote-viewing when the government purse strings were opened. The operational side of things at Fort Meade was cheaper than dirt. Even the furniture was throw-away. This is another reason your author believes the operational program still continues, somewhere. It is just too inexpensive, and occasionally useful, to kill it. When the private sector improves its results, remote viewing will once again see Uncle Sam's dollars.

RV for Commercial Spying

A second prediction is that, both privately and governmentally, the next great target for remote-viewing efforts will be in the arena of industrial espionage. New federal laws abound, new intelligence initiatives are aimed at the prevention and discouragement of industrial espionage. It is a growing threat, as well as a present danger. Remote viewing is a supernatural intelligence-collection tool, which would naturally be used in commercial/industrial spying. It is extremely inexpensive, and probably undetectable, and most likely immune to interference—at least from the overt information available at the time of this writing. (However, certain remote influence experiments, mentioned in the AIR report, give rise to the possibility that biological monitoring may in some way serve as an RV detector.)

No contract security guard, no high-technology intrusion detection system, no barking dog, and no locked filing cabinet can thwart a remote-viewing probe. With an increase in the accuracy of processing psychically obtained intelligence information, it is predicted that remote-viewing may become the industrial spying method of choice. From what we know of the dynamics of remote viewing, we have learned that visual images are more easily acquired than the abstract data of words and numbers. (Although these too have been obtained operationally.) Therefore, we may expect the initial targets of remote viewing for commercial spying purposes to be those industries dealing in design developments: fashion, the automobile industries, architecture, etc. As the techniques improve, and numbers and words are more easily accessed by remote viewing, the industrial espionage targets of psychic spying will increase exponentially. (That is somewhat further into the future.)

From the research, one of the phenomena that often (although not always) occurs in a remote-viewing session is what I label image predominance. In other words, the dominant visual of a scene may be most readily perceived, and have a bias, an analytic overlay effect on what the rest of the viewing session obtains. For example, let's say the target is a picture of the Egyptian pyramids, and a small rubber duck is placed near one of these structures. It is most likely that the buildings will be perceived, and less likely that the bogus bird will come into view. The predominant structure of the target should be the most easily viewed by a remote viewer.

How may this be useful in determining a countermeasure for remote viewing? With a little malice aforethought, one might place large and ludicrous images near a suspected remote-viewing target. Again, by way of example, let us presume we have a poster-sized drawing of the next year's Cadillac model perched on an easel. Our competitors might want to obtain this design by remote viewing. We place a pile of stuffed pink elephants in the immediate vicinity of our drawing, and maybe, just maybe, the remote viewer obtains an astral version of the DTs.

The placement of irrelevant yet attractive symbols and images within the surroundings of a possible RV target needs to be further explored. It might just be a very low-tech, yet highly effective countermeasure. (The government boys in RV have said it wouldn't work against a trained remote viewer, however.)

Thus in our paranormal future, expect to see R&D funding directed to RV countermeasures and detection. Our Soviet friends, back in the 1920s claimed the ability to achieve telepathic intercept, but considering the source, who knows? We haven't been able to specifically chart a remote-viewing attempt via an electroencephalograph, which has direct contact with the viewer's head, so how would we be able to intercept any waves, particles, or whatever might be generated by a remote-viewing attempt at a distance? (Possibly by monitoring the biometric readouts, especially galvanic skin response, of a security guard at a likely target site?)

These suppositions, these suggestions are offered in the partial vacuum created by the present classification of the vast majority of remote-viewing data. Perhaps, locked in some government vault, are the answers to RV countermeasures and detection. If so, they certainly aren't going to publish the results in the Congressional Record.

Psychic spying, countermeasures, telepathic interception—by now, some of the readers must feel they picked up a science fiction novel by mistake. Yet, if the nineteenth-century rational mind read about something like genetic mapping, cloning, and the World Wide Web, would not the owner of that rational mind be guffawing in his gruel? You who read this are probably less than one year away from the third millennium, or are already in it. In this next century you will learn of new developments in nonlethal weaponry, new cures for incurable diseases, anti-aging therapies that make present efforts seem on the Cro-Magnon level, and you also are going to see a different, and more respectful image of paranormal research. (You read it here first.)

The public has a comfortable acceptance of those evolutionary changes that extend the centuries-old Newtonian world view. Merely the making of a more efficient lever, fulcrum, wedge, pulley, etc—science concepts readily replicable and analyzable. But in the field of human performance enhancement, especially in the realms of perception and cognition, many are extremely uncomfortable when the borders of this realm expand. Many are downright hostile. This will end, however. Of necessity, it must.

As the quantum and rate of information transfer increases, so must the cognitive and perceptual abilities of man's mind evolve. Imagine one of our geniuses from ancient Greece faced with fax machines, the Internet, and cellular phones. His sanity would soon melt like goat cheese on a hot Aegean day. Yet we, in the late twentieth century, take it all in stride—although it is a stride with a faster and longer step. Our technologies are not in evolution, but revolution, and last year's hot new development is now floating in the tar pits with the rest of the dinosaurs. Our mental development must parallel this revolution; serious study and significant funding of paranormal research will be keys to this development.

In our next century, what is now paranormal will be normal. Every possible technique promising enhanced human mental and physical performance and perception must be openly explored, for our survival as a race depends on it in the next millennium.

Remote Influence

Stepping down from this spiritual soapbox, we return to predictions about the future military-occult complex. The next area for research and development is also the most frightening. Remote influence, or telepathic projection. We have already learned of experiments in the AIR review which dealt with physiological changes in a visually monitored person. If remote influence can effect the galvanic skin response in a subject, which it seems to be able to do, what else, with further research, might it be able to effect physiologically? Blood pressure, heart beat, respiration? Will we eventually be able to heal or kill via remote influence? The reader will remember the tale in a past chapter about how Heinrich Himmler tried to mentally influence a German general to tell the truth at his trial. Obviously the Nazis weren't all that successful in the field of remote influence, as many of their leaders became disenchanted with the party and its Führer. Nevertheless, the field of remote influence must be explored, because it might become a reality in the twenty-first century. After all, remote influence via mechanical means has existed along with newspapers, radio, and television. Of course, what we will be talking about in the next millennium is remote influence that is covert, and not directly perceived by those being influenced.

We have already read about supposed developments in pulsed microwave audiograms; using microwave technology as a carrier to directly implant into the mind words that will seem to originate from the thoughts of the target. If these tales are true, we may expect to see further research in this area, along with methods of detection and countermeasures—perhaps some stylish Faraday Cage we can wear on our heads?

We know for sure, and have known for some forty years, that sound waves can affect the body and the mind. Those parts of the spectrum known as infrasound and ultrasound can heal or kill when properly targeted. As we learn more about neuroscience, as our brain wave measurement devices improve, as our electromagnetic research continues, we may find ourselves in the twenty-first century with the ability to literally remotely control the mind of another.

What really gets interesting in this paranormal tributary is research to try remote influence without any mechanical means. In other words, pure, unadulterated telepathic projection. This may not seem so ridiculous as it first appears, when we consider studies in telepathic reception have been going on for most of the twentieth century. If reception is possible, and the research seems to indicate that it is, then logically, projection must also be possible. The sexy part comes when we try it with an unknowing or unwilling subject. That will be really interesting.

If remote influence can be achieved and perfected we can throw out most of our war toys. Why bother with tanks and stealth bombers when you can think an enemy into submission? As war policy and planning is a job for very few individuals, these would be the likely targets of remote influence. Ergo, the manpower and materials that would be dedicated to remote influence would be minuscule, and therefore, inexpensive. The only thing we have left to do is get it to work. (Perhaps in some super-secret underground government facility, that is exactly what is going on.)

Social Stratification

The social implications of remote viewing and remote influence are staggering. Individual privacy, already moribund in this age of instant electronic information, will be a fond memory in an age where remote viewing and influence have been practically developed. George Orwell's *1984* will read more like Thomas More's *Utopia* when Big Brother has become Mr. Wizard. One might envision the traditional den in the home being replaced by an electromagnetically shielded "thinking" room, where one might keep the contents of his mind from interception by others. (Unfortunately, from the available information, even such a room probably wouldn't be an effective countermeasure, for there are many instances of ESP functioning despite such electromagnetic shielding.)

It gets scarier. While the research shows most or all people have some degree of psychic functioning, and my interviews with Joseph McMoneagle, our top psychic spy, confirm this, there is a wide difference in human paranormal ability. Ergo, those individuals who can more successfully remote view, and remotely influence others, have the potential to become a psychic Mafia that would make the more worldly version look like a bunch of pikers. Imagine the effect of remote viewing and remote influence on the financial markets. (Several of the remote viewers from the SRI days performed quite admirably in the silver futures market when Delphi Associates used the paranormal to gather profits.)

At this early stage, the above predictions may seem amusing. However, we are still less than thirty years into the scientific research initiated by psychic spying. Besides an end to privacy and manipulation of financial markets, a cadre of highly developed psychic warriors might start to think of themselves as a new Master Race. We have seen, in Eastern Bloc Olympic training, the widespread use of suggestion, imagery, and mental rehearsal to enhance sports performance. We will probably see this trend continue in the military of the third millennium to create Super Soldiers. (Remember Project Jedi of the 1980s, under the auspices of General Albert Stubblebine?) The conscious creation of a superior military force will result in those participants becoming consciously aware of their superiority. Add ego to weapons access, mix with superior psychic spying skills, and *Voila!* we have a new SS that makes Himmler's boys look like the Cub Scouts. A corps of psychics could turn the traditional military hierarchy upside down. Instead of fragging an unpopular lieutenant, he could be remotely influenced to blow himself up. The implications are significant, the possibility of it all becoming true is real.

Perhaps a happy prognostication of a psychic-soldier future will be the lowering of military expenditures and the ability to divert these monies into more socially useful channels. When military men can accurately remotely spy, and have significant remote influence on enemy strategists, we won't need to manufacture so many stealth bombers and submarines. Control the mind that controls the finger that pushes the button or pulls the trigger, and you don't have to make more missiles and rifles than the other guy.

Will the future see the same kind of political and social resistance to the paranormal as it now exists? We predict a negative answer. The generation who fought World War II is close to extinction. The Korean War types are well into senior citizenship. Coming more into power is the generation that grew up in the 1960s and 1970s, exposed to alternative lifestyles, mysticism, and the paranormal. They will be less resistant to research on the frontiers of man's self concept. They will be mindful of a president whose schedule was dominated by an astrologer's advice. They will be mindful of a later presidency that was dominated by financial and sexual scandals, and yet survived as long as it did. The giggle factor in all areas will be greatly reduced, as our country will have seen it all, heard it all, done it all.

Thus we have a future milieu of technological revolution, a sophisticated neuroscience, and a more tolerant attitude towards the unusual, including the paranormal. In this particular melting pot, we will see remote viewing (and perhaps remote influence) developing in ways that will directly challenge man's self image, just as his science has diminished the stature of his God. Until this shadowy concept has become largely irrelevant, man's journey into paranormal research will expand his self-image and his concept of what he is and what he might become.

The SRI research and the operational activities of the Fort Meade remote-viewing unit have demonstrated that extrasensory perception is not only real, but it can be useful. (Read the Kress report on Psychic Spying in the appendix.) As the knowledge of the research becomes more widespread (via books such as the one you now hold in your hands), as the research leads to new discoveries about the perceptual potentials of man, perhaps the ultimate benefit of the psychic spying program will be the elimination of the military and the termination of the intelligence establishment as man's self-respect grows. Perhaps the seed money granted to our spies and soldiers, which grew the remote-viewing unit, will sprout into a wonder weed that will choke the life out of the Pentagon, and the Company. Perhaps the paranormal is our springboard from which we will eventually jump from war into an everlasting peace. We may become too precious to kill. Perhaps not. There is always the possiblity of development of anomalous perturbation, psychokinesis, or more plainly put, mind over matter. There have been experiments conducted to test the ability of a human mind to affect a computer's operation. The results are not too dramatic, but there is an indication that such ability might be extant.

If there are significant developments in the field of anomalous perturbation, the world will be chock full of new destructive potential—and cheap too. The world is run by computers. Cars, planes, businesses, armies. The ability to mess with those busy little electrons in those busy computers could make all current military weapons (at least the ones we know about), obsolete. Why destroy the tank or shoot down the plane or missile? Use the mind to cause the computer to malfunction, and victory is yours. So as not to unduly scare the credulous reader, or allow the skeptical one to die laughing, anomalous perturbation seems to be the weakest paranormal power tested—if it even really exists.

The history of the military-occult complex has come full circle. What started out as magic has again ended up as magic. The names have been changed to protect the professors, politicians, and parapsychologists. Today's magic wand might control microwave radiation instead of demonic hordes, but the goal is still the same. Control, command, conquest.

We are a bloodthirsty animal, a territorial animal with the most dangerous weapon on the planet, a highly developed cerebral cortex. From this has sprung both our creation of medicines and massacres. The paranormal realm is the next step in the mental development of man, and with it will come new benefits, new wonders, new dangers, and new disasters.

In the 1951 science fiction classic *The Thing,* the movie ends (after the monster is destroyed) with a journalist, warning his companions, warning the world, to "keep watching the skies." This writer, this journalist of the paranormal history of the military-occult complex offers a similar warning. Keep watching the mind. Keep watching.

A CHRISTMAS WITH
JOSEPH MCMONEAGLE

I found myself in that Hades of interstate ground transport, the Amtrak waiting room at New York's Pennsylvania Station. It was the week before Christmas 1998, and the huddled masses of students, grand-mothers, thugs, and the occasional theologian waited to board the rail-road cars that would take them to points south.

The young faces radiated enthusiasm and excitement for their trip to hearth and home. They were not yet immune to the mystical mis-direction of retailers known as Christ's Birthday. The old faces mostly sagged in the expression of some dimmer feelings—perhaps in contem-plation of the remnants of joy and pain that were left to them before check-out time.

Me? I was middle-aged, middle class, and a middleman between the worlds of rationality and the supernatural. I was the litigation attorney who was also the tarot reader, a writer who had just completed the first history of Man's use of psychics for military and intelligence pur-poses.

I stood next to my 1950s-vintage Samsonite suitcase and thought of the purpose of my trip.

I am no fan of the Romanized festival of the Persian sun god, Mith-ras. Nor were there any loved ones to visit; those who might be referred to as such had long been dust or ashes. I was going to pay a flying visit to the most competent psychic spy ever fielded by United States Intelligence—U.S. Army (Ret.) Warrant Officer Joseph McMoneagle. He had been of great assistance to me in writing what was to be my first published book, and the first history of its kind.

I stood on the platform, waiting for The Crescent, the train that, on its rumbling way to New Orleans, would deposit me at Charlottesville, Virginia, at the foothills of the Blue Ridge Mountains. The train arrived fifteen minutes late, which by Amtrak standards was almost on time. Traveling first class, I was ushered into my private compartment by a smiling attendant. I immediately closed myself in, and the rest of my fellow passengers out, to inspect my quarters. There was a fold-down sink and toilet, a pull-down bed, an LCD television screen, and a panel of lights that could be dimmed from a convenient switch panel.

This sleeper reminded me of the CHEC facilities I had written about in my book. These were Controlled Holistic Environment Chambers located at the Monroe Institute, which was a stone's throw from where I was headed. It was at Monroe in the early 1980s that America's psychic spies learned to investigate and exploit altered states of consciousness, prior to assuming their duties at Fort Meade as practitioners of ESPionage. Some of the men achieved out-of-body experiences. Some had mystical insights. One went stark, raving mad. It was McMoneagle's wife Nancy who had trained them.

As the train bumped and bounced its way southward, I thought of the other expedition I had just completed, the writing of what is perhaps the most unusual history book ever penned. I had started out on this journey of a thousand miles with the first step of a rational skeptic. I finished wearing the worn shoes of a true believer. Psychic spying was real, did take place, and when it worked, it worked amazingly well.

As I looked out at the passing panorama of rust, debris, and dead vegetation that makes southeastern rail travel such a scenic inspiration, I realized that I had, in part, written a history that dealt more with the future than the past. Man's abilities were far beyond what he had been taught, what he had been told. This was not a revelation that our government was anxious to have shouted from the rooftops. The CIA, three years before, had sponsored a monumental document of disinformation produced by the American Institute of Research, which declared that while there was some evidence of psychic functioning, it was operationally useless. It was a lie.

A touch of paranoia invaded my mind in that sleeper compartment. Little old lawyer and writer me was letting the world in on the real story of psychic spying. Perhaps the CIA would not approve. Perhaps they might express their disapproval in ways not consistent with my continued good health. Of course, I dismissed this as melodrama and fantasy . . . until dinner time.

As I was paying an outrageously expensive fee for my first class travel, I wanted to take advantage of all the perks. Meals were included when you traveled in a sleeper car; when they announced the start of dinner service, I quickly walked to the half-empty dining car. Although there were plenty of empty tables, a well-dressed man in late middle age sat down next to me. He noticed my Masonic ring, and related to me that he too, was a traveling man.

After exchanging pleasantries about our respective pedigrees, this man on his own initiative turned the topic of conversation to matters of intelligence. He waxed eloquent about his involvement with cold war spying, and opined that Gary Powers, the unfortunate U-2 pilot who had provided target practice for the Soviet Union, should have swallowed his cyanide capsule, thereby permanently keeping his mouth shut. He cast doubts about Powers's patriotism, and broadly hinted that the pilot's later demise was not accidental.

I smiled, nodded, and otherwise showed my agreement, meanwhile wondering why the hell this guy was telling me this. Was this meeting more than serendipitous? Was this dinner diversion a message delivered? Did somebody in the government actually give a damn about what I was writing? The possibility was intriguing, and a little bit unnerving.

I exchanged goodbyes with my dinner companion and went back to my compartment with little inclination for a post-prandial nap. Mel Riley, former psychic spy, had told me he believed the government monitored those who showed undue interest in the government remote-viewing unit (what psychic spies were called). Was it possible that the CIA had monitored my Internet research, my phone calls, my e-mail? After all, those who log on to CIA's home page are basically told that they're being monitored while on the site, although not quite in those words. These thoughts occupied me for the rest of the train trip. Eventually, and late, of course, I arrived in Charlottesville. I took a taxi to the inexpensive and musty-smelling hotel room I had booked. Little was happening at the hotel that Friday night; there was no bar, no restaurant, and only the cockroaches were stirring. I slept well.

On Saturday morning, I met with McMoneagle. The man who could accurately and psychically describe nuclear submarine construction, Chinese nuclear devices, and hostage locations, did not look like James Bond, James Randi, Svengali, or Superman. He looked perfectly normal, physically unremarkable. In short, he was the perfect real spy. The only thing out of the ordinary that could be perceived about McMoneagle (by someone with the proper background) was the quiet and frozen calm of a man who had seen—and perhaps caused—violent death. Picture your mailman as a Zen swordmaster, and you'll get the idea.

We exchanged greetings and ventured out—not into the supernatural, but to the supermarket. McMoneagle was in search of enlightenment, not by meditation or magic, but by the purchase of a forty-watt bulb. This genius of extrasensory espionage had difficulty finding the right aisle in the supermarket where the bulbs were sold, proving that even a psychic spy is no match for the wily ways of a supermarket stockboy. Eventually we located said bulb, and McMoneagle, myself, and the light bulb drove over the winding rural roads to his home in Nellysford.

We were greeted by Christmas cooking smells, his charming astrologer wife, Nancy, and a handful of quadrupeds of dubious pedigree. During that weekend visit, we ate, drank, and had traditional holiday discussions about whether or not magical murder was caused by micro-psychokinesis or telepathic projection. Like people at Christmastime everywhere, we pondered the use of bio-sensors as a remote-viewing detection device, and what countermeasures to psychic spying might exist. There was also some talk about the research efforts that we would undertake. Yes, my humble efforts would join with McMoneagle's mastery in a new research organization to be formed. I had started my journey into psychic espionage as a mere scribbling observer, and finished as a possible participant in what will come to be the Intuitive Studies Institute.

The trip was emotionally and intellectually enjoyable. While waiting for the train back to New York, I wondered if perhaps, in some small way, I might bring some future light to the potential that dwells in the darker corners of man's mind. Possibly, I was meant to make both the literary and literal journey I had undertaken, to be a fellow-explorer beyond the borders of dimensionality, penetrating into the final frontier of mind.

May this be both a prayer and a prognostication: *Man, in his greeting the dawn of the third millennium, will experience a cosmic expansion of his concept of self, and his sentience. Stay tuned.*

An Interview with Joseph McMoneagle
Summer 1998

Several authors on remote viewing claim to have interviewed the acknowledged expert on remote viewing, Joseph McMoneagle. They did not. I set out to interview the man and to ask the questions that needed to be asked, and get the answers straight from the source's mouth.

During the summer of 1998, McMoneagle, his wife Nancy, and I developed a cordial working relationship, first by telephone, then in person. (Nancy was to construct and analyze my horoscope.) Joe McMoneagle was kind enough to take the time to answer the following questions about remote viewing, and the reader is reminded that nobody knows more about remote viewing than Joseph McMoneagle.

The following interview took place in late August, 1998.

WAM: Joe, you had various designations while working in remote-viewing. You were number 518, you were number 001, 372, etc. Did these designations have any specific meanings?

JWM: Actually, none. The number 001 was assigned to me by the special project at Fort Meade and the number 372 was assigned by the research facility, Cognitive Sciences Laboratory at SRI-International. They were primarily to protect us viewers as sources from those outside the project. Towards the later part of my time at Meade, end of 1982 through mid-1984, as many as five sets of numbers were used to identify my work. Some of them were numbers that had been used to identify other viewers who had subsequently retired or had left the project. The reasons for this are not material.

WAM: You have spent twenty-one years on the cutting edge of paranormal research. This book is about the entire history of the use of the paranormal as a military and intelligence tool. The Romans, the Egyptians, the Bible tribes all appear to have used extrasensory perception in their armed conflicts. Are we any better at it now than they were?

JWM: Yes and no. If you are asking specifically about remote viewing as originally applied by the Cognitive Sciences Laboratory and the U.S. Army, yes. If you are asking about paranormal methodologies applied in any other context, no. To date, nearly all of the commentaries that have appeared in interviews, magazine articles, newspaper clippings or television presentations, domestic or foreign, which have ever been about remote viewing, I can't think of many which have differentiated between that which is scientifically validated and that which isn't.

In other words, no one seems to care about the differences between remote viewing as applied under strict double blind conditions, and a one-on-one cold reading. There may be some historical merit to a soothsayer giving a cold reading to King Alexander before a battle, but what is actually happening probably isn't paranormal. I live for the day when a clear distinction is maintained between what has been proven by science, and that which seems to raise everyone's giggle factor.

WAM: You are of the opinion that natural talent, not training, is the key requisite in a remote viewer. Are there specific areas of training—artistic, psychological, verbal—that might be incorporated in the methodology that would enhance psychic functioning?

JWM: In my observation, every human being who ever walked into a lab and was subjected to a properly orchestrated remote viewing experience under the appropriate controls, demonstrated some degree of psychic or remote-viewing ability. I believe the reason why is that, under a controlled circumstance, we are seeing another sense being demonstrated, much like sight or hearing. Which means that every human possesses some degree of talent.

Training of any sort implies that someone does something that helps to develop and display a measurable improvement in any kind of skill. Applying the appropriate methodology, learning the rules of the road, developing a creative or specific style in anything will show what appears to be improvement. In the case of remote viewing, it is no different.

Having said this, I must also say that in my twenty-one years of experience, only in the rarest of occasions have I seen someone display a significant improvement in remote viewing following any kind of training. In the cases where this occurred, the individual already seemed to possess a significant talent for it from the outset, which was the very reason they were encouraged to pursue it. Very much like professional athletes or musicians, they had the talent to begin with and what the training did was polish it. There are numerous other reasons dealing with such issues as self-selection, lack of statistics, nor formal studies, etc. Which I won't bother to go into.

WAM: During the remote-viewing years, was there any contact, either in the real world or the "ether" with your Eastern Bloc counterparts?

JWM: In reviewing transcripts, one could say there probably was. However, such contacts, if they were real, were reported as a purely subjective experience. So it is one of those experiences that is impossible to verify one way or another. Since they can't be verified, most observers would put them into the category of viewer imagination, creativity, or science fiction. The only proper way to ask this question really, would be to ask how real the experiences seemed to the viewer who might have had such an experience. Speaking only for myself, I had them, and they seemed very real at the time. But since they were never verified, they could have been flights of fancy.

WAM: Did our Russian or Chinese friends have a different methodology and protocol than the U.S. remote viewers?

JWM: To my knowledge, yes and no. In my talks with both Russian and Chinese experimenters who were and still are pursuing investigations into remote viewing, many of their methods are different. Some of them are clearly operating within the boundaries of good science and some of them are not. I would have to assume that since their interest in my methods is as strong as my interest is in theirs, they at least know about and have replicated the methods which I am familiar with. The difficult part is in determining which methods have merit and which don't. One also has to assume that no one shares everything.

WAM: During RV sessions, were polygraph-type biological measurements, i.e., blood pressure, respiration rate, galvanic skin response taken? If so, were there any correlations between these biometric readings and successful remote-viewing sessions?

JWM: We have gone to excessive extent to biologically measure or model human thoughts or consciousness while doing successful remote viewing. To my knowledge, no specific parameter, effect, or measurement has yet been produced that would differentiate a bad remote-viewing from a successful remote-viewing, other than post hoc analysis of the targeted material. Essentially, a successful remote viewer is neither unique biologically nor mentally from any other human being. However, we have found a very strong indication of where just such a measurable difference might lie within the human brain/mind and we are vigorously pursuing it.

WAM: In today's market, there are a variety of pulsing-light goggle-mind machines to help us achieve altered states of perception. Do any of these have value in RV?

JWM: Again, yes and no. Some of them may have merit in that they help you to control what is going on inside your head. As an example, Stephen LeBerge, a researcher who investigates sleep at Stanford University, invented a pair of goggles that sense when one enters REM or dream states during sleep. They then emit low flashes of light that remind the person sleeping that they are sleeping and in a dream state. This helps the person become lucid in their dream. Eventually they are able to produce lucid dreams at will. While this has no direct effect on RV, it does demonstrate that you can have control over specific mental functions. The more control you can demonstrate over mental functioning, the better you are able to control the processing that takes place during RV. So what you learn to do isn't as important as the degree of control which you develop over mental functioning. Control is everything in RV.

At the same time, a "buyer beware" rule should apply. Many of the machines being advertised do not do what they are advertised to do.

WAM: One of the great post-Cold War threats is bioterrorism. How can RV be effectively used to detect potential threats?

JWM: Remote viewing can be used like any other intelligence collection tool. One should remember, however, like all other forms or other methods of collection, it should never be used in a standalone mode. It is just as effective against bioterrorism as it is against chemical, nuclear or any other kind of terrorism.

WAM: Speaking of terrorists, do you believe RV is being used by them in their intelligence gathering activities?

JWM: Personally, I would automatically assume it. Given the paltry financial resources of most terrorist organizations, it would give them significant bang for the buck. Because many of these terrorist organizations operate on limited dollars or with access to limited technology, there is no reason to assume that they are less sophisticated. Many of their leaders are very well educated and very dangerous people.

WAM: RV research concludes that specific numbers and letters are extremely difficult to remote view. Do you feel this is because numbers and letters are more left-brained and RV involves more right hemisphere activity?

JWM: This is clearly an assumption which is probably not based in fact. In my opinion, in terms of function, remote viewing is just as left-brained as it is right-brained. Whether it is more one than the other probably has no bearing on the targeting of letters and numbers. For the sake of discussion, there have been more than a few significant demonstrations in the targeting of specific words, phrases and numbers, which have taken place both inside and outside of the lab. The difficulty lies in the method of targeting, which is extremely complicated.

WAM: We know that the Soviets experimented with drug-induced psychic research. Do you feel that the controlled use of hallucinogens might be of value in RV training and operations?

JWM: Absolutely not. Drugs, whether they are hallucinogens or otherwise, have no place in remote viewing. Experience has taught us that mental control is everything. Drugs have never been known to enhance mental control. Drugs have a direct effect on the mind. This may be a positive effect or may make someone feel like they have more control, where in reality they do not. Lack of control over one's mental processes is very destructive to remote viewing.

WAM: Have you remote viewed any future developments in non-lethal weapons technology that you might care to share?

JWM: Sorry, I can neither confirm nor deny any such work.

WAM: I understand, Joe. It is reported that the funding of RV research from the government side is dead. Do you foresee any attitudinal changes in the near future that again might get Uncle Sam's funds flowing into paranormal research?

JWM: Yes, funding of research by the U.S. government has been terminated. I can see no changes in future attitudes that might alter this situation. I personally would rather see funding for such research coming out of the public domain, where everyone can share in the harvest. What one should not assume is that because the government does not wish to fund such research, that it isn't valuable or necessary. There are lots of things the government doesn't fund which have changed the face of the planet.

WAM: True. Do you believe the various books on RV and the paranormal—yours, *Mind Trek*, Jim Schnabel's *Remote Viewers*, or mine, for that matter—will have sufficient impact to perhaps get the government to rethink its position on paranormal research funding?

JWM: No. I can't imagine why they would. In my opinion, the government doesn't operate that way. Historically, our government reacts defensively in support of our security, maintains close communication with other nations on our behalf, and otherwise attempts to carry out the desires and wishes of the American people. These desires and wishes are demonstrated through the power of politics, as influenced by votes and representative special interest groups. If remote viewing is seen as directly beneficial to these efforts, then they will use it. But the funding for research should come from people interested in discovering more about human nature. Such knowledge belongs to humankind.

WAM: A profound statement. With respect to RV, were any studies done on the effect of diet upon ability and accuracy?

JWM: Yes. I am aware of studies, which were personal in nature, by some of the viewers. These addressed both diet as well as the use of certain vitamins. Diet is important, since the effects of food on the body and body metabolism impact on how alert someone might be, how well one is able to concentrate or focus, and on specific meditation techniques. However, these studies are personality-dependent. If someone felt less effective when eating meat, then they didn't eat meat before remote viewing. If someone felt uncomfortable drinking caffeine prior to a remote viewing, then they didn't do so. To my knowledge, most of these studies were personally motivated, subjectively evaluated, and not medically formal.

WAM: Can the rigid protocols of RV actually contribute to incidents and the frequency of analytic overlay, and incorrect logical interpretations being placed upon incoming RV data?

JWM: Assuming you really mean protocols here and not remote-viewing methodologies, yes and no. Obviously, when beginning research, protocols are developed which initially appear to be airtight, but which later might be determined to be flawed. This results in changes that directly affect overlay, misinterpretations, etc. The more effective the protocol from a scientific standpoint, the more likely one is to eliminate many of these problems.

In addressing specific methodologies, however, one is looking at how the remote viewer is processing material in his or her head. In this case, there are methods that can be used to effectively reduce analytic overlay by the viewer, or eliminate some of their interpretive mistakes, but always at a cost on the other end. By necessity, many of these methods are draconian, which makes them very effective within a training scenario. However, once training has been completed, continued use of such methods can be very destructive to continued growth or an expansion of ability.

Many of these methods have been born out of an assumption that people can be taught to produce information with little or no internalized processing. Unfortunately, this is probably not an accurate assumption. We are cognitive beings and we process everything. Teaching someone to bury this processing instead of learning to control it will not make it go away.

WAM: You are not an advocate of the sole use of the Swann methods of Coordinate Remote Viewing. Are training and methodology really significant, or are the protocols of data recordation and analysis more important?

JWM: They are probably equally important. As regards training and methodology, you are right. I'm not an advocate of the sole use of any methodology. In my observation, every human being is completely different, especially in the way by which we process information. We've learned this from the many attempts at modeling remote viewing by studying good remote viewers.

For me, remote viewing has always been more a martial art than anything else. Specific methodologies are important at the outset, when you are trying to understand the reasons for something. By studying the style of those who are masters at something, you gain a greater insight into why something is done or not done. You would be cutting off a great deal of information by studying only a single style. Once you have gained a greater insight through understanding many styles, you can then apply them to your own strengths and weaknesses. What hopefully develops is a style that is most effective for you.

Data recordation and analysis require a great deal of competence. It is very easy to make a mistake in this area. How data is recorded, what is recorded, and the subsequent analysis is far trickier an issue than most are capable of dealing with. Many researchers have deluded themselves into thinking something is true when it actually isn't, simply because they erred in a final analysis of the data. If you doubt this, spend an afternoon with a professional statistician.

WAM: Posted around Independence Day 1998 on the Internet is what purports to be the DIA manual for coordinate remote viewing. Have you seen it, and if so, do you believe this manual is authentic?

JWM: I will leave the authentication to others.

WAM: I understand completely. You have used your talents for a variety of governmental entities, including the DEA. Do you know if remote viewing was used to attempt to locate the DEA agent Enrique Camarena in 1985?

JWM: I can neither confirm nor deny the use of remote viewing in this case.

WAM: Okay, I heard that. Joe, what do you think of the future of RV in the military and political world of the future?

JWM: If remote viewing continues to be bastardized by certain segments of the public, irresponsibly maligned within the press and media, and if people continue to try and rewrite its history for personal, monetary, or misinformation purposes—then I see no future for RV in its original form anywhere. It will drift into the same nebulous cloud as current opinions regarding UFOs and crypto-zoological animals. People with courage, integrity, and a healthy skepticism are required if we are to learn the realities underlying the remote-viewing phenomena. Unfortunately, such people are becoming a rare commodity in today's world.

WAM: Nevertheless, there are some of us. One of the darker facets of RV is the fact that a lot of the people involved with the government program have had fatal or near fatal diseases. Pat Price died in 1975 from what was claimed to be a massive heart attack. Your fellow remote-viewer, Mel Riley, told me of how he "died" of a heart attack at his wife's feet, only to be revived later. You have experienced several close calls. Do you think there are any inherent physical dangers involved in continuous RV taskings?

JWM: There are two hypotheses. One dictates that there is something very dangerous about it. There are at least a couple of researchers who seem to think that this is so. They point out the high levels of hypertension within people who deal with the paranormal in general, and remote viewing specifically. I personally don't think enough data has yet been collected to support this theory.

In my own observations, I've noticed that, generally speaking, people who make good psychics and remote viewers are people who are also very dynamic in their lives otherwise. They seek out the controversial and difficult problems and participate in the cutting-edge kinds of problems where innovative or special abilities seem to be required.

In the military, they are the same kind of people who like to walk point, do the long-range reconnaissance behind the lines, or deal with spies in back rooms and alleys. Simply put, they are the kinds of people who like the rush of adrenaline that comes along with taking on a seemingly impossible challenge or mission. Of course, with this comes all the pressures and hypertension associated with cardiovascular disease. In other words, they are a self-selected group, and heart disease just happens to occur right along with everything else.

WAM: What advice would you give the readers of this work vis-à-vis further study and experimentation in RV? Specifically, what is your opinion of the training courses presently being touted to the public?

JWM: Don't believe everything you read or hear. Understand that it ultimately requires a great deal of personal effort, time, and energy. Much of what you learn about yourself, you learn from yourself, not others. I think you can garner valuable instruction from just about anything that is currently being offered, provided you don't believe any one thing or person to be the ultimate source of knowledge. Mostly, don't take any of it so seriously that you are not having any fun doing it.

WAM: Joseph McMoneagle, thanks for sharing.

Analysis and Commentary

The reader has just been party to an interview that took place with a man who has the most experience in the field of the military and intelligence use of remote viewing. Not a word has been changed from the original interview.

We have learned that there is no one training method for the development of remote-viewing skills. We have learned that natural ability is the controlling factor, although it might be spruced up a bit. Perhaps the most frightening bit of information is McMoneagle's quite rational belief that the technique is incorporated in the arsenal of today's terrorists. This bears further discussion and analysis.

It appears that in the area of international terrorism, the most advanced technology has become irrelevant, or superfluous. The hostile introduction of chemical or biological agents into American society is not expensive, high-tech, nor difficult. It is potentially devastating. The technology of the suitcase-sized atomic bomb is old. But the above are capable of some detection and perhaps interdiction.

What is terrifying is psychic terrorism. If the methodologies and protocols of remote viewing are used by the numerous potential psychics that must exist among terrorist groups, they have achieved a potentially effective, low-cost intelligence collection device that cannot be thwarted or detected. (Unless there exist such methods now that are still classified.)

McMoneagle has told us that there have been specific instances of psychic perception of specific words and numbers in remote viewings both in and out of the laboratory. If these methods can be improved, then what we have are a bunch of low-budget terrorists who can obtain high-budget classified information without leaving the comfort of their tents.

The reader should be aware that, given the nature of the subject matter, the confidentiality commitments of the parties involved, and the confidences that exist independent of reporting and publishing, the entire story of remote viewing cannot yet be told. Some of what has occurred in the field of the military-occult complex must yet remain truly occult from the eyes of the public.

However, there has been enough revealed, there has been enough information declassified, to allow even the most dedicated but intelligent skeptic to wonder—*Is this stuff for real?*

McMoneagle has walked this beat for twenty-one years at the time of this writing. Your author has performed his own paranormal investigations since 1970, and is both a practicing attorney, card-carrying skeptic, and former intelligence professional. In your author's opinion remote viewing IS real.

It may become the most economical and valuable intelligence collection tool of the twenty-first century or, with appropriate amounts of apathy, ignorance, and cowardice, it can die a premature death . . . and both the military-occult complex and the world at large will be the poorer for its demise.

THE KRESS REPORT
Parapsychology in Intelligence

A PERSONAL REVIEW AND CONCLUSIONS
Dr. Kenneth A. Kress

In 1996, after the dissemination of the CIA-sponsored report of the American Institute of Research evaluation of the remote-viewing program, the following report from 1977 was declassified. This report, "Parapsychology in Intelligence," was an official admission of the existence of psychic spying and a revelation of the potential operational utility of remote viewing as an intelligence collection tool. It appeared in the Winter 1977 issue of Studies in Intelligence, *an in-house publication of the CIA.*

The Central Intelligence Agency has investigated the controversial phenomenon called parapsychology as it relates to intelligence collection. The author was involved with many aspects of the last such investigations. This paper summarizes selected highlights of the experiences of the author and others. The intent is not historical completeness. Files are available for those interested in details. Instead, the intent is to record some certainly interesting and possibly useful data and opinions. This record is likely to be of future benefit to those who will be required to evaluate intelligence-related aspects of parapsychology.

The Agency took the initiative by sponsoring serious parapsychological research, but circumstances, biases, and fear of ridicule prevented

CIA from completing a scientific investigation of parapsychology and its relevance to national security. During this research period, CIA was buffeted with investigations concerning illegalities and improprieties of all sorts. This situation, perhaps properly so, raised the sensitivity of CIA's involvement in unusual activities. The "Proxmire Effect," where the fear that certain government research contracts would be claimed to be ill-founded and held up for scorn, was another factor precluding CIA from sensitive areas of research. Also, there tend to be two types of reactions to parapsychology: positive or negative, with little in between. Parapsychological data, almost by definition, are elusive and unexplained. Add a history replete with proven frauds and many people instantly reject the subject, saying, in effect, "I would not believe this stuff even if it were true." Others, who must have had personal "conversion" experiences, tend to be equally convinced that one unexplained success establishes a phenomenon. These prejudices make it difficult to evaluate parapsychology carefully and scientifically.

Tantalizing but incomplete data have been generated by CIA-sponsored research. These data show, among other things, that on occasion unexplained results of genuine intelligence significance occur. This is not to say that parapsychology is a proven intelligence tool; it is to say that the evaluation is not yet complete and more research is needed.

Attention is confined to psychokinetics and remote viewing. Psychokinetics is the purported ability of a person to interact with a machine or other object by unexplained means. Remote viewing is akin to clairvoyance in that a person claims to sense information about a site or person from an unknown sensory link.

Anecdotal reports of extrasensory perception (ESP) capabilities have reached U.S. national security agencies at least since World War II, when Hitler was said to rely on astrologers and seers. Suggestions for military applications of ESP continued to be received after World War II. For example, in 1952 the Department of Defense was lectured on the possible usefulness of extrasensory perception in psychological warfare. Over the years, reports continued to accumulate. In 1961, the reports induced one of the earliest U.S. government parapsychology investigations, when the chief of CIA's Office of Technical Service (then the Technical Services Division) became interested in the claims of ESP. Technical project officers soon contacted Stephen I. Abrams, the Director of the Parapsychological Laboratory, Oxford University,

England. Under the auspices of Project ULTRA, Abrams prepared a review article which claimed ESP was demonstrated but not understood or controllable. The report was read with interest but produced no further action for another decade.

Two laser physicists, Dr. Russell Targ and Dr. Harold E. Puthoff, reawakened CIA research in parapsychology. Targ had been avocationally interested in parapsychology for most of his adult life. As an experimentalist, he was interested in scientific observations of parapsychology. Puthoff became interested in the field in the early 1970's. He was a theoretician who was exploring new fields of research after extensive work in quantum electronics.

In April of 1972, Targ met with CIA personnel from the Office of Strategic Intelligence (OSI) and discussed the subject of paranormal abilities. Targ revealed that he had contacts with people who purported to have seen and documented some Soviet investigations of psychokinesis. Films of Soviets moving inanimate objects by "mental powers" were made available to analysts from OSI. They, in turn, contacted personnel from the Office of Research and Development (ORD) and OTS. An ORD project officer then visited Targ, who had recently joined the Stanford Research Institute (SRI). Targ proposed that some psychokinetic verification investigations could be done at SRI in conjunction with Puthoff.

These proposals were quickly followed by a laboratory demonstration. A man was found by Targ and Puthoff who apparently had psychokinetic abilities. He was taken on a surprise visit to a superconducting shielded magnetometer being used in quark (high energy particle) experiments by Dr. A. Hebbard of Stanford University Physics Department. The quark experiment required that the magnetometer be as well shielded as technology would allow. Nevertheless, when the subject placed his attention on the interior of the magnetometer, the output signal was visibly disturbed, indicating a change in the internal magnetic field. Several other correlations of his mental efforts with signal variations were observed. These variations were never seen before or after the visit. The event was summarized and transmitted to the Agency in the form of a letter to an OSI analyst and as discussions with OTS and ORD officers.

The Office of Technical Services took the first action. With the approval of the same manager who supported the ESP studies a decade previously, an OTS project officer contracted for a demonstration with the previously mentioned man for a few days in August 1972. During this demonstration, the subject was asked to describe objects hidden out of sight by the CIA personnel. The subject did well. The descriptions were so startlingly accurate that the OTD and ORD representatives suggested that the work be continued and expanded. The same Director of OTS reviewed the data, approved another $2,500 work order, and encouraged the development of a more complete research plan.

By October 1972, I was the project officer. I was chosen because of my physics background to work with the physicists from SRI. The Office of Technical Service funded a $50,000 expanded effort in parapsychology. The expanded investigation included tests of several abilities of both the original subject and a new one. Curious data began to appear; the paranormal abilities seemed individualistic. For example, one subject, by mental effort, apparently caused an increase in the temperature measured by a thermistor; the action could not be duplicated by the second subject. The second subject was able to reproduce, with impressive accuracy, information inside sealed envelopes. Under identical conditions, the first subject could reproduce nothing. Perhaps even more disturbing, repeating the same experiment with the same subject did not yield consistent results. I began to have serious feelings of being involved with a fraud.

Approximately halfway though this project, the SRI contractors were invited to review their results. After careful consideration of the security and sensitivity factors, the results were shared and discussed with selected Agency personnel during that and subsequent meetings. In February 1973, the most recent data were reviewed; thereafter, several ORD officers showed definite interest in contributing their own expertise and office funding.

The possibility of a joint OTS/ORD program continued to develop. The Office of Research and Development sent new project officers to SRI during February 1973, and the reports which were brought back convinced ORD to become involved. Interest was translated into action when ORD requested an increase in the scope of the effort and transferred funds to OTS. About this time, a third sensitive subject, Pat Price, became available at SRI, and the remote-viewing experiments in which a subject describes his impressions of remote objects or locations began in earnest. The possibility that such useful abilities were real motivated all concerned to move ahead quickly.

The contract required additional management review before it could be continued or its scope increased. The initial review went from OTS and ORD to Mr. William Colby, then the DDO. On 24 April, Mr. Colby decided that the Executive Management Committee should pass judgment on this potentially sensitive project. By the middle of May, 1973, the approval request went through the Management Committee. An approval memorandum was written for the signature of the DCI, Dr. James Schlesinger. Mr. Colby took the memorandum to the DCI a few days later. I was soon told not to increase the scope of the project and not to anticipate any follow-on in this area. The project was too sensitive and potentially embarrassing. It should be tabled. It is interesting to note that OTS was then being investigated for involvement in the Watergate affair, and that in May, 1973, the DCI issued a memorandum to all CIA employees requesting the reporting of any activities that may have been illegal and improper. As project officer, clearly my sense of timing had not been guided by useful paranormal abilities!

During the summer of 1973, SRI continued working informally with an OSI officer on a remote-viewing experiment which eventually stimulated more CIA-sponsored investigations of parapsychology. The target was a vacation property in the eastern United States. The experiment began with the passing of nothing more than the geographic coordinates of the vacation property to the SRI physicists who, in turn, passed them to the two subjects, one of whom was Pat Price. No maps were permitted: and the subjects were asked to give an immediate response of what they remotely viewed at these coordinates. The subjects came back with descriptions which were apparent misses. They both talked about a military-like facility. Nevertheless, a striking correlation of the two independent descriptions was noted. The correlation caused the OSI officer to drive to the site and investigate in more detail.

To the surprise of the OSI officer, he soon discovered a sensitive government installation a few miles from the vacation property. This discovery led to a request to have Price provide information concerning the interior workings of this particular site. All the data produced by the two subjects were reviewed in CIA and the Agency concerned.

The evaluation was, as usual, mixed. Pat Price, who had no military or intelligence background, provided a list of project titles associated with current and past activities, including one of extreme sensitivity. Also, the codename of the site was provided. Other information concerning the physical layout of the site was accurate. Some information, such as the names of the people at the site, proved incorrect.

These experiments took several months to be analyzed and reviewed within the Agency. Now Mr. Colby was DCI, and the new directors of OTS and ORD were favorably impressed by the data. In the fall of 1973, a Statement of Work was outlined, and SRI was asked to propose another program. A jointly funded ORD and OTS program was begun in February 1974. The author again was the project officer. The project proceeded on the premise that the phenomena existed; the objective was to develop and utilize them.

The ORD funds were devoted to basic studies such as the identification of measurable physiological or psychological characteristics of psychic individuals, and the establishment of experimental protocols for validating paranormal abilities. The OTS funds were to evaluate the operational utility of psychic subjects without regard to the detailed understanding of paranormal functioning. If the paranormal functioning was sufficiently reproducible, we were confident applications could be found.

Before many months had passed, difficulties developed in the project. Our tasking in the basic research area proved to be more extensive than time and funds would allow. The contractors wanted to compromise by doing all of the tasks with less completeness. The ORD scientists insisted that with such a controversial topic, fewer but more rigorous results would be of more value. The rigor of the research became a serious issue between the ORD project officers and SRI, with myself generally taking a position between the righteousness of the contractor and indignation of the researchers. Several meetings occurred over that issue.

As an example of the kinds of disputes which developed over the basic research, consider the evaluation of the significance of data from the "ESP teaching machine" experiments. This machine was a four-state electronic random number generator used to test for paranormal abilities. SRI claimed the machine randomly cycled through four states, and the subject indicates the current machine state by pressing a button. The state of the machine and the subject's choice were recorded for later analysis. A subject "guessing" should, on the average, be correct 25 percent of the time. SRI had a subject who averaged a very significant 29 percent for more than 2,500 trials.

I requested a review of the experiment and analysis, and two ORD officers quickly and skeptically responded. They first argued that the ESP machine was possibly not random. They further argued the subjects probably learned the non-random machine patterns and thereby produced higher scores. During this review, it was noted that whether the machine was random or not, the data taken during the experiment could be analyzed to determine actual machine statistics. The machine randomness was unimportant, because the subject's performance could then be compared with actual machine performance. The ORD project officers, however, did not believe it would be worth the effort to do the extra analysis of the actual data.

I disagreed. I had the Office of Joint Computer Services redo the data analysis. The conclusion was that during the experiment "no evidence of non-randomness was discovered" and there was "no solid reason *how* he was able to be so successful." I further ordered the subject retested. He averaged more than 28 percent during another 2,500 trials. This information was given in written and oral form to the ORD project officers, who maintained there must be yet another flaw in the experiment or analysis, but it was not worth finding. Because of more pressing demands, the issue could not be pursued to a more definite conclusion.

Concurrent with this deteriorating state of affairs, new directors of ORD and OTS were named again. Since neither director had any background or experience in paranormal research, the new director of ORD reviewed the parapsychology project and had reservations. I requested a meeting in which he said he could not accept this reality of paranormal functioning, but he understood his bias. He said that inasmuch as he could not make an objective decision in this field, he could simply follow the advice of his staff. The ORD project officers were feeling their own frustrations and uncertainties concerning the work and now had to face this unusual kind of skepticism of their new director. The skepticism about the believability of the phenomenon and quality of the basic research adversely affected the opinions of many people in the OTS. Support for the project was vanishing rapidly.

As these pressures mounted, the first intelligence collection operation using parapsychology was attempted. The target was the Semipalatinsk Unidentified Research and Development Facility (URDF-3, formerly known as PUTS). The experimental collection would use our best subject, Pat Price. From experience it was obvious that Price produced bad data as well as good. Borrowing from classical communications theory concepts, this "noisy channel" of information could nevertheless be useful if it were characterized. An elaborate protocol was designed which would accomplish two characterization measurements. First, we needed assurance the channel was collecting useful data. I reviewed photos of URDF-3 and chose two features which, if Price described them, would show the channel at least partially working. Referring to Figure 1a, these features were the tall crane and the four structures resembling oil well derricks. It was agreed that if Price described these structures, I would be prepared to have him sign a secrecy agreement, making him willing, and collect more relevant intelligence details. Secondly, after a working channel was thus established, a signal-to-noise or quality characterization was required. This would be done by periodic tests of the channel—that is, periodically Price would be asked to describe the features of URDF-3, which were known. The accuracy of these descriptions would be used to estimate the quality of the data we had no obvious way of verifying.

The experiment began with my branch chief and me briefing Targ and Puthoff in a motel. Later, at SRI, Price was briefed by Targ and Puthoff presumably knew nothing about URDF-3. This protocol guarded against cueing and/or telepathy. Initially Price was given only the geographic coordinates, a world atlas map marked with the approximate location of URDF-3, and told it was a Soviet RD&E test site. Overnight, he produced the drawing on the bottom right of Figure 1b. Price further mentioned that this was a "damned big crane" because he saw a person walk by and he only came up to the axles on the wheels. This performance caught my attention, but with two more days of work, we never heard about the derricks. Eventually, a decision was needed. Because the crane was so impressive, my branch chief and I decided the derrick's description requirement should be relaxed and we should continue.

When the decision was made to make Price willing, I decided to test him. My branch chief and I sat in a conference room while Targ and Puthoff brought a smiling Pat Price into the room. I was introduced as the sponsor, and I immediately asked Price if he knew me.

Yes.

Name?

Ken Kress.

Occupation?

Works for CIA.

Since I was then a covert employee, the response was meaningful. After having Price sign a secrecy agreement, and some discussions, I confronted him again. I rolled out a large version of Figure 1a and asked if he had viewed this site.

Yes, of course!

Why didn't you see the four derricks?

Wait, I'll check.

Price closed his eyes, put on his glasses (he "sees" better that way) and in a few seconds answered "I didn't see them because they are not there any more." Since my data were three or four months old, there was no rejoinder to the implied accusation that my data were not good. We proceeded and completed a voluminous data package.

In a few weeks, the latest URDF-3 reconnaissance was checked. Two derricks were partially disassembled, but basically all four were visible. In general, most of Price's data were wrong or could not be evaluated. He did, nevertheless, produce some amazing descriptions, like buildings then under construction, spherical tank sections, and the crane in Figure 1b. Two analysts, a photo interpreter at IAS and a nuclear analyst at Los Alamos Scientific Laboratories agreed that Price's description of the crane was accurate; the nuclear analyst wrote that "one: he, the subject, actually saw it through remote viewing, or two, he was informed what to draw by someone knowledgeable of URDF-3." But, again, since there was so much bad information mixed in with the good, the overall result was not considered useful. As proof of remote viewing, the data are at best inconclusive. The ORD officers concluded that since there were no control experiments to compare with, the data were nothing but lucky guessing.

I began to doubt my own objectivity in evaluating the significance of paranormal abilities to intelligence collection. It was clear that the SRI contractors were claiming success while ORD advisors were saying the experiments were not meaningful because of poor experimental design. As a check on myself, I asked for a critique of the investigation from a disinterested consultant, a theoretical physicist with a broad intellectual background. His first task was to evaluate the field of parapsychology without knowledge of the CIA data. After he had completed this critique, I asked him to acquaint himself with the CIA data and then to reassess the field. The first investigation produced genuine interest in paranormal functioning as a valid research area. After being acquainted with CIA data, his conclusion was, "a large body of reliable experimental evidence points to the inescapable conclusion that extra-sensory perception does exist as a real phenomenon, albeit character-ized by rarity and lack of reliability." This judgment by a competent scientist gave impetus to continue serious inquiry into parapsychology.

Because of the general skepticism and mixed results of the various operational experiments, a final challenge was issued by OTS manage-ment: OTS is not in the research business; do something of genuine operational significance. Price was chosen, and suggestions were solic-ited from operational personnel in both OTS and the DDO. An in-triguing idea was selected from audio collection systems. A test to determine if remote viewing could help was suggested. The interiors of two foreign embassies were known to the audio teams who had made entries several years previously. Price was to visit these embassies by his remote viewing capability, locate the coderooms, and come up with information that might allow a member of the audio team to determine whether Price was likely to be of operational use in subsequent oper-ations. Price was given operationally acceptable data such as the exte-rior photographs and the geographical coordinates of the embassies.

In both cases, Price correctly located the coderooms. He produced copious data, such as the location of interior doors and colors of marble stairs and fireplaces that were accurate and specific. As usual, much was also vague and incorrect. Regardless, the operations officer in-volved concluded, "It is my considered opinion that this technique—whatever it is—offers definite operational possibilities."

This result was reviewed within OTS and the DDO, and various suggestions for potential follow-on activities were formulated. This package of requirements, plus the final results of the current contract, were reviewed at several meetings within OTS and ORD. The results of those meetings are as follows:

1. According to the ORD project officers, the research was not productive or even competent; therefore, research support to SRI was dropped. The director of OTS felt the OTS charter would not support research; therefore, all Agency funding in paranormal research stopped.
2. Because of the mixed results, the operational utility of the capability was considered questionable but deserved further testing.
3. To achieve better security, all the operations-oriented testing

with the contractor was stopped, and a personal services contract with Price was started.

4. Since I was judged to be a positively biased advocate of paranormal functioning, the testing and evaluation of Price would be transferred to a more pragmatic OTS operations psychologist.

The OTS psychologist picked up his new responsibilities and chose to complete an unfinished DDO requirement. The origin of the requirement went back to the fall of 1974 when several OTS engineers became aware of the parapsychology project in OTS and had volunteered to attempt remote viewing. They passed initial remote viewing tests at SRI with some apparent successes. To test these OTS insiders further, I chose a suggested requirement to obtain information about a Libyan site described only by its geographic coordinates. The OTS engineers described new construction which could be an SA-5 missile training site. The Libyan Desk officer was immediately impressed. He then revealed to me that an agent had reported essentially the same story. More coordinates were quickly furnished but were put aside by me.

The second set of Libyan geographic coordinates was passed by the OTS psychologist to Price. A report describing a guerrilla training site was quickly returned. It contained a map-like drawing of the complex. Price described a related underwater sabotage training facility site several hundred kilometers away on the seacoast. This information was passed to the Libyan Desk. Some data were evaluated immediately, some were evaluated only after ordering special reconnaissance. The underwater sabotage training facility description was similar to a collateral agent's report. The Libyan Desk officer quickly escalated the requirement to what was going on inside those buildings, the plans and intentions, etc. The second requirements list was passed to Pat Price. Price died of a heart attack a few days later, and the program stopped. There have been no further CIA-sponsored intelligence collection tests.

Since July, 1975, there has been only modest CIA and intelligence community staff interest in parapsychology. The Office of Scientific Intelligence completed a study about Soviet military and KGB applied parapsychology. During November of 1976, Director George Bush became aware that official Soviets were visiting and questioning Puthoff and Targ at SRI about their work in parapsychology. Mr. Bush requested and received a briefing on CIA's investigations into parapsychology. Before there was any official reaction, he left the Agency. Various intelligence community groups, such as the Human Resources Subcommittee on R&D, have exhaustively reviewed parapsychology in CIA, DOD, and the open research, but have failed to conclude whether parapsychology is or is not a worthwhile area for further investigation. Several proposals from SRI and other contractors were received by CIA but none were accepted. There are no current plans for CIA to fund parapsychology investigations.

Postscript

At this point, I have traced the action and reaction of various elements of CIA to what is certainly an unconventional and highly controversial subject. Also of interest are the concurrent reactions of other agencies to parapsychology. In August, 1972, parapsychology was discussed with several members of DIA. The DIA people were basically interested in the Soviet activities in this area, and expressed considerable interest in our own fledgling results. Numerous meetings have occurred during the past several years. DIA remains interested on a low priority basis.

The Army Material Command learned of CIA interest in the paranormal. We discovered the Army interest was generated by data which emerged from Vietnam. Apparently certain individuals called point men, who led patrols into hostile territory, had far fewer casualties from booby traps and ambushes than the average. These point men, needless to say, had a following of loyal men and, in general, greatly helped the morale of their troops under a brutal, stressful situation. The Army gave extensive physical and psychological tests to a group of unusually successful point men and came to no conclusion other than perhaps that paranormal capabilities may be the explanation!

The Army was most interested in CIA results and wanted to stay closely informed. After a few more follow-up meetings, the Army Materiel Command was never heard from again.

The Defense Advanced Research Projects Agency (DARPA) reported that they had not only a showing of interest but a hostile response as well to the subject area. At one time, we felt we had the strong interest of some people at DARPA to discuss our data. The SRI contractors and I went to a briefing where we had a several-hour confrontation with an assemblage of hostile DARPA people who had been convened especially to debunk our results. After a long, inconclusive, emotional discussion, we left. Contacts with DARPA stopped for several years.

The Navy reviewed part of the work and became interested. Some groups developed strong interest, and minor funding was provided to SRI by Navy to replicate one of SRI's earlier experiments under more controlled conditions. The experiment was replicated. Then the Navy asked SRI to repeat the same experiment under different conditions. An effect was observed, but it was not the same as the previous observations. About this same time, the Navy became very concerned about this research being "mind-warfare"–related. Funding was stopped.

The active funding for parapsychology now has shifted to the Air Force's Foreign Technology Division with the addition of modest testing being completed by another group at DARPA. These investigations are not yet completed, but a second phase is funded by the Air Force. The Air Force project is attempting to evaluate whether signals and communications can be sent and received by paranormal functioning. Also aircraft and missile intelligence which can be verified is being gathered and evaluated. To date the results are more consistent than those seen during the CIA research, but still they are mixed. Some simple experiments seemed very impressive and conclusive. The more complex experiments are difficult to assess.

In the non-government world, an explosion of interest in unclassified parapsychology research occurred after the first publication of CIA-sponsored projects. Books have been written, prestigious professional societies have had sessions on parapsychology, and several national news reports have been broadcast and printed. Director Turner revealed publicly that CIA has had operational interest in parapsychology. The open publication of these investigations is generally healthy and helpful. It shows a reduction of associated emotionalism and bias. These publications will also stimulate other scientific investigations into parapsychology.

There is a less positive aspect to open interest and publications. Before adequate assessment was made by CIA and others, we may have allowed some important national security information out into the public domain. It is my opinion that, as it relates to intelligence, sufficient understanding and assessment of parapsychology has not been achieved. There are observations, such as the original magnetic experiments at Stanford University, the OSI remote viewing, the OTS-coderoom experiments, and others, done for the Department of Defense, that defy explanation. Coincidence is not likely, and fraud has not been discovered. The implication of these data cannot be determined until the assessment is done.

If the above is true, how is it that the phenomenon remains controversial and receives so little official government support? Why is it that the proper assessment was never made? This state of affairs occurs because of the elementary understanding of parapsychology and because of the peculiarities of the intelligence and military organizations which have attempted the assessments. There is no fundamental understanding of the mechanisms of paranormal functioning, and the reproducibility remains poor. The research and experiments have successfully demonstrated abilities, but have not explained them nor made them reproducible. Past and current support of parapsychology comes from applications-oriented intelligence and military agencies. The people managing such agencies demand quick and relevant results. The intelligence and military agencies, therefore, press for results before there is sufficient experimental reproducibility or understanding of the physical mechanisms. Unless there is a major breakthrough in understanding, the situation is not likely to change as long as applications-oriented agencies are funding parapsychology. Agencies must commit long-term basic research funds and learn to confine attention to testing only abilities which at least appear reproducible enough to be used to augment other hard collection techniques (example: use parapsychology to help target hard intelligence collection techniques and determine if the take is thereby increased). Parapsychology, like other technical issues, can then rise or fall on its merits and not stumble over bureaucratic charters and conjectures proposed by people who are irrevocably on one side or the other in the controversial area.

APPENDIX 2

Supernatural Counterinsurgency in the Congo

WITCHCRAFT, SORCERY, MAGIC, AND OTHER PSYCHOLOGICAL PHENOMENA AND THEIR IMPLICATIONS ON MILITARY AND PARAMILITARY OPERATIONS IN THE CONGO

In 1964, the United States Government issued a report on the use of the supernatural as a psychological warfare tool in the Congo, prepared by the Army.

This report has been prepared in response to a query posed by ODCS/OPS, Department of the Army, regarding the purported use of witchcraft, sorcery, and magic by insurgent elements in the Republic of the Congo (Leopoldville). Magical practices are said to be effective in conditioning dissident elements and their followers to do battle with Government troops.

Rebel tribesmen are said to have been persuaded that they can be made magically impervious to Congolese army firepower. Their fear of the government has thus been diminished and, conversely, fear of the rebels has grown within army ranks.

The problem, therefore, which CINFAC was asked to explore is the role of supernatural or superstitious concepts in a counterinsurgency in the Congo.

Any reply to this question involves consideration of several factors. It is necessary to examine the nature of general African beliefs about magic, insofar as this may be done on the basis of published studies.

It is also necessary to gain some insight as to the roles played by magic in other African revolutionary upheavals. And finally, it is suggested that today's insurgency situation should not be studied in a vacuum, but should be considered as part of a continuum stemming from the pre-independence Belgian administration, the impact of Western culture upon African tribal systems, the circumstances of the birth of the Congo Republic, and the nature of the struggle for power within the Congo since 1960.

A review of the available literature indicates that in Africa, uprisings embodying supernatural practices have tended to occur generally whenever the continued physical safety or internal power structure of a tribe or tribes has been seriously threatened. Manifestations of witchcraft and sorcery in these instances can be said to reflect, in part, a return to traditionalism. A tribe unites more readily when a threat is explainable and solutions are propounded in terms of tribal common denominators of belief. In order to determine the degree to which such a generalization is applicable to the current situation in the Congo, a brief recapitulation of certain aspects of recent Congolese history will serve as a useful point of departure.

Origins of Congolese Political Instability

The tribal uprisings which have erupted in the Republic of the Congo (Leopoldville) since its independence in 1960 can be traced to situations which appeared to threaten the various tribes both in terms of their physical well-being and their position within the structure of Congolese national society. With independence, these tribes found themselves lacking the basic services which the colonial administration had provided—alimentation, hygiene, medical care, schools, and physical security—while at the same time the future of the tribe and its organization was being debated by the new government at Leopoldville. By and large, however, it was the disruption in government machinery which forced the younger members of the tribes to seek the urban centers in an effort to improve their situation, and pushed the older members back towards traditionalism and beliefs in magic and witchcraft.

The actual disintegration of the Congo was caused by two main factors: the absence of associational groups which could replace the departing colonial administration; and the power struggle that took place between those Congolese political parties favoring centralism and those favoring federalism. This conflict prevented any attempts by Congolese governments to restore some semblance of administrative order.

The apparent docility of the Congolese people had led the Belgian colonial administration to believe its regime would endure, and that it could take its time in preparing the country for an eventual peaceful transfer of power. It was not until the bloody riots of January 5, 1959, that the Belgian government realized that it would have to give freedom to the Congo much sooner than it had envisaged. In the ensuing agreements between Congolese representatives and the Belgian government, provisions were made for the utilization of Belgian colonial civil servants in their former capacities until Congolese replacements could be trained. Such agreements were never implemented. On July 8, 1960, eight days after independence, the Congolese National Army in the capital city of Leopoldville mutinied against its Belgian officers, and in less than three days the mutiny had spread to the rest of the Congo where the position of all Belgian civilians became serious. Kasai province was to follow suit in August. On July 12, Premier Patrice Lumumba called on the United Nations to eject the Belgian troops and help to restore order. In the weeks following the arrival of UN forces, Lumumba's followers made repeated attempts to reimpose central government control on Katanga and Kasai. The attempts, and the high number of casualties resulting from them, precipitated a power struggle between the centralist bloc of Lumumba and the federalist bloc of President Joseph Kasavubu which paralyzed all government activity. Although Lumumba was eventually removed from office by the Army chief of staff, and a more or less federal set-up with a strong executive was established, the government remained virtually paralyzed by its effort to regain Katanga province. Anarchy thus set in, providing Lumumba's followers with opportunities to set up their own political organizations. These were cast along tribal lines, and the trappings of tribalism, including manifestations of beliefs in magic and witchcraft, began again to impinge upon politics at the national level.

Elements of East-West confrontation entered the picture when the situation in the Congo was internationalized. By calling in the United Nations, Lumumba had hoped that it would help him in his efforts to restore central government control over Kasai and Katanga provinces while also helping him train civil service cadres to replace the Belgians who had departed after the July riots. In the UN, Lumumba had received his initial support from the Afro-Asian and Communist Blocs. But when the United Nations refused to accede to all of his demands, he turned against it and accepted the proffered assistance of the Communist Bloc countries, along with that of Ghana, Guinea, and the United Arab Republic. Communist machinations, and subsequent attempts by UN Ghanian troops to disarm the Congolese Army seemed to have prompted General Mobutu to stage the removal of Lumumba. With the overthrow of Lumumba and the ejection of all Communist Bloc missions from the Congo by Mobutu, it appeared that Communist influence in the Congo was reduced to a minimum in spite of the fact that some of Lumumba's left-leaning associates remained active on the scene. The present recurrence of Communist agitation seems, however, to derive its main impetus from the Chinese Communist Mission in Burundi.

The role being played today by tribalism, with its attendant reversion to other aspects of traditionalism, can be understood fully only in light of the effect on the tribes of the transition from colonialism to full independence. Belgian colonial policy was, in general, paternalistic in tone and indirect in administration. The Belgian administration assumed the role of tutor, and dealt with local populations through local indigenous institutions. It was thought that this process would be less disruptive and would condition local societies to accept foreign rule more readily. With particular reference to the tribes, indirect rule resulted in the incorporation of the tribal chiefs into the administrative system. With minor exceptions, the Belgian administration came to control the tribe through its chief, leaving the internal organization of the tribe intact. In a sense, a chief became the principal agent between his tribe and the colonial authorities.

Thus the Belgians accepted the traditional boundaries of the chiefdoms, reemphasized the hereditary character of tribal chieftaincy, and made the chiefs responsible for population registration, public health, tax collection, security, and labor matters within the respective chiefdoms. It was mainly in the field of jurisprudence, and especially punitive actions, that the traditional powers of the chiefs were curtailed. Too, the ability of tribal members to appeal directly to colonial authorities on legal points, and the fact that Europeans could disregard tribal immigration barriers established by the chiefs and recruit labor at will, tended to reduce the overall effectiveness of the chiefs.

Expanding economic opportunities, missionary activity, and the suppression of intertribal warfare contributed in the long-run to the gradual erosion of the role of tribal communities in the social structure of the Congo as a whole. With the establishment of major urban centers, and the close contact between Europeans and Congolese which they afforded, a new class of Congolese began to emerge. The longer they remained in the cities, the weaker became their tribal attachments, until in the post World War II era many were to harbor strongly anti-tribal sentiments. The new class was known as evolues (literally: evolved), and most evolue leaders came to regard the continued existence of a tribal society as typifying backwardness and colonialism.

With independence, most of the evolues, of which Patrice Lumumba was one, became identified with the centralist political bloc, while others, such as Moise Tshombe and Joseph Kasavubu, tribal chieftains in their own right, formed the federalist bloc of political parties. The centralists viewed any federal setup as an attempt to preserve colonial influences and practices, while the federalists viewed centralism as the attempted elimination of the political opposition and the establishment of a dictatorship similar to that of Ghana and Guinea. The power struggle between these two blocs prevented the drafting of a constitution clearly defining the role and position of the tribes, and it was not until recently that this was resolved in the form of a federalist system with a strong executive. This represented a compromise between centralist and federalist points of view. It recognized tribal structures, but underlines the authority of the central government. Unfortunately, the persistence of political chaos and insurgency has hindered the restoration of effective governmental machinery, and until this machinery is restored no objective evaluation of the compromise system will be possible.

Supernatural Aspects of the Present Insurgency Situation

We began this discussion with an observation that threats to the concept or form of tribal structures in Africa tend to generate uprisings characterized by emphasis upon traditionalist elements in African life. The current uprisings in the Congo, and for that matter elsewhere in black Africa, gain impetus from the insurgent practice of employing magical procedures to convince tribal insurgents that no harm can be done to them by forces of the central government.

These tactics are effective, because in the Congo and elsewhere in black Africa beliefs in witchcraft, sorcery, magic, and other supernatural phenomenon are deeply rooted among the people. Although the manifestations of these beliefs vary widely according to tribal and cultural circumstances, magico-religious causes are usually cited to explain misfortunes of any kind, even those of clearly natural origin. If crops are blighted, if a hut caves in and kills its occupants, if the chief becomes unfriendly, or if sudden illness or death occur, bewitching is usually given as the primary cause. The people may understand that in fact the house fell because termites ate away the foundations, but that it fell at the time it did was a result of witchcraft or sorcery. Witchcraft is also cited as a factor in personal disputes, especially where the relationship is inherently subject to tensions—as for example, in the relationship between husband and wife, or between co-wives. In these cases, not only physical or direct remedies, but occult remedies as well are considered necessary to counteract the evil influence.

A distinction drawn by Evans-Pritchard in his *Witchcraft, Oracles, and Magic Among the Azande* (Oxford University Press, 1937) which is helpful for purposes of study is that between witchcraft and sorcery. Although these two concepts often overlap, especially in application (the same person may be thought to practice sorcery as well as witchcraft), they do represent two distinct theories of supernatural behaviour which are shared by practically all African tribal societies.

A sorcerer is one who is thought to practice evil magic against others.

The techniques of sorcery may be learned by anyone, and are usually based upon the use of various organic or vegetable compounds called "medicines" which, when prepared according to stringent ritualistic requirements, are believed to acquire magical properties enabling them to work the will of the sorcerer.

The reciprocal to the concept of sorcery, or the practice of evil magic, is the concept of the use of magical rites or medicines for socially approved purposes. These include everything from the protection of personal safety, to improvement of soil fertility, to success at the hunt or in battle. In short, "good" magic may be invoked to stimulate good results in any phase of the life cycle. Again, strict and proper ritual must be observed in the preparation of the necessary medicines, and

these rituals—which include taboo observance, verbal formulae, etc.—
are idiosyncratic to particular tribes, and even differing schools of
thought within the same tribe or sub-tribe.

Witchcraft, on the other hand, is said to be an inborn trait which
enables its possessor to harm other people merely by wishing to do so.
"Medicines" play no part in true bewitching operations. Some tribes
believe that witchcraft power is activated by feelings of hostility or envy
even without conscious decision on the part of the witch—or even
without the witch's knowledge that he contains witchcraft power within
him. In the Congo, belief that the witchcraft was embodied as a physical substance in the belly was so widespread that the Belgian authorities had to ban the practice of tribal elders' performing autopsies upon
the bodies of suspected witches. In 1924 the colonial administration
also banned use of the poison ordeal—the other universally accepted
method of screening witches. (Ritually-prepared poison was adminis-
tered to suspects in the belief that the innocent would survive and the
guilty perish.)

Although Africa's infrastructure of supernatural beliefs and practices
has been subjected to concentrated assault by Europeans—primarily
missionaries—for as many as five hundred years in some areas, few
lasting inroads have been made against ingrained traditions. In the
Congo, practically all education since 1878 has been in the hands of
various Catholic and Protestant missionary groups. Missionary activities
have succeeded in establishing rather substantial church organizations
and church membership, but closer examination reveals that to the
extent that Christian and other European influences have taken root in
the Congo, they have also often been modified so as to merge with,
not supersede, the traditional foundations of the country and its people.
Europeanized Congolese may carry amulets and charms, consult oracles
about the advisability of business transactions, and observe other rituals
learned in childhood. Others hold both traditional and Christian fu-
neral ceremonies. Institutionally, many syncretic sects—often pseudo-
Christian—stand between Christianity and tradition, started by
prophets who believed they were divinely inspired. Most began as messianic cults but developed nationalistic and anti-European characteristics along the way.

Among the people, there is little evidence that traditional beliefs in
witchcraft, sorcery, and magic have been diminished by Western influences. The evidence is rather that the practice of secret magical rites is

on the increase. History indicates that beliefs in witches and magic die hard in all societies. And because of Africa's particular cultural setting, it is unlikely that these beliefs will disappear other than as a result of generations of careful and gradual education in the Western mold. Western education is not, however, an immediate solution. In Africa beliefs in magic and witchcraft are used to explain ultimate causations—the existence and origin of fortune and misfortune. Western secular education does not provide unequivocal answers to questions of such a fundamental nature.

Western institutions have, as a matter of fact, served in some ways to increase tensions and anxieties in African societies, especially as these relate to superstitious beliefs and practices. The control of witches and sorcerers is of paramount importance to people who believe in magic. Yet the imposition of political systems of a Western type upon African tribes has resulted in the elimination of the most efficacious witch-control measure—the poison ordeal. In addition, the execution of convicted witches and sorcerers is no longer allowed. As a result, many Africans feel that Western political systems such as the modern state have aligned themselves on the side of evil because from their standpoint, the "civilized" elimination of traditional control measures work to protect witches and sorcerers from retaliation by their innocent victims. The African man-in-the-bush is, therefore, much more at the mercy of those who wish to harm him by supernatural means than ever before. He thus tends to rely more and more upon the witch-doctor who, in the absence of the poison ordeal and other drastic sanctions, provides the main source of protection from evil.

Counterinsurgency Analysis

In the context of the current insurgency situations in Kivu and Katanga, where insurgents rely upon "medicines" and ritualistic observances to protect them from firepower, the suggestion to devise and employ magical practices in counterinsurgency operations is obvious and tempting. Before adopting this course of action, however, the U.S. counterinsurgency planner should give serious consideration to several pertinent factors.

A. In the event that the U.S. role, if any, in the Congo will be of an advisory character, the advisors must rely upon the extent of their influence upon Congolese counterparts. U.S. policy recommendations must, therefore, be acceptable to Congolese leaders. The Congolese leadership class is driven almost exclusively from a small elite group who, having obtained Western education under the Belgians, have become "Europeanized" (a concept virtually equivalent to "civilized") to the extent that they are known as evolues. Kasavubu, Lumumba, Kalonji, Adoula, Mobutu, and Tshombe are all evolues and as such are fiercely proud of their civilized status and image. These evolues can be expected to resist any association with policies that might reflect endorsement of "uncivilized" behavior, even though they themselves might be to some extent dependent upon secret charms or other superstitious beliefs or practices.

B. Although beliefs in witchcraft, sorcery, and magic are endemic throughout sub-Saharan Africa, these beliefs vary considerably in detail according to tribe or sub-tribe. Literally, one man's charm may be another man's poison, depending upon particular tribal beliefs. It follows that the counterinsurgency planner, should he desire to exploit the psychological potential of superstition, must be able to compile and analyze a large quantity of specific and detailed information embracing the entire spectrum of superstitious beliefs and other values of the specific ethnic group with which he is concerned. This tends to relegate the use of magic to limited tactical objectives rather than broad strategic concepts or solutions to fundamental problems. By the same token, however, the prevalence of superstitious beliefs in Africa suggests that the counterinsurgency planner requires considerable information about these beliefs for intelligence and counterintelligence purposes alone. A sound understanding of magical concepts, practices, and mannerisms is necessary for defensive purposes should they play any role of importance in any insurgency situation.

Knowledge of the specific uses of charms, medicines, bodily scarification, and the like, will help to identify membership in a particular cult, or will enable patterns of activity to be defined. Failing complete and detailed information of this type, both operational and counterintelligence planning will be unrealistic. Unfortunately, such information may not be quickly acquired about the more than 200 reported tribes in the Congo, but must be painstakingly gathered and evaluated over a long period of time. Detailed studies of supernatural beliefs of specific tribes are limited. The secrecy inherent in most magical rituals presents a formidable obstacle to the outside investigator, whether he may be a scientist or an intelligence agent.

C. And finally, the tactics employed to counter current insurgencies in various parts of the Congo must be evaluated in terms not only of their immediate effectiveness against the short-term military problem, but in terms also of the positive or negative influence upon the long-range problem of establishing a viable political system.

It cannot be denied that the exploitation of superstitious beliefs by insurgent leaders is a double-edged weapon. Fear of magic and witch-craft can be reversed and used with telling effects against the insurgents. If reliable and detailed operational intelligence can be gathered, counterinsurgency planners will be able to concoct "medicines" and other devices within the superstitious framework of the target group, with which to neutralize and overpower the magic spells cast by insurgent witch-doctors. These procedures could well involve a continuing duel of thrust and parry, because the witch-doctors could also be counted on to devise counter-counter measures, and so forth. But there is little doubt that counter-magic tactics properly conceived and imaginatively executed could be quite effective in achieving short-run victories. A broader question is whether the exploitation of superstition in this fashion is not also a triple-edged weapon, in that superstition itself, rather than the central government, may become, in the long-run, the main beneficiary. Since tribalism and superstition, so closely related to each other, have provided a fertile seedbed for political instability in the Congo, and measures which enhance the divisive and destructive aspects of tribalism simply lay additional obstacles in the already cluttered path toward Congolese nationhood. Should the central government successfully use occult methods to defeat a movement based upon such methods, the very concepts of sorcery and magic which lend impetus to the insurgencies of the moment may gain strength and acquire even greater troublemaking potential for the future. In other words, the more successful the counterinsurgency campaign, if that campaign is based upon a counter-magic approach, the more ominous the outlook for the future. Any thesis that an insurgency inspired or sustained by magical concepts may be defeated more easily and at less cost and trouble by employing counter-magic is therefore questionable on these grounds.

Nor does the current situation in the Congo represent anything new in the history of insurgency insofar as the use of magical practices is concerned. History is replete with instances wherein uprisings have been reinforced by magic spells. The T'ai P'ing rebellion in China was led by a man who represented himself as the younger brother of Jesus Christ. The Boxer cultists believed that they could cause cannon to fall apart at great distances by psycho-kinetic means. Those who took Mau Mau oaths in Kenya were taught that oath violation would be instantly lethal. African history contains numerous other examples of similar phenomena (the "Maji-Maji" rebellion in Tanganyika, the Makombe uprising in Portuguese East Africa, etc.). Current problems in the Congo as well as the Lumpa uprising in Northern Rhodesia today exemplify the same superstitious manifestations.

Any study of historical examples of uprisings supported by superstitious practices, however, will reveal that vigorous military countermeasures of a conventional nature have produced optimum results in suppressing the insurgency. If there are substantial political or economic motives behind the uprisings, these naturally must be taken into account. The reference here is to military tactics and their effects against magic.

Despite the ingrained quality of superstition throughout black Africa, there is a certain core of pragmatism immediately applicable to the present problem. The history of messianic movements and especially those movements whose primary function in the detection and/ or neutralization of witchcraft and sorcery reveals that Africans easily recognize and accept concrete proof of the ineffectiveness of a particular magical rite or charm. Such recognition and acceptance in no way affect the basic pattern of belief in magic. The opposite is in fact true, as is proven by the continuing succession of short-lived anti-witchcraft cults throughout Africa. Africans are quite prepared to admit that they have been fooled by a particular practitioner or cult. The pattern then is to reject the "false" cult and accept one which, until events prove otherwise, is the "real thing." The same type of mental processes seem to apply to witch-doctors themselves. Informed opinion is that most witch-doctors believe themselves as individuals to be clever charlatans, since they are aware that they really have no magic power. But an individual witch-doctor is also likely to believe that he alone is a charlatan and that his colleagues do indeed have magical abilities.

In the Congo, as elsewhere in black Africa, there is every reason to believe that disciplined troops, proficient in marksmanship, and led by competent officers, can handily dispel most notions of magical invulnerability. It is quite true that the raising of such a force may pose more problems in the Congo than in some other areas, but the problem is by no means insoluble. The elite gendarmerie organized by the Belgians to offset the ill-disciplined Force Publique gendarmerie is an example of what can be done in the Congo. The same concept of the gendarmerie was employed, together with foreign mercenaries, by Moise Tshombe in the Katanga secessionist movement. Tshombe's forces were generally conceded to be highly effective, and were suppressed only with great difficulty by the United Nations.

The immediate military problems related to the Congo's fundamental problems of instability and chaos appear more susceptible to lasting solution by conventional methods than by reliance on purely psychological or occult phenomena whose values are limited to support functions in tactical situations and whose implementation is fraught with long-run risks. Drawing upon the Belgian experience as well as that of Tshombe in Katanga, it would appear that a more flexible approach to the military problem is to be found in the concept of elite troops: troops which are carefully trained and disciplined, and which are well-commanded. Unit morale and the confidence engendered by good training, knowledge of weaponry, and, above all, dynamic and competent leadership, can go far to counteract superstitious fears.

NOTES

Chapter 2

1. P. Vandenberg, *The Mystery of the Oracles* (New York: Macmillan, 1979), p. 273.
2. Ibid., pp. 215–219.
3. Ibid., pp. 222–224.
4. Ibid., pp. 224–225.
5. B. Cunliffe, *The Celtic World* (New York: McGraw-Hill, 1979).
6. *The Mystery of the Oracles*, p. 259.
7. Ibid., p. 260.
8. Ibid., p. 271.
9. *The Celtic World*, p. 108.
10. Ibid., p. 83.
11. L. Spence, *Encyclopedia of Occultism* (New York: University Books, 1968), p. 97.
12. Ibid.
13. *The Celtic World*, p. 137.
14. 1 Samuel 28:7.
15. *Encyclopedia of Occultism*, p. 126.
16. Ibid., p. 214.
17. Ibid., p. 281.

Chapter 3

1. E. A. Budge, *Egyptian Magic* (New York: Dover, 1971), pp. x-xi.
2. Ibid., p. 6.
3. Ibid., pp. 73–77.
4. Ibid., p. 215.
5. Ibid., p. 91–93.

6. Ibid., p 216.
7. *Encyclopedia of Occultism*, p. 130.
8. Ibid., p. 130.
9. Ibid., p. 338.
10. Ibid.
11. Ibid.
12. Ibid.
13. Ibid., p. 84.
14. Ibid., p. 93.
15. Ibid., p. 110.
16. Ibid., p. 125.
17. Ibid., p. 130.
18. Ibid., p. 176.
19. Ibid., p. 251.
20. Ibid., p. 252.
21. Ibid., p. 274.
22. Ibid., p. 363.
23. Ibid., p. 205.
24. Paracelsus, *The Archidoxes of Magic* (New York: Samuel Weiser, 1975), pp. 62–63.
25. *The Sworn Book of Honorius*, translated by D. Driscoll (New Jersey: Heptangle Books, 1983), p. 70.
26. Ibid., p. 82.
27. Ibid., p. 85.
28. Ibid., p. 99.
29. *Fourth Book of Occult Philosophy*, translated by R. Turner (London: Askin, 1978), p. 45.
30. Ibid.
31. Ibid., pp. 2–63.
32. Peter De Abano, *Heptameron* (London: Askin, 1978), p. 94.
33. *Arbatel of Magic* (London: Askin, 1978), p. 197.
34. Ibid., p. 216.
35. *The Sixth and Seventh Books of Moses* (Chicago: The DeLaurence Co., n.d.), p. 47.
36. G. James, *The Enochian Evocation of John Dee* (New Jersey: Heptangle Books, 1984), p. xxi.
37. Ibid., p. 81.
38. *Encyclopedia of Occultism*, p. 181.
39. Ibid., p. 238.
40. Ibid.
41. Ibid.
42. *The Greater Key of Solomon*, translated by S. Mathers (Chicago: The DeLaurence Co., 1914), p. 68.

43. Ibid., p. 68.
44. *A Treatise on Angel Magic*, ed. A. McLean (Michigan: Phanes Press, 1990), p .112.
45. Ibid., p. 54.
46. Ibid., p. 55.
47. Ibid., p. 58.
48. *The Lesser Key of Solomon*, translated by S. Mathers (Chicago: The DeLaurence Co., 1916), p. 26.
49. Ibid., p. 27.
50. Ibid., p. 34.
51. Ibid., p. 35.
52. Ibid p. 36.

Chapter 4

1. "Exercise Physiology" article on the web site of Defense and Civil Institute of Environmental Medicine, Canada.
2. Teachings of Tibetan Yoga, translated by C. Chang (New Jersey: Citadel Press, 1977), p. 79.
3. Ibid., p. 80.
4. A. Kim, *Ninja Mind Control* (Colorado: Palladin Press, 1985), p. 34.
5. C. Martin, *The Boxer Rebellion* (New York: Abelard Schuman, 1968), p. 42.
6. "Hypnosis Comes of Age," *Science Digest*, April 1971, pp. 44–50.
7. Ibid.
8. E. DeShere, "Hypnosis in Interrogation," *Studies in Intelligence*, CIA, 1960.
9. Ibid.
10. D. Sklar, *The Nazis and the Occult* (New York: Dorset Press, 1977), p. 100.
11. P. Levenda, *Unholy Alliance* (New York: Avon, 1995), p. 148.
12. J. Alexander, et al., *The Warrior's Edge* (New York: Morrow, 1990), p. 10.
13. Ibid., p. 13.
14. R. McRae, *Mind Wars* (New York: St. Martin's Press, 1984), pp. 120–121.
15. Ibid.
16. Ibid., p. 122.
17. J. Dunnigan, *Digital Soldiers* (New York: St. Martin's Press, 1996), pp. 222–223.
18. Ibid., p. 284.
19. Ibid., p. 285.
20. Ibid., p. 291.
21. Ibid., p. xviii.
22. "Carbohydrate Electrolyte Solution Effects on Physical Performance of Military Tasks," *Aviation & Space Environmental Medicine* (1977), pp. 384–391.

23. A. Toffler, *War and Anti-War* (New York: Little, Brown & Co.), pp. 93–94.
24. Ibid., p. 121.
25. Ibid., p. 120.
26. "Advanced Technologies Can Aid Future Naval Forces," NRC press release 8/26/97.
27. Ibid.
28. Moscow *Times* article 7/11/95.
29. Article in *Newspeak* 1996, p. 129.

Chapter 5

1. D. Friedel, et. al. *Maya Cosmos* (New York: Morrow, 1993), p. 33.
2. Ibid., p. 34.
3. Ibid., p. 36.
4. B. Keeny, *Shaking the Spirits* (New York: Station Hill Press, 1994), p. 125.
5. Ibid., p. 23.
6. Targ Puthoff, "Information Transmission Under Conditions of Sensory Shielding," *Nature* 252 no. 5476 (10/18/74), pp. 602–607.
7. *Shaking the Spirits*, p. 63.
8. Ibid., p. 81.
9. Ibid., p. 63.
10. Ibid., p. 51.
11. R. Broughton, *Parapsychology The Controversial Science* (New York: Ballantine Books, 1991), p. 28.
12. Lynn Monahan, "Peru Shamans Pray to End Crisis," *Washington Post* 1/6/97.
13. Ibid.

Chapter 6

1. C. Wood, *The Quest For Eternity—Manners & Morals In the Age of Chivalry* (Hanover, NH: University Press of New England, 1983), p. 67.
2. Ibid., p. 67.
3. Ibid., p. 101.
4. E. Bradford, *The Shield and the Sword* (Boston: E.P. Dutton, 1973), p. 101.
5. Ibid., p. 18.
6. Ibid.
7. "A Short History of the Knights Templars" on the Templars home page on the web, http://intranet.ca/magicworks/knights/contents.html
8. Ibid.
9. "Initiation into the Order" on the Templars home page on the web.

10. "Popes and their Effect upon the Order" on the Templar home page on the web.
11. "Daily Live" on the Templars home page on the web.
12. "Rome and the Templars" on the Templars home page on the web.
13. "The Excavation of Solomon's Temple" on the Templars home page on the web.
14. "The Legend of the Skull of Sidon" on the Templars home page on the web.
15. W. Nogaret, "List of Accusations," A.D. 1308.
16. Ibid.
17. Ibid.
18. Ibid.
19. "Templars vs. The Assassins" on the Templars home page on the web.
20. Ermoul the Frank, "Account of the Battle of Hattin," A.D. 1187.
21. Ibid.
22. *Encyclopedia of Occultism*, pp. 38–40.
23. Ibid.
24. *The Shield and the Sword*, p. 97.

Chapter 7

1. R. Turner, *Elizabethan Magic* (Boston: Element Books, 1989), p. 16.
2. S. Berg, *Elizabeth I*, (Oxford: Oxford University Press, 1988), p. 63.
3. C. Erickson, *The First Elizabeth* (New York: Summit Books, 1983), p. 362.
4. Ibid., p. 26.
5. *Elizabethan Magic*, p. 17.
6. *Elizabeth I*, p. 226.
7. M. Howard, *The Occult Conspiracy* (MJF Books, 1989), p. 53.
8. *The First Elizabeth*, p. 356.
9. Ibid., p. 357.
10. Ibid., p. 334.
11. Ibid., p. 337.
12. Ibid., p. 356.
13. *Elizabeth I*, p. 267.
14. *The Occult Conspiracy*, p. 52.
15. Ibid.
16. Ibid., p. 53.
17. Ibid., p. 54.
18. *Encyclopedia of Occultism*, p. 116.
19. Ibid., p. 117.
20. Ibid.
21. Ibid.

22. Ibid., p. 115.
23. Ibid., p. 116.

Chapter 8

1. *The Occult Conspiracy*, p. 80.
2. Ibid., p. 82.
3. E. Cook, *Eminent Men in Secret Societies* (1880), pp. 12–27 (publisher unknown).
4. A. McCoy Roberts, *Freemasonry in American History* (1985).
5. J. Lowe, *Freemasonry and the Civil War* (http://www.nemason.org/book/civilwar.htm, 1995) p. 2.
6. *The Occult Conspiracy*, pp. 62–63.
7. Ibid., p. 65.
8. "Customs of the Secret Society" on the Edo home page on the web.

Chapter 9

1. R. Miller, *Rasputin: The Holy Devil* (New York: Viking Press, 1928), p. 171.
2. Ibid., pp. 12–15.
3. Ibid., p. 32.
4. Ibid., p. 37.
5. Ibid., pp. 114–15.
6. Ibid., p. 125.
7. Ibid., p. 140.
8. Ibid., p. 142.
9. Ibid., p. 115.
10. *The Occult Conspiracy*, pp. 101–102.
11. Ibid., pp. 118–119.
12. A. DeJonge, *The Life & Times of Grigorii Rasputin* (Coward McCann & Geoghegan, 1982) p. 26.
13. Ibid., p. 254.
14. Ibid., p. 341.
15. *Rasputin: The Holy Devil*, p. 202.
16. Ibid., p. 165.
17. Ibid., p. 341.
18. Ibid., p. 163.
19. Ibid., pp. 158–159.
20. *The Life and Times of Grigorii Rasputin*, p. 256.
21. Ibid., p. 257.
22. Ibid., p. 257.
23. Ibid., p. 292.
24. Ibid., p. 247.

25. Ibid., p. 128.
26. *Rasputin: The Holy Devil*, p. 332.
27. Ibid., p. 306.
28. Ibid., p. 238.
29. Ibid., p. 162.

Chapter 10

1. Biography on Gurdjieff on www.gurdjieff.org.
2. *The Occult Conspiracy*, pp. 128–129.
3. *Tomorrow* 9 no. 6 (February 1950), pp. 20–25.
4. *The Occult Conspiracy*, p. 134.
5. *Magick Without Tears*, ed. M. Motta, (Ordo Templi Orientis, 1983), p. 140.
6. Ibid., p. 7.
7. Ibid., p. 459.
8. Ibid., p. 456.
9. *The Occult Conspiracy*, p. 134.
10. G. Suster, *The Legacy of the Beast* (Maine: Samuel Weiser, 1989), p. 219.
11. *Unholy Alliance*, pp. 88–91.
12. Ibid., pp. 227–233.
13. *The Occult Conspiracy*, p. 135.
14. A. Lyons, *Satan Wants You* (New York: Mysterious Press, 1988), p. 80.
15. C. Wilson, *The Nature of the Beast* (Northamptonshire, UK: Aquarius, 1987), p. 111.
16. Ibid., p. 103.

Chapter 11

1. A. Constantine, "The OTO and the CIA," 1996, on Doc Hambone's web page.
2. *Unholy Alliance*, p. 112.
3. *The Occult Conspiracy*, p. 11.
4. S. Llewellyn Flowers, *Fire and Ice* (St. Paul, 1990), pp. 186–187.
5. A. Crowley, *Magical Diaries of the Beast 666* (London: Duckworth, 1972), pp. 7–8.
6. Ibid., pp. 17–18.
7. *The Occult Conspiracy*, p. 133.
8. Ibid., p. 134.
9. *Magick Without Tears*, p. 15.
10. Ibid., p. 447.
11. *Unholy Alliance*, p. 271.
12. Ibid., p. 272.

13. M. Staley, "The Babalon Working," http://freespeech.org/magick/koenig/staley11.htm
14. Ibid.
15. *Nazis and the Occult*, pp. 28–43.
16. K. Anderson, *Hitler and the Occult* (New York: Prometheus Books, 1995), p. 42.

Chapter 12

1. *The Occult Conspiracy*, pp. 124–125.
2. Ibid., p. 125.
3. Ibid.
4. R. Grunberger, *Hitler's SS* (New York: Dorset Press, 1970), p. 13.
5. Ibid., p. 14.
6. Ibid., p. 49.
7. *The Occult Conspiracy*, p. 131.
8. *Hitler and the Occult*, p. 212.
9. Ibid., p. 215.
10. *The Occult Conspiracy*, pp. 137–138.
11. A. Rosenberg, *Der Mythus des 20. Jahrhunderts* [*The Myth of the Twentieth Century*] (1930).
12. *Hitler and the Occult*, p. 178.
13. *Unholy Alliance*, p. 179.
14. *The Occult Conspiracy*, p. 182.
15. *The Myth of the Twentieth Century*.

Chapter 13

1. Ostrander, et al. *Psychic Discoveries Behind the Iron Curtain* (New York: Bantam, 1970), p. 104.
2. Ibid., p. 105.
3. Ibid., p. 106–108.
4. "The *Nautilus* Affair," article on the World Wide Web.
5. Ibid.
6. *Psychic Discoveries Behind the Iron Curtain*, p. 115.
7. "The Operational Potential of Subliminal Perception," *Studies in Intelligence*, CIA, 1958.
8. *Psychic Discoveries Behind the Iron Curtain*, p. 131.
9. Moscow *Times* article 7/95 by Owen Matthews.
10. L. Vilenskaya, "From Slavic Mysteries to Contemporary Psi Research." On the web.
11. Ibid.
12. M. Ebon, "Amplified Mind Power," http://www.resonate.org/places/writings/larissa/myth.htm

13. *Psychic Discoveries Behind the Iron Curtain*, pp. 253–254.
14. Ibid.
15. "Controlled Offensive Techniques," DIA declassified report 1972.
16. "Amplified Mind Power," op. cit.
17. Barker Testimony, 11/97, to Senate Subcommittee.
18. T. Rifat, "Military Development of Mind Control Technology." On the web.
19. Lt. Col. Thomas Bearden biography on Doc Hambone's Web Page, http://www.io.com/~hambone/arch/bearden.html
20. Ibid.

Chapter 14

1. J. Elliston, "PsyWar Terror Tactics." On parascope.com.
2. Ibid.
3. "The Use of Superstitions in Psychological Operations in Vietnam," 5/10/67 JUSPAO Saigon.
4. Ibid.
5. Ibid.
6. Ibid.
7. U.S. Army, "Witchcraft, Sorcery, Magic . . . In the Congo," 1964.
8. Ibid.
9. Ibid.
10. C. Galdiano Montenegro, *Palo Mayombe—The Dark Side of Santería* (New York: Original Publications), p. 6.
11. Ibid., p. 89.
12. "Witchcraft Sorcery, Magic . . . In the Congo."
13. Ibid.
14. Ibid.
15. Ibid.
16. Ibid.
17. *Al Hayat Al Jadidah* 12/1/97 article by Fuad Abu Hijla.
18. *Al Ayam* 11/22/97.
19. Ibid.
20. *Al Hayat Al Jadidah* 9/2/97.
21. "The Divine Wind—Japanese Kamikazes" by R. Germinsky, www.chinfo.navy.mil.

Chapter 15

1. G. Thomas, *Journey into Madness* (New York: Bantam, 1989), pp. 269–285.
2. Ibid.

3. Ibid.
4. Ibid.
5. H. Puthoff, "CIA initiated remote viewing at SRI," www.biomindsuper powers.com.
6. Ibid.
7. Ibid.
8. Ibid.
9. Ibid.
10. *Journal of Scientific Exploration* 10 no. 1, "Remote Viewing at SRI," R. Targ.
11. Ibid., "An Assessment of Evidence for Psychic Functioning," J. Utts.
12. Ibid.
13. Ibid.
14. Ibid.
15. Ibid.
16. *Mind Wars*, p. 102.
17. Ibid.

Chapter 16

All quotes from K. Kress, "Parapsychology in Intelligence," *Studies in Intelligence*, Winter 1977.

Chapter 17

1. "The Use of Psychics Clouds CIA," *Newsday*, 12/3/95.
2. Ibid.
3. "Parapsychology in Intelligence."
4. "Navy To See If Ditched Copter Can Be Raised," *Newsday*, 11/28/91.

Chapter 18

1. "Major Dames Sets the Record Straight," on the Firedocs web page, www.firedocs.com
2. Conversations with Joseph McMoneagle, Summer 1998.
3. "Point by Point Response to Ed Dames," Firedocs web page.
4. "Statement on CIA's Involvement with CRV," Ed Dames, 12/7/95, Firedocs web page.
5. "Paul Smith's Response to Ed Dames," Firedocs web page.
6. Conversations with McMoneagle, Summer 1998.
7. Dame's Psi-Tech brochure on the web, www.trv-psitech.com.
8. Ibid.

9. Ibid.
10. Conversations with Mel Riley and Joseph McMoneagle, Fall 1998.
11. Dames on Art Bell's radio show 1/30/97.
12. Ibid.
13. Ibid.
14. Ibid.
15. Ibid.
16. Ibid.
17. Ibid., 1998.
18. Ibid.
19. J. Schnabel, *Remote Viewers* (New York: Dell, 1997), p. 297.
20. C. Wilson, *The Psychic Detectives* (San Francisco: Mercury House, 1985), pp. 4–11.
21. "What Do You See in a Session," on the P-S-I website of Lyn Buchanan.
22. Ibid.
23. Ibid.
24. "Did Star Gate Use Biofeedback?" on the P-S-I website of Lyn Buchanan.
25. Ibid.
26. Ibid.
27. *The Psychic Detectives*.
28. D. Morehouse, *Psychic Warrior* (New York: St. Martin's Press, 1996), p. 42.
29. "An American Hero" Schnabel, J. On the web.
30. *Psychic Warrior,* p. vii.
31. Ibid., p. 70.
32. Ibid., p. 95.
33. Ibid., p. 111.
34. Ibid., p. 154.
35. Ibid., p. 155.
36. Ibid., p. 157.
37. "An American Hero Part 2" Schnabel, J. On the web.
38. *Psychic Warrior*, p. 170.
39. "An American Hero Part 2" Schnabel, J. On the web.
40. Ibid.
41. Ibid.
42. "A Personal Remark," Lyn Buchanan, on the Firedocs web page.
43. "Theft of Book Manuscript." Notice on the web by Morehouse.
44. Ibid.
45. *Sightings on the Radio*, with Jeff Rense, host, 6/1/97 show.
46. *Magical Blend Magazine*, issue no. 52, McMoneagle interview.
47. Ibid.
48. "Mind Trek" excerpt on Firedocs web page.
49. *Washington Post* interview with McMoneagle, 12/4/95.

50. On-line conversation on Compuserve 1/4/96.
51. *Sightings on the Radio*, 6/1/97 McMoneagle interview.
52. Ibid.
53. Ibid.
54. Ibid.
55. Ibid.
56. Conversations with McMoneagle, Summer '98.
57. 1992 Stubblebine Lecture at UFO Convention.
58. Ibid.
59. *Remote Viewers*, pp. 275–276.
60. Ibid., pp. 279–280.
61. Ibid., p. 311.
62. Ibid.
63. Ibid.
64. 1992 Stubblebine Lecture at UFO Convention.
65. Ibid.
66. Ibid.
67. Ingo Swann biography on Doc Hambone's web page.
68. *Remote Viewers,* pp. 88–89.
69. "The Real Story of Remote Viewing, Ch 53," on Swann's web page.
70. Ibid.
71. Ibid.
72. Ibid.
73. "Front Matter" on Swann's web page.
74. Ibid.
75. Ibid.
76. Remote Viewing vs. The Skeptics, 1/20/96 Swann statement on the web.
77. Ibid.
78. Ibid.
79. Ibid.
80. Ibid.
81. Ibid.
82. *Satan Wants You*, pp. 127–131.
83. J. Parker, *At the Heart of Darkness* (New York: Citadel, 1993), pp. 264–269.
84. Ibid.
85. Aquino complaint *Aquino v. Electriciti Communications*, Superior Court San Francisco, Case no. 984751.

Chapter 19

1. "Sorcery at the Pentagon" *New York Times*, 2/23/84.
2. Ibid.

3. "Pentagon Is Said To Focus on ESP for Wartime Use," *New York Times*, 3/84.
4. Ibid.
5. Ibid.
6. Ibid.

Chapter 20

1. Robert Allan Monroe biography on Monroe Institute web site.
2. "CHEC Unit," article on Monroe Institute web site.
3. "The Hemi Sync® Process," by F. Atwater. On Monroe Institute web site.

Chapter 21

1. "Remote Viewing Archives" on Doc Hambone's web pages.
2. *Remote Viewers*, p. 27.

Chapter 22

1. DIA Training Manual for Remote Viewing 5/1/86.
2. P.E.I. Bonewitz, *Real Magic* (San Francisco: Creative Arts, 1970), p. 135.
3. DIA Training Manual for Remote Viewing.
4. *Real Magic,* p. 131.
5. Ibid., p. 138.
6. DIA Manual.
7. H. Irwin, *An Introduction to Parapsychology*, 2 ed. (North Carolina: McFarland, 1994), p. 286.

Chapter 23

All quotes are from DIA Training Manual for Remote Viewing.

Chapter 24

1. "Nancy's Star-Crossed Secret," on the web at parascope.com.
2. Ibid.
3. "Bad Times for Bonzo," on the web at parascope.com.
4. Ibid.
5. "So Speaks the Soothsayer," on the web at parascope.com.
6. Ibid.
7. Ibid.

292 ✺ NOTES

1. CIA Executive Summary of AIR report 9/95.
2. "An Evaluation of the Remote Viewing Program," AIR 9/95.
3. Ibid.
4. Ibid.
5. Press Release, Edwin May Society for Scientific Exploration, 3/22/96.
6. "An Evaluation of the Remote Viewing Program."
7. Edwin May Press release.
8. "An Evaluation of the Remote Viewing Program."
9. Ibid.
10. Edwin May Press Release.
11. Ibid.
12. "An Evaluation of the Remote Viewing Program."
13. Edwin May Press Release.
14. "An Evaluation . . ."
15. Edwin May Press Release.
16. Ibid.
17. "An Evaluation . . ."
18. Ibid.
19. Edwin May Press Release.
20. Ibid.
21. "An Evaluation . . ."
22. Ibid.
23. Edwin May Press Release.
24. "An Evaluation . . ."
25. Ibid.
26. Ibid.
27. Ibid.
28. Ibid.
29. Ibid.
30. Edwin May Press Release.
31. "An Evaluation . . ."
32. Edwin May Press release.
33. "An Evaluation . . ."
34. Ibid.
35. Ibid.
36. Ibid.
37. Ibid.
38. Ibid.
39. Ibid.
40. Edwin May press release.
41. "An Evaluation . . ."

42. Ibid.
43. Ibid.
44. Ibid.
45. Ibid.
46. "An Evaluation of the Remote Viewing Program," AIR 9/25.
47. Press release of 3/22/96 from the Edwin May Society of Scientific Exploration.
48. Ibid.
49. Ibid.

INDEX

Abano, Peter de, 34
Aberdeen (Maryland), 50
Abrams, Stephen I., 254–55
Adams, John, 77
advertising, mind control by, 120
Africa, superstition and magic in, 3, 125–28, 267–78
Agrippa, Henry Cornelius, 33–34
AIR. *See* American Institute of Research
Air Force, U.S., 145, 265
alchemy, 69, 102
Alexander I (Czar of Russia), 84
Alexander II (Czar of Russia), 84
Alexander III (Czar of Russia), 84
Alexandra (Czarina of Russia), 83–84, 86
Alexander, John, 46–47
Alexei (Czarevich), 83, 86–88
altered states of mind, 34, 86, 154, 171
    machines to achieve, 245
    sound frequencies in, 191–93, 196
American Institute of Research (AIR)
    report, 141, 157, 173, 183, 197–98, 214–16
    as disinformation, 216–27, 239
American Revolution, Freemasons in, 76–77
American Society for Psychical Research, 6, 38, 180
angelic communication, 71–73
animism, shamans and, 56
anomalous perturbation and cognition, 142, 236
    of Thule Society, 102
Aquino, Michael, 184–87
Arafat, Yasir, 128–29
Arbatel of Magic, The, 34–35
architecture, remote viewing and, 230

Army, U.S.
    Congo report by, 267–78
    Human Engineering Laboratory, 50
    Monroe Institute and, 191–92
    Satanism in, 185–86
Army Materiel Command, 264
Army Security Agency, 154, 170
Arnold, Benedict, 77
"Aryan race," 103, 108
assassins, the, 66–67
Assigned Witness Program, 162
Association of Former Intelligence
    Officers, 54
astral projection. *See* out-of-body
    experiences
astrology, 28–29, 69, 82, 90, 91, 94, 102, 103, 124, 197
    British World War II use of, 109–10
    CIA, 132
    1583, predicted doom by, 70
    Hess's belief in, 109
    in interwar Germany, 111
    Reagans' interest in, 211–13
Atwater, Franklin Holmes, 193
augurs, 19, 21
automobile industry, remote viewing and, 230, 231
autosuggestion, 44, 45
Aztec psychics, 28

Babalon Working, 100
Babylon, 28, 31
Badmaev (healer), 83
Bearden, Thomas E., 121
Bell, Art, 158–60

295

Saul, 13, 21
Scanate project, 135, 181
Schlesinger, James, 257
Schnabel, Jim, 168, 181, 192
Schroeder, Lynn. *See* Ostrander, Sheila
Scientific Engineering Institute, 131
SCUD missiles, 184
sealed-container experiments, 133, 256
sealed envelopes. reading contents of, 143
séances. *See* spiritualism
Sebottendorf, Baron Rudolf von, 102
secrecy agreements and clearances, 165, 166, 181, 184, 261
secret service, psychics and, 74
secret societies, 75–81
  Hitler's outlawing of, 103, 110
Semipalatinsk (Soviet Union), 136, 144, 259–61
Severodvinsk (Soviet Union), 173–74
sex-magic, 91, 97–99
shamans, 53–57, 114
  animistic, 56
  circumambulation of, 34
  techno-, 46
Shaolin Temple monks, 79–80
"shew-stone" (crystal), Kelly's, 35, 71–73
Shriners, 76
Six and Seventh Books of Moses, The, 35
Skotpsi sect, 84
Skull of Sidon, 62
Skylab, 173
sleep deprivation, 28
smart bombs, 49
Smith, Arden, 150
Smith, Marianne, 150
Smith, Paul H., 157, 196, 209
Socialist League, 97
soldiers
  of the future, 235
  possible elimination of, 236
  training of, 40–52
sound
  altered states of mind produced by, 191–93, 196
  to heal or kill, 233
Soviet Union
  fall of, 118
  psychic research in, 2, 113–22, 134, 181, 201, 255
  remote mind-control studies in, 118–19

  remote viewing by CIA of, 136, 144,173–74, 259–61
  superstitions studied in, 132–33
  telepathy in, 113–17, 120, 231
Spain, English spies in, 70
Spanish Armada, 72
special forces, 75
spell-books (grimoires), 23, 31–35, 37–38
Spence, Lewis, 72–73
spies, sorcerers and, 89
spiritualism
  in Russia, 84, 87, 88
  of Thule Society, 106
  in White House, 213
sports performance, enhancing of, 235
SRI. *See* Stanford Research Institute SS
  (Schutzstaffel), 46, 107–9, 186
  Ahnenerbe, 62
  of the future, 235
Stalin, Joseph, 114
Stanford Research Institute (SRI), 54, 133–45, 154–55, 163, 171–71, 180, 181, 183, 189, 200, 223, 234, 236, 242, 255–58, 260–62
  as separate from Stanford University, 48, 125
Stargate Program, 149, 151, 195, 197, 218, 228
Stilbides, 17
stones, magical, 30–31
Stubblebine, Albert, III, 162, 177–80, 191, 193, 196, 197, 235
subliminal influence. *See* remote influence
Sufi, 102
suicide ritual, 129
Sun Dance, 45–46
Sun Streak program, 165, 166, 197
Sun Tzu, 47–48
superstitions
  in the Congo, 3, 125–28, 267–78
  in Philippines, 123–24, 127
  university courses in, 132–33
  in Vietnam, 124
Swann, Ingo, 133–34, 142–43, 155, 180–84, 203
swastika, 102, 103, 107
Sworn Book of Honorius, 32, 33
symbols
  in dream interpretation, 27
  human need for, 104
  in magic, 24, 33
  in psychically obtained input, 155–56